Elektra Paschali

Masculinities in Politics

Elektra Paschali

Masculinities in Politics

On Gender Constructions within Political Youth Organizations in Greece

LIT

Cover image: Matt Manley, 'arboretum'

Bibliographic information published by the Deutsche Nationalbibliothek
The Deutsche Nationalbibliothek lists this publication in the Deutsche Nationalbibliografie; detailed bibliographic data are available in the Internet at http://dnb.d-nb.de.

ISBN 978-3-643-90460-7
Zugl.: Freiburg i.Br., Albert-Ludwigs-Universität, Diss., 2012

A catalogue record for this book is available from the British Library

Klosbachstr. 107
CH-8032 Zürich
Tel. +41 (0) 44-251 75 05
Fax +41 (0) 44-251 75 06
E-Mail: zuerich@lit-verlag.ch
http://www.lit-verlag.ch

LIT VERLAG Dr. W. Hopf
Berlin 2014
Fresnostr. 2
D-48159 Münster
Tel. +49 (0) 2 51-62 03 20
Fax +49 (0) 2 51-23 19 72
E-Mail: lit@lit-verlag.de
http://www.lit-verlag.de

Distribution:

In Germany: LIT Verlag Fresnostr. 2, D-48159 Münster
Tel. +49 (0) 2 51-620 32 22, Fax +49 (0) 2 51-922 60 99, E-mail: vertrieb@lit-verlag.de

In Austria: Medienlogistik Pichler-ÖBZ, e-mail: mlo@medien-logistik.at
In the UK: Global Book Marketing, e-mail: mo@centralbooks.com
In North America: International Specialized Book Services, e-mail: orders@isbs.com
e-books are available at www.litwebshop.de

Acknowledgments

I would like to thank all the people who talked to me openly and interestingly and who gave me any kind of helpful material for the completion of this work, the people I interviewed and talked to during my fieldwork.

I have to thank my both parents and most important, Iro, for all the clever suggestions, ideas and remarks. Also Jens, especially for his patience to listen to my presentations and his technical skills.

Many thanks to IGA Freiburg for the financial support, without which I never would have been able to complete the thesis.

Thanks to InterGender for the inspiring courses.

Also lot of thanks to Dr. Georg Winter who supported the publication of this book.

Every time I will be reading this work in the future, I definitely will remember StaBi Berlin and all the days I have spent there surrounded by books and a mystic atmosphere.

Inhalt

A General Introduction To This Work 1

1 A Critical Epistemology of 'Gender' and 'Masculinities' 9

1.1 Theorizing Gender: From Structures to Agency 14

1.2 Between Structures and Relations: Gendered Subjectivities 16

1.3 What Are Masculinities Studies about? 17

1.3.1 History of Research on Masculinity 19

1.3.2 Hegemonic Masculinities: a Useful Tool for Analysing Relations of Power 22

1.3.3 Critique of Hegemonic Masculinity and the Issue of Agency and Identity 28

2 Constructing Gender and Political Identities in Organized Politics 41

2.1 Ideology and Identity 45

2.2 Theorizing Ideology 49

2.2.1 Political Parties, Hegemony, Masculinities and Feminist Critique 54

2.2.2 The Character of Modern Democracy, the Role of the Parties and the Demands for Broader Representation: a Feminist Challenge 58

2.3 From Masculinities to the Political 60

2.3.1 On Political Culture 63

2.3.2 On Greek Political Culture 65

2.3.3 On Political Socialization of Children and Young Adults 66

2.3.4 Young People in Greek Political Culture 69

2.3.5 'Gender Equality': Participation of Women in Greek Politics 74

3 Methodological Approaches-Epistemological Assumptions 79
3.1 From Feminist Theory to Feminist Political Demands 80
3.2 Knowledge and Power 82
3.3 Feminist Standpoint Epistemology for a Study on Masculinities 85
3.4 Focus Groups Discussions 89
3.5 The Role of the Researcher in the Research Process 90

4 Let's talk politics: Discourses on Utopia, Ideology, Active Political Participation, Gender Equality and Difference 97
4.1 Talking about the Art of Politics 97
4.2 The Men and Women of the Research: Talking in Groups about Politics 100
4.3 Reading Modern Political Narratives 101
4.3.1 About Utopias 102
4.3.2 History and Tradition 106
4.3.3 On Active Political Participation 109
4.3.4 Building Up a Political Identity-The Role of Ideology 116
4.3.5 The Gender Variable in Discourse 117
4.3.6 The 'Common Good': Further Discussions around Citizenship, Politics and Society 120
4.3.7 Talking about Quotas 128
4.4 A Brief Note on Equality and Difference 130
4.4.1 Equality-Difference, Theories and Political Scenarios 132
4.4.2 From Feminist Theories to Politics: Linking Equality and Difference to Citizenship and Political Involvement 134
4.4.3 Talking about Difference 136
4.5 Masculinities and Femininities in Political Youth Organizations 140
4.5.1 Masculinities and Sexuality: Sexual 'Normativities' in Politics 144
4.5.2 The 'Sexualization' of Political Life 147
4.5.3 Heteronormativity, Homophobia and Exclusion in Political Youth Organizations 150

4.6 'Waving Their Testosterone as a Flag': Patterns of Masculinities 154
4.6.1 Models of 'Political Hegemonic Masculinities' 155
4.6.2 Theorists vs. Activists: Structural Divisions within Political Youth Organizations 160
4.6.3 Skill: a Class and Gender Related Variable of Differentiation within Political Youth Groups 161
4.6.4 Practicing Masculinity in Politics 162
4.6.5 Collective Masculinities: the Negotiations of Hegemonic Masculinities in the Group 165
4.7 Violence as a Structure Forming Political Masculinities 167
4.8 Concluding 173
5 Epilogue 175
6 Bibliography 179

List of Tables

Table 4.1	Discourses on politics, utopias, gender relations	115
Table 4.2	Discourses on equality and difference in politics	119
Table 4.3	Contextualizing violence	168

A General Introduction To This Work

This work offers a critical analysis of the construction of masculine subjectivities within political youth organizations in contemporary Greece. The whole analysis is an attempt to reveal interrelations between socio-political structures, the political culture and masculinities. The main focus is on power dynamics that form gender and gender relations within political organizations. The character of the Political as well as of politics and political culture is influenced by the intersection of social, political, economic and cultural structures with gender patterns and is formed by power relations developed within organizational structures and practices. Gender and gendered power relations are major features of political organizations (Hearn, 2001:4). Gender relations within political organizations reflect the broader social, economic and political structural relations. Gender becomes a major variable of the Social and the Political, so that the gendered character of political organizations reveals crucial aspects of the morphology of the dominant political system, insights of the landscape of contemporary political culture and the character of democracy.

Through a structural analysis that connects the broader picture of the political culture as formed by social, economic, political and cultural processes, structures and practices in contemporary Greece with the specific micro-picture of the construction of gender subjectivities as formed through dominant gender relations within political youth organizations, this work attempts to combine within a single conceptual framework notions of gender with the Political and reveal the gendered character of political organizations and its influence upon the individuals as well as upon the whole of Greek political culture.

The dissertation is looking at the construction of masculine subjectivities that emerge from the intersection of political ideology and political practices, within the framework of political youth organizations in the contemporary Greek socio-political context. The work attempts to reveal the gendered character of political organizations in Greece by combining two views: first, of specific individual and collective gender constructions; and second, of patterns of socially constructed gendered relations of power. Consequently, the study focuses on political youth organizations attached to political parties that participate in the Greek parliament. Within political organizations, it examines the tension between patterns of 'hegemonic masculinity' and alternative models of masculine subjectivities, as they are formed by institutional structures, ideological discourses and political practices. For that purpose, the work engages with the concept of hegemony and its modules – power, violence, ideology and utopia.

The theoretical concept of hegemonic masculinity (Connell 1987, 1990, 2005), although it has come under scrutiny (Donaldson, 1993; Demetriou, 2001; Whitehead, 2002; Hearn, 2004; Howson, 2006, 2009), has proved very helpful analytically for this work. Hegemonic masculinity remains a critical way of theorizing gendered power relations among men and groups of men and helps to understand the effectiveness of masculinities in the legitimation of the gender order (Connell, 2005:xviii).

Drawing from critical theory and theories of practice, the work further examines the gender ideologies that emerge in relation to political ideologies, as expressed on a representational level (collective imaginaries, dominant discourses), a personal level (*Weltanschauung*, personal discourses) and a structural level (organizational structures, practices). The empirical analysis will be based on qualitative discourse analysis of group discussions with members of political youth organizations supported by a theoretical framework that deals with the impact of mainly ideological and organizational structures on gendered subjects within politics. The theoretical analysis will draw from theory of hegemony by A. Gramsci, feminist state theories, hegemonic masculinity theory by R.W. Connell, feminist critique of political theories, feminist standpoint theories, post-positivist realist identity theories and other relevant theories.

The choice of political youth organizations is based on the assumption that organizations are places where social relations are organized and structured. Political organizations engage, give directions and solutions and draw lines and policies around crucial social issues at a given historical moment. Youth organizations have a special educational role, offering young people a political socialization and a chance to participate in the political arena and take an active role in the political procedures that are happening at local, regional, national and international levels. Access to power, hierarchy, organizational structure and ideology shape and form any kind of relation within these spheres.

The focus on gender is a 'sine qua non' for a critical analysis of political organizations. Gender is a defining variable of the character of almost all organizations. Organizations are not just embedded in gender but pervaded and constituted by and through gender. Furthermore, at the same time, organizational realities themselves construct, sustain and sometimes subvert dominant gender relations and even gender itself (Hearn, 2001:4).

The major assumption that guides the whole analysis is that hegemonic and other masculinities within political youth organizations are formed by power relations that reflect the power relations that are dominant in the broader political, social and economic structures in contemporary Greece. This hypothesis will be discussed in the first two chapters of the work and will constitute the theoretical part of the analysis. The first chapter deals with the issue of gender and gender relations through a theoretical analysis of masculinities. The theory of hegemonic masculinity by Connell will offer the basis for a further theoretical analysis of masculinity constructions within political organizations. Furthermore, political identity will become an analytical concept through which the variables of political ideology and political practice will be connected to gender, structuring a theoretical analysis around the question of the intersection between political ideologies and gender identities.

The second chapter will focus on the dynamics that shape the dimensions of the Greek political culture and consequently the character of the political youth organizations. The notions of power and hegemony and their effect on gendered and political power relations will set the framework for where masculinities, politics and power relations will meet, thus revealing the character of the Political in Greece.

In the light of this theoretical analysis, the focus will be shifted in the 3rd chapter on the methodological approaches and epistemological assumptions that the theoretical and empirical research has been based on. In this context, how feminist standpoint epistemology and methodology contributes to an analysis of masculinity constructions in political youth organizations will be discussed. Moreover, some reflections on the role of the researcher in the research process will be presented.

The discussion in the 4th chapter focuses on the political youth organizations and the collective and individual political and gendered subjectivities in them. The discussion will include an analysis of the empirical material. For this analysis, the main point to be proved is that discourses on politics, utopias, state, violence and gender relations reflect the dominant ideologies, traditions and formal lines of the parties, influencing accordingly the formation of masculine subjectivities within political organizations. In addition to that, the everyday political practices, which are informed by the general power relations, form collective and individual masculinities, accordingly. The analysis will try to trace within the discourses on ideologies, utopias, politics, state, violence and gender relations, as re-constructed in the group discussions, the power and hegemonic relations that influence not only dominant and official political ideologies but the individual and collective political/ideological identities of the members. Parallel to the hegemonic sites, ruptures, negotiations and brakes and their influence on the construction of gender subjectivities will be discussed. Through the discursive re-construction of collective and individual everyday organizational political practices, connections will be drawn to the formation of collective and individual forms of masculinities, and the question how they respond to hegemonic ones will be analyzed.

The main assumption of the empirical analysis is linked to the main hypothesis of the theoretical part in the way that both refer to broader structures that are etched upon the organizations and their members and to their influence on the gendered character and gendered subjectivities of both organizations and individuals.

The analysis of the empirical material concentrates on individual and collective narrations on utopias and political traditions, the issue of the active political participation and on ideology and its influence on the construction of political and gender identities. Especially the connection between political identity and gendered identity as formed in the space of political youth organizations will be stressed and explained, drawing from discursive reconstructions of the informants and relevant theory. As K. Sliverman (1992) and J. Hearn (1996) suggest, 'if ideology is to successfully command the subject's belief, then it must necessarily intervene at the most profound level of the latter's constitution' (Silverman, 1992:6), including, 'the constitution of the subject and male subjectivity themselves' (Hearn, 1996:615).

Furthermore, the empirical analysis will concentrate on discourses around the quota system in Greek electorate and politics and will take a closer look at the issue of equality and difference in contemporary politics, linking it to relevant feminist theories.

Shifting to the agency and practices of masculine and feminine subjects within political organizations, the analysis will focus on 'political' masculinities and femininities and the intersection of gender with class, sexuality, violence, education, body and ideology. Nevertheless, the intersections of gender with the previous structures and processes will be analytically connected with the different levels and areas of political involvement and gender consciousness, variables that also influence the construction of gender subjectivities within political youth groups. Concentrating more on masculinities, a presentation of hegemonic forms of masculinity and alternative ones and their relation to femininities and to the whole political culture will follow. In conclusion, the issue of the normalization and negotiation of violence through gender constructions in organized politics will be presented.

In the framework that the above issues are set and analysed, two major questions appear central:

a) How do political ideologies form relevant gender ideologies?
b) How are collective and individual masculinities formed within political youth organizations?

The two questions, aside from trying to combine structures with relations on a theoretical and empirical analytical level, bring three major categories of critical analysis on gender and organizations together: gender (referring to gender relations); class (referring to political ideologies and practices); and age (referring to youth organizations). In my opinion, these (and especially the first two) variables influence the character of the Political and politics the most.

In a work that has as its major focus power dynamics that form gender and gender relations within politics, gender gets accordingly conceptualized. In this analytical context, *gender* is defined as, 'a primary way of signifying relations of power' (Scott, 1986:1056), and *gender relations* as, 'fundamental regulating relations in all social forms' (Haug, 2001:284). Furthermore, the notion of *gender regime* describes, 'the state of play in gender relations in a given institution' (Connell, 1987:99). In this case, the institutional site of political youth organizations and *gender order* signifies, 'the state of play in gender relations in a society wide scale', which refers to ordering relationships between gender regimes (Connell, 1987:98). By adopting the concept of 'play', as appears in the definition of Connell, the attention is turned to the notions of complicity and consent that are implied and which lead to the institutionalization of dominant patterns of gender relations and the de-legitimization of alternatives, processes which are also reflected in Gramsci's analysis of hegemony.

In order to show the connections between broader power relations and gender constructions within political youth organizations, we have to introduce to the discussion four important variables, the analysis of which will structure the whole work. The first variable is *gender* and the analysis will focus on hegemonic masculinities and the negotiation of alternative masculinities within political youth organizations, as well as the relation between masculinities and femininities. Especially on the relation between masculinities and femininities, a theoretical discussion around the issue of equality and difference will set the framework in which the impact of hegemonic political masculinities on the formation of political femininities will be examined on the basis of the empirical material.

Talking about *political youth organizations*, we introduce the second analytical variable, which is the Greek *political culture*, of which the political youth organizations are certainly a part. In the analysis of the political culture, political identity becomes an important analytical variable that influences the construction of gendered subjectivities within political organizations. Political identities, as mentioned above, are formed through the interaction of dominant political ideologies and organizational practices. The fourth variable, crucial to the whole analysis, is the notion of *power*. The various forms and aspects of power and its effect on gender relations are revealed through the discourses and the practices which members of political organizations are parts of and which are re-constructed and negotiated in the process of the group interviews.

The notion of power is not integrated in the analysis as a static, ahistorical and overarching notion that affects the lives and *Weltanschauungen* of individuals and social groups. Power has a material as well as symbolic impact on the everyday lives of people and on the broader structures that shape the Economic, Social, Political and Cultural of a given society at a given historical moment. Power is structured via hierarchies, differentiations, struggles and ambivalent dynamics and in turn produces inequalities, marginalization and domination. The access to power as well as the influence of power relations on individuals and groups varies from the economic and material conditions of life to the social, political and cultural context of life. In connection to 'power', the notion of hegemony implies different poles and positions inside the matrix of power relations and categories such as class, gender, ethnicity, and age become crucial analytical tools for the understanding of gender inequality and oppression.

The four variables, mentioned above, mark the content of analysis of each chapter and reveal various aspects of the constructions of masculinities within political youth organizations in contemporary Greece.

Through the process of analysing, evaluating and systematizing the empirical material and trying to engage in a theoretical discussion around gender relations, political structures and power, it becomes clear that these attempts are not enough to grasp the roots, character and meaning of phenomena such as sexism, homophobia, suppression and domination within political organizations as well as society as a whole. This analysis takes off from looking at structures, institutions, discourses and practices and their influence on gendered subjectivities. During the analysis it becomes obvious that men and women are social categories formed to fit in a given gender system compatible to a certain economic, social, political and cultural system, but they simultaneously become collective and individual agents of social practices and discourses. Although the focus of the analysis is put on the first aspect, in no way is the second aspect ignored or rejected.

The question that remains open and to which this work offers a partial answer is how far gendered subjects can release themselves, their discourses, their imaginations and their utopias from the given system of discourses and practices that are dominant within various institutional sites. The broader structures remain highly determining of gender notions and constructions that affect individual and collective gender formations. Although individuals offer different, sometimes contradictory and antagonistic interpretations of relations and structures, they usually seem unable to see the world beyond and outside of them. That proves among all the inability to form unique and affirming notions of social and personal utopias in their discourses (referring to the group discussions analysed in this work) or the reflection of formal political organizational lines upon personal views and discourses. This is not meant to imply that there is no way out of the power matrix that forms the gendered selves and bodies; on the contrary, this work hopes to establish a first step towards change. In order to fight systemic and systematized oppression and domination, we have to recognize it, identify the mechanisms and acknowledge our roles (compliance, resistance and above all, agency) inside it.

Problems of Method, New Directions, Further Research

This particular work has two distinct analytical parts, one theoretical and one empirical. The theoretical analysis offers the necessary framework through which the empirical data can be connected to the broader picture of general social, economic, political and cultural gendered relations. The empirical part offers a local focus and rich detail on the specific situation of political youth organizations in contemporary Greece. However, the analysis misses a global dimension, which would offer the opportunity to understand masculinities on a world scale and to grasp the global relations and structures involved. This gap is bridged through the theoretical analysis on power, state, political ideologies and political organizations. The theoretical and empirical analyses could be read separately from each other; however, together they offer a combined view of the macro and the micro level of politics and gender.

This work offers a critical view of masculinities and political organizations and can be integrated into more general analyses of social change. It surely has potential for further development, but as a synthesis of ideas and empirical understanding it will hopefully trigger a dialogue with broader contemporary discourses in a constructive way.

1 A Critical Epistemology of 'Gender' and 'Masculinities'

Talking about a structural analysis of gender relations in a given society, certain historical moment or period, we should define what we mean by social structures and locate the character of the analysis based on that definition.

Structure usually draws lines of a frame, within which practices are (re)produced by social actors. The restrictive character of a clearly defined framework implies a kind of limitation that indicates that practices within a structural framework might change but can never escape it. Connell (1987:97) conceives social structure as 'the pattern of constraint on practice inherent in a set of social relations'. Usually, structures are not obvious, although they are mostly influential in the ways interactions and institutions are organized. The relation between structure and practice is central in an analysis of gender relations and many attempts to analyse their connection to each other are reflected in theories of practice. P. Bourdieu's 'habitus' and A. Giddens 'theory of structuration' are two major theoretical models that are used in sociological analyses of gender. The problem with these theories is that they do not correspond to the notion of history and do not involve the aspect of change. Practices can often express a resistance to or rejection of the structural causes and so a kind of reversion happens. Practices then form existing structures without being able to produce new ones. Feminist thought has focused on structural analysis tending however to look at a single structure (women's oppression by men) in an attempt to explain complex gender relations. Issues such as ideology, the state and production have been analysed as manifestations of the subordination of women to men.

Over the last decades, research has focused on two underlying structures of the relationship between the genders, the division of labor (meaning the organization of housework), childcare, the division of paid and unpaid work, unequal wages and additionally the issue of reproduction, which is often treated as a distinct structure[1] or as practice related to the division of labor. The second major structure is related to authority and control, meaning the hierarchies of the state, institutional, interpersonal and domestic violence, and surveillance. These structures interweave but often follow different directions as they develop historically and affect differently the formation of masculinities and femininities.

Connell (1987) introduces in his theory of practice, alongside a structural model that includes the structures of division of labor, power and cathexis, a structural inventory that aims to investigate more deeply the current interplay of gender relations at all levels and dimensions. He borrows from J. Matthews (1984) the 'gender order' that describes systematically the patterns of power relations between men and women and the definitions of masculinity and femininity of an entire society (Connell, 1987:99).

The concept of 'gender relations' is central to an analysis of gender. Connell has noted that masculinity can only be understood within a framework of gender relations (Connell, 1995:44). I. Rösing (1999) describes the 'gender' allocations of space, time, field and public offices as aspects of formation of gender relations. According to that definition she concludes that, 'the fundamental, everyday division of labor, family life and sexuality are affected by symbolic genderness (Haug, 2005:29). N. Fraser (1989), in her critique of J. Habermas's analysis of modern society, introduces a new picture of private and public realms of gender relations where fields of material and symbolic reproduction take new places (Haug, 2005:297). Accordingly, Fraser urges an understanding of the 'citizen' as a gender-political concept. R. Becker-Schmidt and A. Knapp (1995:18) talk about the 'arrangement of genders' instead of gender relations and understand them as 'cultural, political and economic'. They relate them to exchange in labor, performances, satisfaction of needs or to exclusion from spaces, terrains of praxis, resources and rituals (Becker-Schmidt and Knapp in Haug 2005:298). To this definition of gender relations there is the underlying notion of power that stresses their asymmetrical and unequal character. Here, I. Lenz's (1995) definition of power as determination over processes and resources draws back to the exchange and exclusion paradigm of Becker-Schmidt and Knapp and explains the multiplicity of gender relations, the phenomena of complicity or resistance of gendered subjects towards hegemonic discourses and patterns of masculinity and femininity. Connell (1995:48) stresses here that definitions of masculinity are profoundly interwoven with

[1] See J.Mitchell's *Woman's Estate* (1971)

economic structures and the history of institutions. Finally, we can agree with the definition of F. Haug for gender relations 'as fundamental regulating relations in all social formations' (Haug, 2005:294).

The focus of recent feminist theory on institutions is an attempt to deal with the gender blindness of mainstream sociological analyses of states and other major institutions. Connell names the actual situation in gender relations in a given institution as its 'gender regime' (Connell, 1987:120). Within institutions, patterns and models of hegemonic masculinity reign, in relation to which other forms are subordinated. However, formal and informal organizations differ in the character of gender regimes, without escaping from the model of hegemonic-marginalized gender patterns with hegemonic masculinity setting the character of most institutions.

The state represents for some feminist theorists the ultimate institutionalization of gender (*Ibid*, 126). Except the obvious sexual division of labor and access to the state apparatuses (state elites preserved by men, the military and state ideologies and policies that promote force and aggressiveness), the state promotes popular ideologies on sex and gender through birth control, sexual anti-discrimination laws, equal opportunities policies, pre-natal policies, anti-natal policies, intervening in the sexual division of labor and regulating families, schools, workplaces (*Ibid*). The state has a regulating, sustaining and intensifying role in gender relations. A. Touraine (1981) writes that the state, rather than guaranteeing the social order, has the role of the agent of a historical collectivity, 'situated in relation to other communities and to its own transformation' (Connell, 1987:127). This collectivity can be defined in gender as well as in class terms (*Ibid*).

One theoretical approach that tries to draw the connection between the two views on the state is that of state as a class state producing effects on sex and as a gender state in pursuit of class interests. Theorists such as M. McIntosh (1978) introduce political economy as the maintaining of men's subordination of women through class divisions (Connell, 1987:129). Another theoretical perspective conceives the state as a patriarchal institution. C. McKinnon (1982) looks at state action as the institutionalization of a male point of view. C. Pateman (1983) sees the development of the liberal state as an outcome of a new form of patriarchy in civil society developing in the seventeenth and eighteenth centuries (Connell, 1987:128).

The gendered character of the state becomes obvious when we look at the state's mechanisms of repression. The most frequent and fierce uses of state force are perpetrated by men against men. This reflects certain politics of masculinity. The state tries to legitimize and sustain hegemonic masculinity through legal violence and on the other hand attempting to control it. The state also promotes other forms of masculinities that are related to each other: the masculinity of the technocrats, the leaders, the planners, the operators etc.

As Connell suggests, the state is not patriarchal from the beginning but develops historically, adopting different forms of patriarchal order in an open political process. In this regard the state can afford controversies, re-arrangements of the patriarchal order and it is open to including groups and policies that used to be contrary or marginalized. That explains the funding of feminism through programmes and organizations supported financially by the state. Patriarchy is one aspect of the character of the modern state that supports and cooperates with its capitalistic character, where shifts of interests can lead to coalitions and inclusions with the ultimate aim of sustaining its interests and the interests of the dominant groups that profit from it.

As Connell writes, 'power in the state is strategic because there is more at issue than a simple distribution of benefits' (Connell, 1987:130). The state has a central part in the constitution of social categories of the gender order through the constitution of marriage and motherhood and by creating subsequent categories such as wives, mothers, fathers etc. (*Ibid*, 130). So the state constitutes interests at play in sexual politics. As mentioned above, the state can be seen not as the center of patriarchy but the set of power relations and political processes where interests of hegemonic aspects of domination, including patriarchy, are structured and contested. Pateman sees a direct connection of the change in patterns of masculinity with the changing character of the modern state. Women are considered as 'equal citizens', but this has not managed to reshape party politics, and apart from a number of women politicians and some women's organizations within the parliament and the parties that are considered part of the usual political processes, women as citizens are considered as direct consumers of state services. As S. Shaver (1983) notes, when welfare and taxation are considered as systems of transfer, the state is taking from women as individuals and is distributing to them as mother, wife etc. (Connell, 1987:132).

The division of labor, the power relations between men and women within political organizations and the institutionalized gendered character of organizations, aside from having roots in the conventional images of man-as-breadwinner, public-men, men-in-the-leadership, also have a strong material base.

Focusing on the power relations between men and women within the framework of socialist feminism, the focus of Marxist analyses is on the connection between women's oppression and the capitalist system. K. Millett (1970) is cited in H. Hartmann (1979:11): 'Our society...is in patriarchy. This is obvious when we look at the centers of power in the society, including the repressive power of the police that is distributed absolutely only in male hands'.

Women's subordination is central to unequal class relations and relations of production. Analyses have focused on the level of family and have shown how the family is maintained by women's oppression, which in turn maintains capitalism. Consequently, the gender inequality problem is directly connected to the class inequality problem and can only be solved if the class issue is solved. In this framework the priority of the class struggle was criticized as 'a dogma' by theorists such as C. Delphy (1977), who revealed in particular the unexplained and weak connection between patriarchy and capitalism, as women's subordination existed before capitalism and continued to exist in non-capitalist countries. In the 1970s, there was a shift in the analysis in the same direction but through a structuralist Marxist perspective. The gender relations were seen as an aspect of the reproduction of the 'relations of production'.

Reproduction was primarily understood as bearing children to cover the needs of the production but also as a matter of socialization making people fit into the capitalist mould. Mitchell (1971) therefore saw patriarchy as a sphere of ideology, forming people to meet the needs of the production processes. She clearly theorizes patriarchy as the basic ideological structure, exactly as capital is the basic economic structure of the society (Hartmann, 1979:10). This 'social reproduction theory' reveals a systemic connection between women's oppression and economic exploitation that leads to unequal social relations within a capitalist social organization.

Critiques of the stable character of the social structure have been made on the basis that in history social structure should and is constantly constituted rather than reproduced unchanged. As groups privilege through the reproduction of structures that secure their power, they develop strategies of re-arrangement and re-adjustment to maintain power in an ever-changing process. Social reproduction is therefore an 'object of strategy' (Connell, 1978:44). Still, it is not clear what this reproduction of power should be based on and/or if it produces sexual hierarchy and oppression.

Here, social reproduction theory meets J. Lacan's psychoanalysis and C. Levi-Strauss' cultural anthropology and semiotics. Social reproduction of the patriarchal order dwells entirely in the realm of ideology and becomes disconnected from the sphere of production. This theoretical view has led to a perception of gender relations as a part of class relations and as a truncated structure (*Ibid*, 45), while works focusing on the women's material world, wage rates and unionism have revealed that gender is a basic part of the 'relations of production' and not just included in their reproduction. Theorists such as M. Dalla Costa (1975) argued that in order to view women's exploitation as the basis for the building up of class exploitation, we have to consider the social importance of housework and its practical necessity for Capital (Hartmann, 1979:6), while N. Hartsock argued for a reconsidering of the category of class through a gender lens.

Major works such as H. Hartmann's *The unhappy marriage of Marxism and Feminism* (1971) introduced the idea of a 'dual system theory' stressing the argument that capitalism and patriarchy are two distinct but intertwined systems of social relations. As she explains, the economic production (what Marxists used to view as modes of production) and the production of people in the sphere of sex/ gender are determining together what F. Engels called, 'the social organization of a certain historical time and country' (Hartmann, 1971:10). Accordingly, the whole society can be understood if the two kinds of production and reproduction, of people and things, are considered. She explains that it is impossible for 'pure' capitalism or 'pure' patriarchy to exist, as they have to co-exist in order for each one of the both systems to exist at all, in a formation that Z. Eisenstein (1979) calls 'capitalist patriarchy'.

1.1 Theorizing Gender: From Structures to Agency

A theoretical turn towards the focus of agency within the systems of gender relations is the theory that provides a general analysis of social interaction (Connell, 1987:48). The basic idea is that through socialization into certain (mostly established and reproduced) female and male roles, individuals actively build their 'womanhood' or 'manhood'. Often these roles meet social expectations and are promoted by media images and repeated by individuals in an almost ritualized way, as B. Friedan described in her *Feminine Mystique* (1963). Sex role theory tries to give an alternative to the central issue of connecting social structure and human agency by introducing the individuals into the social structures. However, what is actually achieved is an accounting of differences between the sexes rather than a revealing of the relations between them. Furthermore, the notion of 'role' proves problematic to define. It imposes both voluntarism and trapped reaction towards models of femininity and masculinity. The individuals have the agency to reproduce existing models or not or they cannot but adopt the existing models. In the sex role theory the notion of structure has been replaced by the category of sex, which is biologically determined. Inevitably, the discussion of sex roles leads to accounting of sex role differences that reproduce the binaries of man/woman, male/female. Above all, the concept of power between the roles is absent, as male roles and female roles are treated equally. The whole role paradigm falls back to creation of 'normativities', describing male or female roles, what is supposed to be or what is mostly observed in society. This, on the other hand, can give an informative insight into powerful discourses that inform the constructions of femininity and masculinity. Sex role theory cannot give attention to social institutions and social structures, nor can it adequately describe the power relations within them.

In contrast to sex role theory that focuses on individualism, there are other theories that give a broader picture of gender relations on a world scale. The main notions are power and conflict of interests, as in S. Firestone's (1971) concept of 'sex class', which derived from Marxian analysis. The relation of direct domination is central in theories that investigate the relations between categories, such as in M. Daly's theory of global patriarchy. However, the theorization of phenomena as linked to gender categories, such as the environmental problems derived from masculinity (where masculinity is seen as environmentally destructive) misses the hegemonic arrangement of certain kinds of masculinity that form certain social arrangements and does not give causal explanations of the construction of this kind of masculinity.

In this theoretical framework it is possible to introduce further categories other than gender, such as class, race, ethnicity, and to show their cross-classifications. But as Connell points out, 'the logical cross-classification does not correspond in any simple way to the constitution of a social interest' (Connell, 1987:60).

Theories based on practice focus on what people do as they constitute social relations based on gender, as well as other categories. They try to give an explanatory framework of how gender relations are structured and organized as a condition of related practices (*Ibid*, 63). Within certain historical frameworks, it becomes possible to trace the dominance and hegemony of certain social interests. So, femininity and masculinity as structures that form gender subjectivities have to be seen as historically mutable (*Ibid*).

1.2 Between Structures and Relations: Gendered Subjectivities

The real material conditions of men and women are as different, among certain generations and social classes, as the social meanings that define the different genders. The differentiated evaluation of 'male' and 'female' in all the domains of social life refers to power relations that determine the gender relations (Pantelidou- Malouta, 1992:10). These are processes that give a particular content and meaning to different social categories, by defining the limits and distances between them and creating a dynamic in which different interests are influencing identity and organizing action. These processes are defining 'gender', and we can trace them on three levels. On the representational level, we have to consider the differentiated shaping of genders in their cultural definitions as having developed historically in new directions alongside the formation of notions of 'masculinity' and 'femininity'. These notions are always determined by the gender relations within a certain historical context and accordingly inform the particular constructions of femininity and masculinity, so that categories of men and women are constantly (re)defined on a collective and individual level. Within these general categories, many conflicting interests with material bases in unequal relations of power and resources are expressed, though the general tendency is the repetitive constitution of these categories by individuals and groups. Moments of resistance and breaks in the cyclical process of reproduction lead to collective social processes that initiate historical action (Connell, 1987:139). The conflict of interests forms a hierarchical ordering of general categories and of relationships between institutions, generating hegemonies. On a structural level, interests define the access to institutional resources that bear on gender relations and form the organizational character of institutions. Here we have to consider also the development of the division of labor, domination and the forms of ideological legitimization (Haug, 2005:288).

So, gender is an active process that links social practices and the structures of the practices in certain ways around organizing social life (Connell, 1987:140). This becomes obvious when we speak of 'gendered subjectivities'. The organization of the structures of the practices happens in a 'cyclical' way that contains the notion of repetition, reproduction and parallel development in history and leads to the constitution of institutions. It is important, too, to stress the fact that the institutionalization of gender is linked to the systemic reproduction of cyclical practices that constitute it (*Ibid*, 141).

1.3 What Are Masculinities Studies about?

When doing sociological research on gender, it is necessary to set the theoretical framework of the analysis, which will become the theoretical explanation of the empirical phenomena. The perspective from which we view gender is determining for the character of the analysis. Focusing on social structures, gender serves as a social-structural category. If the analysis is set within the theoretical framework of interactive constructivism, then gender is analysed as produced interactively. Within the framework of 'discourse de-constructivism', gender is viewed as a categorizing principle on the level of meanings. These perspectives are often combined and intertwined and serve to give answers to the central questions of sociological research on gender. Which social structures set the framework of phenomena, such as gender inequality and the practices resulting from them? Which identities, possibilities and limitations appear through interactions of individuals within the above social framework and how are these phenomena and processes reflected on the level of symbolic representations? Each question can be answered through all three theoretical perspectives. While the structure oriented sociological analysis aims at a social critique and demands the abolition of all social inequalities, the interactive constructivist perspective focuses on the individual level and tries to reconstruct identity concepts and processes empirically. In contrast, the discourse orientated de-constructivist perspective moves on the level of theories that are parts of discourses, institutionalized and regulated, and the frameworks that enable their development within and above social structures. These discourses produce not only meanings but also (re)produce the social reality, and so they have a strong performative character (Degele, 2008:18). All these perspectives serve for the building up of theories that enable a meaningful analysis of empirical data. In short we can say that according to the different theoretical stands, gender takes a different meaning, remaining a fluid and ever-developing notion: gender as social category, gender as doing gender (interaction), gender as discourse and narration, gender as history.

Still, gender remains a vague notion that gets a different meaning according to different theoretical and empirical analyses based on a variety of perspectives. This poses an opportunity to define some certain common issues that are almost always included in analyses of gender:

'Gender denotes a hierarchical division between women and men embedded in both social institutions and social practices. Gender is thus a social structural phenomenon but it is also produced, negotiated and sustained at the level of everyday interaction.' (Jackson; Scott, 2009:1-2). Apart from that, feminist and gender theoretical analysis agrees that sex (our 'maleness' or 'femaleness', the biological basis of gender differentiation) causes gender (culturally ascribed notions about femininity and masculinity) (Stanley, 2003:31). A very important aspect of the character of the notion of gender is what J. Butler (Butler, 1990:13) states in the *Gender Trouble*: 'Gender has not an essential basis; there is no original 'authentic' femininity or masculinity located in male and female bodies or in our inner selves', further establishing the independence of gender from sex, a core idea of feminist theory.

This work views gender mostly as the primary way of signifying and legitimizing power relations (Scott, 1997:309). As such, gender constructs social relations and gives meaning to difference among individuals. Through this perspective, gender is transformed from an object of study to a political and epistemological position that marks the location of the subject under analysis (for example, masculinity constructions in political youth organizations) within the empirical reality of politics. In this way, gender serves as a tool to problematize power differentials, social inequalities and hegemonic discourses based on sex/gender division, the priority of sex over gender, established social gender norms (for example, heteronormativity), popular gender imaginaries, social practices, institutional practices and discourses, and furthermore it critiques political structures that are intensifying rather than soothing social and political inequalities based on gender and on its intersections with class, ethnicity, age, sexuality etc.

This work takes elements from the three theoretical and methodological perspectives mentioned above, trying to analyse the construction of masculine subjectivities on three levels. First, on the representational level, there is an attempt to reveal the connection of dominant political ideologies and hegemonic masculinities, the negotiations, alterations, interruptions and subversions within, in between and outside them. Second, on the identity/subjectivity level, the focus is on the members of political youth organizations and the formation of their masculinities within this context through the analysis of discourses on ideology, power, violence, utopia, subjectivity and gender relations. Third, an analytical approach to the structural/organizational level will reveal the connection between organizational practices that (re)form and intensify the gendered character of organizations and the gender identities of the members.

Through this analytical model, this work aims to criticize the male domination and much more the 'masculinization' that concerns institutions and which (re)produces power relations based on gendered symbolic relations, gendered practices and gender subjectivity formations. In this respect, it is assumed that masculinities formed within political organizations are informative about general gender relations and therefore a strong analytical and empirical tool for research on masculinities and politics.

When doing sociological research on men, the subject under analysis is actually gender relations. The sociological framework of such research is set by various gender configurations and the notion of 'man'. Although men's studies move theoretically and analytically around established binaries, such as man/woman, the pluralities and relationalities of gender, when set under critical light they reveal a commonality between gender and queer studies. Masculinities are spoken of and not masculinity (Connell, 2005). Masculinity is first and foremost defined by its relation and distinction to and from the feminine. In this context, masculinity is always discussed in relation to femininity, and these notions refer to concepts and not individual persons. We can think about masculinity without talking about men and the same is valid for femininity. Various masculinity constructions are defined in opposition and relation to other masculinities and femininities within a complex network of class and race positions (Schössler, 2008:137), as well as further categories like age, political ideology, etc.

1.3.1 History of Research on Masculinity

Research on masculinity was the outcome of an epistemological turn to the research of gender. In the framework of gender studies, men have been researched as gendered subjects, constructed through social relations, practices, symbols and representations. Through this perspective the research on masculinity is not as much a distinctive field as an analytical prism through which somebody can examine issues that are inscribed in the fields of anthropology, history, sociology, etc. Above all, all research on masculinities refers to the research on gender and sexuality. Gender and masculinities are linked by looking at masculinity as a relational phenomenon in the context of gender relations and analysing it as a structuring principle of social constellations (Bereswill; Meuser; Scholz, 2007). The turn of the sociological interest to the different formations of gendered subjects and the negotiation of gendered relations was enforced by the rise of gender as an analytical tool for sociological research.

In the last decades, research on masculinity has focused on the multiple ways of being a man, and this multiplicity of masculinity has been a main focus in the theoretical aftermath of sex role theory and diverse notions of patriarchy (Connell, 2000, 2002; Whitehead, 2002). Masculinity came to be an issue of merely individual character, in contrast to the Marxist perspectives on gender that were concerned primarily with power (Eichler, 1980 in Mellström, 2007:244).The pluralizing of masculinity responded to the psychological determinism of some early feminist works where men are depicted as one-sided and one-dimensional (Chodorow, 1978). Eventually, there was a turn towards differentiation and difference of gender configurations during the 1980s. Masculinity studies and critical men's studies, with concepts such as hegemonic masculinity, take their starting point in investigating subordinated gender forms (not only women) and also take into consideration the expressed desires of men to go beyond heteronormative expressions of sexuality (Connell, 1993). The sexual politics of the gay and lesbian activism have been of immense importance to the research on masculine gender configurations (Mellström, 2007:243).

Although anthropologists as well as sociologists have shown soon enough of an interest to examine sexual practices and behaviors in many different societies, this attempt was restrained for a long period by the collection of empirical facts around phenomena which they characterised as 'sexual'. However, through this approach sexuality as an universal phenomenon unrelated to various aspects of social life continued to be generally accepted by researchers. The first research attempts on sexuality have been influenced by the theory of social construction, very dominant in the 1970s.

The questioning of the natural character of sexual behavior has as an outcome the switch of interest on the multiple ways sexuality is related to different socio-economic, political, cultural and embodied desires. Under the influence of queer studies, gender itself was seen as a result of performance according to certain obligatory rules of heterosexuality.

The men's studies define masculinity as gender and as a paradoxical narrative construct that is determined through factors such as femininity, class, ethnicity, religion, age, etc. Masculinity is a developing and ever-changing analytical model. Men's studies focus on issues such as power, working relations within a global world, men's associations, military, family and state institutions that bring the attention of gender research to public processes. Parallel to that, it, like queer studies, turns away from the binding world of heterosexuality and brings into the picture alternative, marginalized and transgressing gendered subjectivities (Schößler, 2008:142).

In the history of the research on men, there are two major frameworks that set the context of research analysis, the socio-psychological gender roles theory and the feminist critique on patriarchy. In the analytical context informed by the male sex role, in focus was the process of socialization into certain male gender roles and the consequences of the recent changes in gender relations for men (Pleck, 1987). One of the new points was that through the rigid gender roles, the socialization of men was suppressed, pointing to the impact of male sex roles on the male psyche.

The theory of socialization into gender roles (Harrison, 1978) has introduced a linkage between the notions of sex difference and social role, which in the 1950s suggested that gender is not a biologically related characteristic but an outcome of social conditions, introducing the metaphor of society as a theatrical scene and the idea of human life and action as theatrical roles. The notion of role, referring to social behaviors, starts by connecting the idea of a certain position within a social structure and the actions that are expressed by the occupier of that position. So, the idea that masculinity translates to an internalized male role was intended to include an idea of change. As the gendered roles are informed by and express social realities, so could they change through certain political and social practices, something that would presuppose that institutions that promote and enable socialization would change orientation and men would claim different roles.

The contribution of the theories of socialization according to different gendered roles was that they underlined the fact that gendered differences are not an outcome of only biological factors but result from the socialization within institutions that are dominating and suppressing for both genders (Pleck, 1981). The weak point is that it gave to the process of 'engendering' a mechanistic character, suggesting the subjects as passive receivers of their gendered socialization and not as active subjects that participate in the construction of their gendered subjectivity. It failed to acknowledge that subjects are able to manage the social and institutional orders they receive, forming the given social system of ideas and beliefs.

Most importantly, the theory of gender roles does not take into consideration the processes of negotiation, resistance, rejection and re-consideration that take place during the construction of gendered identities. The gendered subjects express and create forms of masculinity and femininity, as they are formed by them in a dialectical process. The subjects try mostly to balance the social orders and their desires, designing what they can actually be.

The theories of gender roles have been criticized as reproducing gender stereotypes and as failing to include and discuss critically issues of power and as simply explaining subordination as a conflict between the role and the self (Carrigan et al, 1985; Kimmel, 1987; Connell, 1995; Segal, 1997).

From here develops the second theoretical context of masculinity studies, the feminist critique, which by focusing on the notion of power in the gender relations system introduces a critique of domination and subordination in society and tries to show the connection between difference (between men and women, men and men, women and women) and hierarchy.

In an influential work for men's studies, The *Gender of Oppression* (1987), Hearn tries to see patriarchy and capitalism as two interconnected systems of subordination. He underlines that the oppressive power of patriarchy is addressed towards men as well as women and that relations of domination affect women, children, and young people as well as certain categories of men (Hearn; Collinson, 1994:98). The patriarchal hegemony of men is grounded in the exploitation of women's labor force. So, men are – willingly or unwillingly- the gender of oppression. In his analysis, Hearn takes in consideration the consequences for men of the hegemonic relations in organized gender relations systems. He tries to set the consequences of patriarchy for men in a socio-theoretical framework, not by prioritizing the troubles of men but by revealing the power relations that constitute the male gender through its supremacy. This supremacy is analysed by Hearn as system related and as a dynamic that is independent from the intentions of male actors (Hearn, 1987).

1.3.2 Hegemonic Masculinities: a Useful Tool for Analysing Relations of Power

Following the critique on patriarchy, the analysis of Carrigan, Connell and Lee (1985) on the concept of 'hegemonic masculinity' introduces a culture-theoretical perspective that depicts thoroughly the different levels of hierarchization that structure the relations among men. Based on the definition of 'hegemony' by Gramsci, Connell (1987; 1995) sees the male dominance not so much in the subordination through use of violence (symbolic or real) but through the general acceptance of certain cultural values and norms by men and women.

The concept of 'hegemony', deriving from Gramsci's analysis of class relations, refers to the cultural dynamic by which a group claims and sustains a leading position in social life. At any given time, one form of masculinity rather than others is culturally exalted. 'Hegemonic masculinity' can be defined as the configuration of gender practice which embodies the currently accepted answer to the problem of the legitimacy of patriarchy, which guarantees (or is taken to guarantee) the dominant position of men and the subordination of women (Connell, 1995:77).

Similar to the way dominant ideologies work, 'hegemonic masculinity' is not a simple model of cultural control, but is strongly related to the dynamics of structural change and is connected with the mobilization of whole classes (Connell; Messerschmidt, 2005:831). The masculine dominance has a two-folded character, a hetero-social (the dominance of men on women, as social groups) and a homo-social which describes the hegemonic structures within different expressions of masculinity. This shows the double character of hegemonic masculinity as a relational category: it stands in relation to subordinated femininity and in relation to non-hegemonic masculinities. Connell distinguishes here between subordinated, complicit and marginalized masculinities. Although few men fulfil the ideal of hegemonic masculinity, this serves as an orientating model of masculine practices and simultaneously as a generational principle of masculinity (Meuser; Scholz, 2005 in Meuser; Scholz, 2007:11). Connell notes: "Hegemonic masculinity' is always constructed in relation to various subordinated masculinities as well as in relation to women' (Connell, 1987:183). 'Hegemonic masculinity' describes a configuration of gender practices, which guarantees the dominant position of men within the gender relations system. Connell's analysis touches the questions of how the relations are interconnected and how the power and hegemonic relations are related to the hetero-social and homo-social dimensions. These questions open a discussion around the theoretical concepts of complex social inequalities that are related to the categories of race, class and gender (Connell; Messerschmidt, 2005) and that create the crossing of the 'axes of difference' (Knapp, 2005 in Bereswill, 2007:11).

The hegemony of each dominant model of masculinity is based on the notions of power and violence. As Connell clarifies, violence does not directly refer to force, but rather to the forms of economic, political or ideological violence that back up dominant discourses such as 'law', 'order' and 'citizen'. Without the co-operation of other patterns, models and groups, the violent and dominant status of hegemonic masculinity cannot be sustained. The 'interplay' suggests an equilibrium of forces that presupposes the insertion of as many different models of masculinity as possible and their subordination to the hegemonic pattern of masculinity. The different patterns of subordinated masculinity in their plurality and differentiation often rather sustain than endanger the hegemonic pattern of masculinity, making the connections to each other and to it more complex and deep. Hegemonic masculinity as a pattern, a construction model and a gender order feeds itself with as many as possible subordinated, marginalized and cooperative models of masculinity and femininity. That is why often hegemonic masculinity is open to contradicting practices, such as misogyny and heterosexual attraction, tolerance towards homosexual relations and to violence. Mostly hegemonic masculinity is heterosexual, with close connection to the institution of marriage, and so marginalized masculinities are homosexual (Connell, 1987: 186). A considerable amount of cultural ideals form the image of hegemonic masculinity that may correspond to the material and actual conditions of the social, economic, and political life of certain (very few) dominant social groups that the rest of society don't necessarily fulfil and incorporate. As Connell describes: 'The public face of hegemonic masculinity is not necessarily what powerful men are, but what sustains their power and what large numbers of men are motivated to support' (*Ibid*,185).

The ideological aspect of hegemonic masculinity is what actually sustains its dominance as it informs most the dominant discourses that have to do with power and violence. According to Connell, the reason that most men 'agree' to cooperate with the dominant groups of the powerful and sustain hegemonic masculinity without really living it is that they stand to benefit from the subordination of women, and this ascendancy is culturally expressed by hegemonic masculinity and institutionalized by practices that maintain both women's subordination and hegemonic masculinity (*Ibid*). Models of femininity are informed by and correspond with patterns of hegemonic masculinity. Accordingly, there are models of emphasized femininities, feminine masculinities, resisting femininities, etc. that interact at the ideological level but do not really correspond with the material lives of most women. All forms of femininity are constructed based on their subordination to masculinities. There is no model of femininity that has an equal role and function to the hegemonic masculinity. That leaves the social power concentrated in the hands of men (although many women support and profit indirectly from this concentration of power). On the other hand, violence and negation among different patterns of femininity is not thematicized in femininity generally, as it is with hegemonic masculinity and other forms of masculinity (*Ibid*, 187).

The concept of hegemony is based on the notion of ideology, and masculinity becomes an ideological structure, a concept that does not exist in opposition to the materiality of life but stresses how gender as an ideological structure mobilises and reproduces thoughts, morals, cultures and practices. This hegemonic process requires access to and combination with the whole of the superstructures.

This identification of the different structures in which hegemony operates is compatible with the notion of ideology. There are different theories within Marxian analysis about ideology and hegemony. Based on two very known 'aphorisms' of Marx, one in Preface (Marx 1959/1975), 'social being determines consciousness', and the other in the German Ideology (Marx; Engels, 1845/1970): 'the economic structure, the real foundation determines 'a legal and political superstructure', such that the ideas of 'the ruling class are in every epoch the ruling ideas', the notion of hegemony from this perspective embodies both material and intellectual force. It is, however, concentrated on social formation rather than activities of particular classes. A. Gramsci's (1971) concept of hegemony stresses the operation of power and ideology in the cultural and ideological realm. Hegemony encompasses the range of social arenas – material economic, political, cultural, discursive – rather than prioritizing the economic. In contemporary critical analyses of men and masculinities, the notion of hegemony is very central and becomes widened and thus has a broader range of analytical use. In Donaldson (1993:45), this construction is used in order to show the ways in which the ruling class establishes and maintains its domination.

Many feminist critical works view gender as a hegemonic ideological structure (Grant, 1993; Irigaray, 1991) that creates two major divisions of 'mythical' genders, organized hierarchically. The ideology of (the two) gender(s) is being reproduced and reinforced through a system of rules and practices in all institutional sites and all aspects of life.

Drawing from Althusser, ideology is 'a representation of the imaginary relationship of individuals to their real conditions of existence' (Althusser, 1971:162). Definitively, ideology has a material existence and its material forms 'exist in an apparatus and its practice or practices' (*Ibid*, 166).

Turning to gender, Hearn stresses the relationship between material practices and gender as ideology, suggesting the perception of ideology as material practice (Hearn, 1991: 240). Irigaray (1991) also views gender as ideology, describing the feminine and masculine as imaginary and symbolic processes that regulate the workings of a society and culture.

Constitutive structure of all ideologies is the category of the subject. As Althusser writes, 'there is no ideology except by the subject and for the subjects. Meaning, there is no ideology except for concrete subjects, and this destination for ideology is only made possible by the subject' (Althusser, 1971:182). This understanding of ideology as directly linked to the subject in combination with the ahistorical perception of ideology – that 'ideology has no history' (*Ibid*, 161) – is an attempt to see ideology not as a cause of historical processes but as the starting point of history, trying in this way to express a critique of historically established structures of domination that seem ever-present. From this starting point, the subject is both an agent and a receiver of ideology, as ideology cannot exist out of the frame of interpellation: 'ideology interpellates individuals as subjects' (*Ibid*, 169).

The subject that is the constitutive category for all ideologies and is located at the starting point of history forms ideology according to other related categories such as gender, class and ethnicity. Standpoint theory has particularly stressed the importance of the point where the subject is located as a forming criterion for the way subjects 'see the world'. This positionality is also connected to the identity of the subject (as discussed above).

By conceptualizing gender as an ideological structure, we can then follow how gender constitutes subjects 'in its own image' (Grant, 1993:161) and is sustained and reproduced by practices. Consequently, 'we know the world as ideologically constructing and ideologically sustaining gendered subjects' (*Ibid*, 162).

The hegemonic character of gender as ideology leads to the total domination of individuals, and, paradoxically, the complete acceptance of the dominant gender system appears consensual. That explains how hegemonic masculinity becomes gradually but almost completely the general established gender order and how sites of resistance appear immediately deviant.

Connell connects the notion of power with this concept of authority, which is legitimate power, as the main axis of the power structure of gender (Connell, 1987:109). The power of men and the authority of masculinity are concentrated in institutions and established groups, for example in military, in state apparatuses, etc. Connell describes this phenomenon as a manifestation of 'hegemonic masculinity', adding gender to the discussions of power relations based on divisions of class and race. Hegemonic masculinity is a justifying ideology based on the patriarchal order and the subordination of women that requires and reproduces a gender-based hierarchy among men. This hierarchy has three elements: hegemonic masculinity, conservative masculinities (complicit in the collective but moderate in its manifestations) and subordinated ones (*Ibid*, 110) that develop within macro and micro levels of relations of power *(Ibid*, 111).

Remaining within the Marxist theoretical framework, the use of the notion of hegemony is connected inevitably with modes of production and reproduction and the gendered division of labor, and in this way the categories of class and gender intersect and provide an analytical framework that can be used to understand the multiple structures of inequality and oppression. As mentioned before, the concept of the division of labor is primarily linked with the 'capitalist mode of production' that in Marxist theory is seen as a production system fundamentally defined by class relations. Feminist theory has adequately argued that gender divisions are a central feature of production (*Ibid*, 103). Game and Pringle have shown that gender divisions are essential characteristics of the capitalist system and are as fundamental as class divisions. In an attempt to revise the socialist analysis of capitalism, feminist critique, along with the analysis of the Third World radical movements that theorize capitalism as a system of global inequality and imperialism (*Ibid*), view capitalism as partly constituted of the opportunities for power and profit created by gender relations (*Ibid*,104). This gendered character of the capitalist system is based on the gendered logic of accumulation of resources and on what Connell describes as the 'political economy of masculinity' (*Ibid*, 106), which involves significant practices that constitute masculinity as an economic resource. As the author explains, a hegemonic pattern of masculinity that promotes solidarity among men is used as an economic as well as a cultural force. These structural features of capitalism operate on the basis of power. Power is an underlying structure of gender relations that can be traced in personal interactions but also at the institutional and ideological levels. The structure of power accordingly forms social relations and practices. Power can be materialized by creating inequalities as a matter of lack of resources, unequal division of labor or division of decisions at home or within an institution, and it can broker ideological control over groups of people, inside institutions and in the whole society. Through hegemony[2], groups of people, usually men, are empowered in gender relations, but their practices produce their own limits. Power has a dual character: it is a structure, an object of practice, but also becomes its condition.

Connell sees all these practices and their underlying structures that determine gender relations not as unified elements of a system but as elements of a historical composition, a matter of a real historical process of interaction and group formation (Connell, 1978:116). He underlines the idea that structures and practices are 'the outcome of strategy in the historical

---

[2] According to Connell's definition, hegemony expresses the ability to impose a set of terms in which events are understood, issues are discussed, ideas and ideals are formulated asserting hegemony, which is essential part of social power (Connell, 1987:109)).

process of group formation and interaction' (*Ibid*, 117). This strategy often shows a degree of systematicity that reflects the dominance of a group whose interests are served by a particular gender role (*Ibid*, 117). A culturally idealized form, it is both a personal and a collective project, as is the common sense ideas about breadwinning and manhood. It is exclusive, internally and hierarchically differentiated, pseudo-natural and socially sustained. While centrally connected with the institutions of male dominance, not all men practice it, though most benefit from it. Although cross-class, it often excludes working-class and black men. It is a lived experience, and an economic and cultural force, and dependent on social arrangements.

1.3.3 Critique of Hegemonic Masculinity and the Issue of Agency and Identity

In his critique of the concept of hegemonic masculinity, R. Howson (2006; 2008; 2009) concentrates on the existing contradictions between representations and practices, between what men think as masculine and what they actually do. In an effort to understand the conditions of social life framed by hegemony, the author stresses his attention on the antagonisms (what is being done and what should be done) and the dislocations that hegemony combines within a given gender order. At this point, Hearn underlines that in analyses of gender relations of power, hegemonic masculinity can only give a partial understanding of what men think and do and that we have to engage with men rather than stay on the level of masculinity as an ideal. By 'ignoring' men, we fail to underline 'the ambiguity and subtlety, even contradiction, in the self-construction of masculinity and the masculine, hegemonic or not' (Hearn, 2004:59). And he adds, 'it is time to go back from masculinity to men, to examine the hegemony of men and about men'. (Hearn, 2004). In this way, Hearn is stressing the matter of agency within the matrix of structures, placing the topic of men and masculinity within a structure-agency model, a classical critical issue in philosophy and sociology.

Following the Marxist tradition and its reflections in the critique of socialist feminist theory, which concentrates on the core concepts of oppression and domination as universal phenomena, the turn from masculinity to men introduces the notion of difference, embedded in class, history and culture, as well as race, ethnicity, age, and (dis)ability. The establishment of the term masculinities already points to the historicity of the term masculinity but obscures the socially constructed experiences of individuals. As domination, oppression and power relations become structures with a material base, all women (and some men) are oppressed by a gender system of domination that may vary according to the mode of production. What this theoretical line does not explain is how men and women across classes and alongside different economic, political and social interests comply with the general ideal of hegemonic masculinity within different gender regimes. An analysis of hegemonic masculinity (Connell, 1995, 2000, 2005; Hearn, 2004; Howson, 2006, 2009; Donaldson, 1993) can give an answer to this question, as well as to relevant questions such as how hegemonic masculine practices become legitimate and consequently produce homogeneity and stability across particular and universal identities.

Following the line of Hearn and Howson in this work, the discussion focuses on political masculinities trying to put men/women in the context of the certain social relations that take the form of gendered power relations within political youth organizations. In this framework, we cannot say how men generally are and put their thinking about masculinity into patterns, but we can draw a clear connection between political masculinities and private or working masculinities. The general relations of domination, oppression and power (not only those based on gender but also on class, ethnicity and age distinctions) are reflected in the social relations developed in the certain institutional context of the political youth organizations and the (social, organizational) relations of this context influence again the ways men think/do/relate, also outside of the political youth group, at home, the workplace, etc. Of course, each institutional context creates its own culture that only partially affects the ways of thinking and doing of the people inside it, but still, the masculinities inside political youth organizations have a share in the general hegemonic masculine order. In order, however, to avoid 'fixed' patterns of masculinities, trying to fit people in them for the purpose of proving a kind of (non) existing masculine hegemony, we have to look at how political identities are constructed and how power is operationalized within the context of political youth organizations.

In *Challenging Hegemonic Masculinity* (Howson, 2006), it is claimed that hegemony cannot be simply expressed as domination, because nothing distinguishes it then from concepts such as patriarchy. Howson criticizes how on one hand, hegemonic masculinity is constructed in total asymmetry to femininity and other forms of masculinity, and on the other hand, as a 'state of play' and kind of consensus that finally becomes a 'cultural ideal' (Connell, 1987:183-188). Important for Howson is that hegemonic masculinities actually are open to historical change and this change, together with social, economic, political and cultural changes, creates dislocations between hegemonic masculinities and men, between identities and practice, between the symbolic and the material.

In the context of political youth organizations, the gendered subjects themselves, in the process of re-constructing their personal and collective forms of masculinities, have pointed to new forms of hegemonic masculinities that bare some elements of past hegemonic models but entail oppositions to old patterns and enclose contradictions with other forms of contemporary masculinities.

How do we begin to explain this complicity as well as this simultaneous disengagement from hegemonic forms and patterns of masculinity? Howson, similar to Hearn, proposes identity as a starting point. Combining Hegelian thought, Marxist analysis and post-structuralist theoretical lines, Howson continues his critical analysis of hegemonic masculinity by stressing the fact that identity is constructed upon the negation of the negation. Identity is often based on imitations but more so on negations (or oppositions) of certain representations, ideas and is most definitely constructed by the real conditions of life. Masculine subjectivities follow the same line of construction. Hence, hegemonic masculinities do not only exist as an opposition within the materially of the base of social life but work to secure their prolonged existence and do so via mobilizing thoughts, morals and culture. This hegemonic process requires access to the whole of the superstructures (Howson, 2009:13). The hegemonic signification presents authority as an 'ethico-political reality' (*Ibid*, 17). Hegemonic principles determine configurations, practices and relationships that become legitimate and normative, almost natural. These principles 'represent desires, interests and values that the hegemonic is able to extend into social life and thereby expand the hegemony' (*Ibid*, 17). Hegemonic principles as mentioned before are always a historical product and imposed by material and real social relations, practices and consciousness (formed by relative ideologies), never being determined but always 'overdetermined' (Althusser, 1969:97-101; Mouffe, 1985:97-105). Central hegemonic principles in the Western world, even nowadays, continue to be heterosexuality, breadwinning, aggression, involving competitiveness, toughness, authoritarianism, misogyny, physical and verbal violence (Howson, 2006:73). Some of these principles are characteristic elements of political hegemonic masculinities.

However, while there is not only one type of hegemonic masculinity, this one is of the dominative masculinity, ever present in most gender regimes. 'Aspirational masculinity' (*Ibid*, 31) constructs 'a progressive, moral and intellectual hegemonic force' (*Ibid*, 17) that is developed by some certain groups that Howson calls, following Gramsci, 'organic intellectuals' by engaging the people in a moral and intellectual way rather than in a violent and forced way. Ironically, aspirational hegemony promotes consensus and gives recognition to the heterogeneity of the people.

Howson points, however, to the impossible totality created by any kind of hegemony and, in this case, the hegemony of masculinity. As he writes, no gender order is ever able to complete itself because there are always antagonisms and therefore dislocations that in turn limit the real universality of any identity. Masculinity has been shown to represent gender as a whole, as a representation of an ideal or an ideology, and, as such, has to represent the hegemonic principles of the hegemony of men as capable of becoming universal principles. Other gender identities align not so much their practice but their aspiration in order to become hegemonic (Howson, 2009:19). So, hegemonic masculinity achieves the appearance of homogeneity and stability by producing at best complicity and at worst ambivalence to its hegemonic principles. Hegemonic as the empty signifier of gender does not set out the practices that men and women achieve but, rather, what men and women aspire to within a certain historical hegemony (*Ibid*, 21).

A lot of constructive critique has been done on the concept of hegemonic masculinities in an attempt to expand its analytical and epistemological use rather than abandon or dismiss it. H. Brod (1994) has criticized the one-sided character of the concept, as it looks only at men and the relations between them. He proposes, therefore, a consistently relational approach to gender, suggesting that 'masculinity' means primarily a way that men position (relationally) themselves through practices.

S. Whitehead (2002) stresses the weakness of the concept to explain how a minority of heterosexual men legitimate and reproduce their dominance over women and other men. As the author argues, the concept results 'in obfuscation, in the conflation of fluid masculinities with overarching structure and, ultimately, in 'abstract' structural dynamics' (Whitehead, 2002:93-94). Whitehead suggests that rather than concentrating on structures, it is better to focus on discourse as the means by which men come to know themselves and 'practice identity work' (*Ibid*).

L. Archer (2001) tries to show, with his work on identity talk, taking as empirical examples young Muslims in Britain, the construction of masculinities in discourse. He, however, stresses the point that gender relations are also constituted through non-discursive practices, including wage labor, violence, sexuality and domestic labor, as well as routinized actions.

Other authors have concentrated on the possibility of change in gender relations. D. Demetriou (2001) introduces the notion of dialectical pragmatism that captures the influence that various forms of masculinities have on each other, suggesting that hegemonic masculine patterns may change to a more positive direction by incorporating elements from others.

In a recent review of the concept, Connell; Messerschmidt (2005) suggest a more holistic understanding of gender hierarchy, recognizing the agency of subordinated groups. They underline that in a given gender order, gender relations are in tension with each other. The hegemonic model that appears in a certain historical time stabilizes the tensions and secures the establishment of a patriarchal order, often by reconstituting it in new conditions.

In an analytical turn to agency, critical studies on men and masculinities are concerned with men's practices and how these practices have a forming role at an individual or collective level on the general gender order, the hegemonic condition (Connell, 1995) or discursive framework (Whitehead, 2002). While men's practices appear within the framework of powerful ideological regimes shaped by economic, political, social and cultural structures that are central to their lives and their experiences, by responding, adopting, and rejecting these gendered practices men are actually practicing masculinity and simultaneously contributing to the defining of a collective that is men.

Following this path of defining personality as expressed through personal and collective practices, Connell (1995) re-discusses in *Masculinities* hegemonic masculinity, reaffirming the link between the Gramscian analysis of economic class relations through the operation of cultural dynamics (Whitehead, 2007:423). The individual and collective practices of masculinities are now defined rather as 'the configuration of gender practice which embodies the currently accepted answer to the problem of patriarchy, which guarantees or is taken to guarantee the dominant position of men and the subordination of women' (Connell, 1995:77).

In *Gender & Power* (1987), personality was defined as a field where the dynamics of social relations meet, shaped by social interests, institutions and the mobilization of power (Connell, 1987:229). In *Masculinities* (1995, 2005), the author gives more agency to the gendered subjects that individually and collectively actively form, through their practices and discourses, the notion of men and masculinity up to a certain degree.

The shift from identity and agency towards a reformation of structures has been discussed a lot within feminist theoretical discourses. From a feminist theoretical perspective, there are various approaches to identity with regard to 'agency'. According to an essentialist perspective on identity politics, members of oppressed groups have agency through the interpretation of their experience of oppression. That implies, however, that all members of the group have a similar perception of the same experience, something that empirically cannot be true.

On this point, theorist S. Mohanty (2000) links identity to the real conditions of life but stresses the fact that it is not evident or homogeneous and that identity is grounded in the process of interpreting experience (Henze in Moya, 2000:236). Accordingly, agency becomes socially mediated. P. Moya theorizes full agency to individuals as they make sense of their experiences of oppression (Henze, 2000:237). According to realist theorizations of identity that imply a concept of structure and agency, 'individual agency' is defined as the opportunity for an oppressed person to represent and act for herself. But effective political agency towards liberation would prove ineffective in resisting structural apparatuses and institutions which enforce and sustain oppression (*Ibid*). This determined failure against structural oppression seems to be avoided only with collectivity, with individual agency facilitating the process of collectivity formation. It seems then that the resultant collective has greater potential for liberatory political transformation (*Ibid*).

Within a politically formed collective, members participate through their agency in a dialectically developing process, providing evidence that individual agency is necessary in order for an effective political collective to work on behalf of its members.

Individual and collective agency is based on experience and furthermore on the interpretation that agency is predicated on 'personally observing, encountering or undergoing a particular event or situation' (Moya in Henze, 2000:238). It is the theoretical interpretation of every single experience that forms individual identities and shapes the character and direction of agency. It becomes clear that different individuals have different agencies and so it is difficult to assume that people in apparently similar 'social locations' experience and understand their lives similarly.

For this reason, many feminist theorists distance themselves from the universal category of Woman[3] or experience and turn their attention to the

3 The same distance from universal categories applies in critical works on men, where the introduction of the term masculinities enables the differentiations among gendered subjects and the de-construction of the general category gender, as a stable and ahistorical dichotomy.

structure of gender itself, proposing a point of view of liberation from gender as the way to throw light on agency within and away from structures (primarily gender but also class, race, etc.).

The issue of agency introduced within Marxist theorizations the epistemological and methodological necessity of the standpoint. Marx acknowledged that a historical material theory could not talk about a 'universal Man', thus showing that the material category class became necessary. So, the proletariat constituted objectively a class, but not subjectively a revolutionary agent, so Lukács advised theorists and critics to adopt the proletarian standpoint (Grant, 1993:155). This Marxist theoretical problem is analogous to the feminist problem of the 'universal Woman'. Standpoint epistemology and methodology proved useful for the theorization of the oppression of women and led to critical analyses of men, too.

The analytical framework of standpoint theory has proved useful to some extent for this work. Further analysis follows later.

As for now, it is important to focus once more on gender as a central aspect of identity and to concentrate more on the construction of gender identity among young people since the discussion is about the construction of masculinities in youth organizations.

Masculinity *as an aspect of identity* is a notion that does not constitute a certain frame of rules of behavior, which applies to the male nature. It refers rather to a frame of discourses, negotiations that are realised in a dynamic framework of social and political life. The subjects perform their socially constructed masculinity in front of an audience, aiming for its acceptance and accordingly organizing its actions. With this performativity, the subject creates the poetic version of its masculinity, which is informed by the given cultural context and is not mechanistically constructed through a gendered socialization process (Politis, 2006:244). Young men occupy different positions within the multiple discourses and practices of masculinity, getting constructed and re-constructed as multiply positioned gendered subjects, possessing different and alternative ways of defining their gendered selves. This changing character of masculine identities argues for a 'nomadic male subjectivity'. This term was introduced by R. Braidotti (1994) to analyse the notion of female subjectivity. According to the theorist, subjectivity should be perceived as an autonomous and constantly changing and also internalized net of multiplicity and uniqueness (Politis 2006:246).

M. Herzfeld (Herzfeld, 1985:16) connects the 'poetics' with the notion of performance. Studying the construction of masculinity of inhabitants of the Greek island Crete, he suggests that 'to be a good man' is not as important as 'to be good at being a man' and concludes that the personal public performances are part of a theatrical competition with other men.

The term 'masculinities' in plural indicates a shift from the man's role to the men's roles in discussions on gender equality as well as in broader feminist theoretical discourses. It also signifies a turn towards a more complex picture of masculinity in gender scholarship, looking at men's unequal relations to men as well as men's relations to women (Mellström, 2007:245). Masculinities are used as analytical tools for a wide range of social phenomena (Connell, 1987, 1995, 2000). The constitution of masculinities – as well as femininities – happens on the level of certain individual settings, social groups or milieus as well as on the level of the whole society. On this broader level, we can follow the constitution of masculinities if we imagine a hierarchical ladder where an ordering of different but directly related patterns and models of masculinity takes place. This ordering happens in face to face relations, on the institutional level and on the representational level. The 'interplay' (Connell, 1987:183) of masculinities between one another is mostly influenced by their relationship to the hegemonic masculinity model that is dominant in a certain social, political, economic and cultural context at a certain historical moment. According to the hegemonic model of masculinity, the other models of masculinity and femininity are subordinated, marginalized or compliant. Both among masculinities and femininities are developed strategies of co-operation or resistance.

Talking about gender as an element of identity, we have to refer briefly to the issue of agency, especially in terms of masculinities. As Hearn (Hearn, 1987:96ff) has analysed, men have agency, meaning they are, first and foremost, agents of oppression. Furthermore, they respond differently, even contrary to or independently of the demands of structured relations. So, individual men undergo different agencies within dominant structured relations at different times and in different phases of their lives.

While being on the level of identity, we can focus more closely on the construction of gender identities of young people (teenagers and adults), since we will talk about masculinity construction in youth organizations.

Here again, we have to connect the broader, structural macro-level with the individual micro-level in order to understand the 'mechanisms' of gendered identity construction. In the case of youth organizations, the meso-level of the organizational structures play also an important role (see next chapters).

Children's and youngsters' gender development, although happening individually or in smaller groups (peer, school, sport clubs etc.), is embedded in a larger societal context. By adopting a social-structural approach, in order to consider how people's relative status and power in society shape their personal situations, it is able to address the constraints that these institutionalized roles impose on individuals' behavior. Together with gender, there are also other social-structural factors that influence the formation of subjectivity, such as ethnicity, race, class and sexual orientation. Feminist analysis that adopts a social-structural perspective emphasizes the impact of unequal gender relations of power, existing in social and political institutions, including in the labor market and the home (Leaper; Friedman in Grusec; Hastings, 2007:561). In general, socio-structural factors that influence the formation of gender identities include the division of labor and the prevalence of patriarchy in the larger society.

The socialization along the lines of certain gendered social-interaction styles and roles perpetuates traditional adult gender roles as well as power imbalances between men and women (Leaper, 2000). That is, men's dominant status in society and their task orientation are enacted and maintained through the use of self-assertive strategies, such as directive and instrumental communication. Conversely, women's relatively subordinate status, as well as their traditional role as caregiver, is enacted through the use of strategies, such as showing support and agreement (Leaper, 2000:148).

Group analysis has focused especially on communities of men that are formed by common organizational structures, like men's associations or studies on military, football clubs, political organizations, or artists' societies. Very often the character of these associations is defined by its radical opposition to everything soft and female (Sombart, 1996:141). The reference point in these groups is a strong idealism, the charisma of the leader and the relation of the members to it. Usually there is a strict hierarchical structure and a strong feeling of devotion to the collective (Widdig, 1997:236). This attitude can be observed in groups of both boys and adults.

Important here is to stress the impact of collective gender socialization according to given or dominant patterns in youth groups and organizations. At this case, gender construction is based on interaction.

Viewing gender socialization as a social-interactive process, we can borrow ideas from both social cognitive theory and socio-cultural theory. The main focus in this kind of analysis of gender is on children's social interactions as contexts for learning culture. Another important aspect is the repetition of particular behaviors as important influences. As they are repeated over and over again during the course of childhood, gender-typed practices contribute to the development of gender differences in expectations, values, preferences, etc. (Leaper; Friedman, 2007:562). Group socialization processes can have different degrees of impact on individuals' motives, depending on the status and power of one group relative to the other group (or groups). Consistent with the greater status and power traditionally accorded to males in society, boys are likely to initiate and maintain role and group boundaries. Partly for this reason, gender typing pressures tend to be more acute for boys than for girls. With regard to gender, masculine-stereotyped attributes (e.g. independence and assertiveness) tend to be valued more than feminine stereotyped attributes (e.g. nurturing and compassion) in highly male-dominated societies (Hofstede, 2000 in Leaper; Friedman, 2007:563). Although cross-gender-typed behavior can sometimes enhance a girl's status, it typically diminishes a boy's status (Leaper, 1994). Accordingly, cross-gender-typed behavior tends to me more common among girls than boys.

This social-interactive perspective, enriched with psychoanalytical and performative concepts, views masculinity as a masquerade and as doing gender. Masculinity becomes an outcome of diverse inscriptions, processes through which symbols, narrations and performances of the masculine are revealed (Erhart; Herrmann, 1997:16).

The concept of masculinity has also been analysed as history, as a series of heterogeneous narrations on a macrohistorical as well as on an individual level. In the last years, these stories that construct the history of masculinities in modern societies are narrating unstable masculine subjectivities, vague ensembles of performances and heterogeneous narrations. Masculinity as a gender specific category possesses a narrative structure (Erhart, 2001:9)

Focusing on the social (re)production of gender, disconnecting it form the biological sex, we observe that the gender identity of young people is the first important identification and one of the longest and deepest ones, as Millett notes (Millett, 1971:39). Comparing that identity to the political identity, which is often formed during an early age but does not last that long and can change completely or partially, it seems that gender identity is much stronger for a subject. On the other hand, political identity forms a *Weltanschauung* and affects the way a person views almost all aspects of social, political, economic and cultural life. In the following chapters, we will talk about the intersection of gender and political identities as formed within structures, among relations and organizations.

Here, we have to note that sexuality is an important aspect of gender identity and, as such, is not a natural process but has a lot to do with the 'the technologies of the self' that are linked to rules of politics (Foucault, 1997). Sexuality, as Millett underlines, is regulated by power and is therefore political and belongs to the central strategies of self-administrating, through which the subject organises itself according to the hegemonic discourses (Schößler, 2008:108). As Schmerl et al note, the established norms surrounding sexuality were and are the basis of the state and culture; social institutions, state politics and cultural symbolic systems are regulated, so they achieve the channelling and ritualising of specific forms of sexuality.

Consequently, we have to return to the power and power relations that form various gender relations. In the end, the political meaning of writing about masculinity hinges mainly on its treatment of power. This work investigates the masculinized character of the political culture as reflected in the organizational character and practices as well as the political identities of the members of political youth organizations. Parallel to that, it attempts to connect these organizational practices and discourses with broader political, economic and social structures. By concentrating on structures that form gender relations, the work is attempting to go beyond simplistic perceptions of masculinities as 'unrelieved villainy' (Carrigan et al, 2002:100) towards viewing gender as anchored in ideologies, political discourses, organizational practices and as shaped by political, economic and social structures of power.

Talking about masculinities entails entering a space of various political discourses. It goes beyond the discourses around socialization, identity construction and psychology through the far-reaching social structures towards a critique of the existing social order and a design for social change. It should avoid the exaggerating underlining of differences between men and women, the obscuring of class, race, sexuality structures and the ignoring or blurring of the issue of power. Definitions of masculinity, from essentialist to positivist over to normative and semiotic, have tried to find the real meaning of gender by emphasizing either one quality that is apparently central in masculinity, by offering standards of what masculinity ought to be or by dismissing the individual or structural level, concentrating on symbolic differences between men and women, masculinities and femininities. Rather than that, masculinities should be traced simultaneously within the system of gender relations, in the practices that have an effect on bodies, personalities, culture, politics and the structures that frame and underlie these practices. Connell (2005) sets the practices that are related to gender structures in larger units, so that masculinity and femininity become configurations of gender practice. The gender practices are (re)produced as people 'grapple with their historical, social and political situations' (Connell, 2005:72). Masculinities are a set of practices outlined by structures that are embedded in the gender order of a society in a given historical context. Feminist critique has shown the complex character of gender structures by shedding light on the number of different and contradicting logics that are imposed on them. Mitchell and Rubin have argued that gender is a disrupting moment in history, and its configurations (masculinities and femininities) are formed by power and production relations which constitute reality (*Ibid*, 81). To connect gender with sexuality, we have to accentuate the relationship of masculinity to heterosexuality, a relationship that defines men's positioning in a system of social dominance (*Ibid*, 73).

Masculinities are expressed on a structural level (laws, division of labor, institutions, politics, etc.), on the individual level, in how people construct, incorporate and make meaning of their gendered identity, and on an ideological level (values, ideas, models, gender ideologies and gender consciousness). Masculinities are defined often by what they are not, by the opposite and the 'otherness' incorporated by women and other men, and they are formed by categories such as body, sexuality, class, ethnicity, education, age, religion, political ideology and the notions of power, difference and violence. Masculinities are mostly defined by their relation to the gender order, their accordance with or resistance to it. In this regard, they are always redefined and their (re)making constitutes a political process that influences the balancing of interests in society. In order to understand the social dynamics and the direction of social change, we have to set the different coexisting forms of masculinities within the larger structural framework and observe how they fit into it as well as what different positions they occupy.

After analysing the notion of 'masculinities' and its use as an analytical tool in critical works on gender and gender relations, it is time to put the theory in context and talk about masculinities in politics and especially in political youth organizations.

2 Constructing Gender and Political Identities in Organized Politics

How can masculinity be linked with political ideologies, organizational structures and gender representations in the context of political youth organizations?

Masculinity (and, relationally, femininity) goes beyond the materiality of the body and the binary of man/woman, is rooted deep in the social structures and relations, forms the character of organizations, such as political youth organizations, is part of dominant ideologies, reigns in the domain of representations and influences the construction of gendered subjectivities in all social sites and spaces.

Talking about masculinity construction within political youth organizations is talking about gender and politics and the intersections between them. Adopting J. Scott's definition of gender as 'a primary way of signifying relations of power' (Scott, 1997:42-48) that forms gender relations, which can be perceived as fundamental relations that regulate all social formations (Haug, 2001:761) and perceiving politics as relations of power and domination between groups with contradicting interests, we can see that gender constructions are sites and moments of negotiation of power within political processes, structures and practices.

Gender relations as well as politics and the Political are imbued with different meanings in different social, cultural and historical contexts. Coming to the political culture of contemporary Greece and focusing on political youth organizations, which reflect the character and texture of the contemporary political landscape, we will be able to trace the processes of gender constructions as they happen nowadays within the political framework. Researching masculinity construction in political youth organizations is a way to reveal power relations that form both gender relations and politics, a way to link political identity and gender identity, political ideologies with relevant gender ideologies, and organizational practices with processes of gender formation. By launching a critique of the dominant ideologies, power relations and practices within political organizations that sustain the masculinized character of politics and form accordingly the contemporary political culture in Greece, I am not concentrating on the individuals that are involved in the organizations and blaming the masculine character of the organizations on men as carriers of sexist, homophobic and misogynist ideas that form the organizations they belong to.

A feminist critique can go beyond gendered experience and gendered cultural categories, to investigate the ways social institutions are organized according to power dynamics and hierarchical lines that enable or disable (depending on the social group) access to services, information and resources. As I.M. Young suggests, feminists need to pay attention to concrete material conditions and to acknowledge the complexity of social causation (Young, 1997:22-37).

Sexism, homophobia, hegemony and domination go far beyond forming patterns of thought and action, and are replicated in race, class, heterosexism, and other forms of social domination and subordination (*Ibid*, 22ff). They are part of dominant political ideologies and political theoretical traditions; they are rooted in the structures and relations of basic social institutions and the state.

Political parties and youth organizations operate within a political system in the framework of a contemporary democratic state. Feminist state theory early on revealed gender and gender relations as constitutive elements of the state. C. Pateman (1994:739) has suggested that the so-called social contract was rather based on a gender contract that served as the basis of the modern state and legitimized a patriarchal social structure. This structure intensifies the division of the public and private domain and places men in the public and women in the private. Furthermore, this division is sustaining a monopoly on violence that is gender specific and oriented towards the suppression of women. The principles of the state are androcentric (Gerhard, 1997; Sackofsky, 1996) and make the character of the welfare state patriarchal (Gerhard, 1988). Histories of the state as reflected in the a-gendered notion of citizenship can be read as accounts in which men and women have different locations, positions and interests (Hearn, 2001:40), as citizens, workers, politicians, mothers/fathers, professionals, etc. The development of the modern state is fundamental to the construction of men's and women's relations to the complex relations of the state (political, legal and administrative authority) and nation (culture and ideology) (Yuval-Davis, 1997). The rights of national citizenship, including the participation in politics, political organization, and administrative and legislative processes of the state 'are located within a set of complex class, gendered and racialized histories' (Hearn, 2001:41), in which gendered violence in forms of domination, suppression, hierarchization and exclusion has always been central.

Feminist critiques of state theories theorize the state as a men's collective, and E. Kreisky (Kreisky, 1995:215) describes masculinity as a system that inscribes the male interests and life experiences on state institutions. Gendered hierarchies, seniority principle, and gendered division of roles and practices within state institutions are elements of the masculine character of institutions (Sauer, 2001:141) that have an impact on the gender relations in the society and regulate the access to social resources. Feminist state theory goes as far as to show how the state, through its institutions and their structures and practices, is involved in the reproduction of 'masculinity' and 'femininity'. At this point, we have to underline that although there are many forms of masculinities and femininities, there are few forms with certain characteristics that sustain the masculine character of the state and its institutions, and that these are constantly reproduced by marginalizing, suppressing and controlling other forms of masculinity and femininity. Within every institution reigns a certain gender regime that determines the gender order of a certain society at a certain historical moment, which is what Connell names 'hegemonic masculinity' (see chapter 1).

Within the framework of a critique of the exclusive character of the modern state, we can extend the examination to particular organizations and the forms of authority, hierarchies and domination within them (in terms of class, gender, age, ethnicity, etc.) and show how these processes are gendered. As social structures provide the societal context of organizations, so too do they form the context of political organizations. Organizations and, in particular, political organizations reproduce the structural relations and can therefore be understood as 'means of (re)creation of oppression and exclusion' (Hearn, 2001:89). As feminist theorists have analyzed (Hearn, 1978, 2001; Walby, 1990; McKinnon, 1989), the processes that shape the oppressive character of organizations are obvious in the histories of political and economic systems, and a major example is the capitalist system. As capitalism relies on the exploitation of people and other parts of the world, nation-states accordingly have been formed based on competition with others, with men holding the power to rule over women and other men. This is where states and organizations can be understood in a framework of patriarchy and patriarchal relations. As Hearn (2001) underlines, patriarchal systems are based first on domination of men over women but also on some men's rule over other men through organizational hierarchies by age, class, race and other divisions. At this point, it makes sense to introduce theories of hegemonic masculinities as major ideological, organizational and practical patterns that shape relations within political organizations in the analysis.

Going back to the reproduction of masculinities and femininities by the state, Gramsci's state theory and his perception of state power as being operated through hegemony can provide some useful insights to gender constructions in the framework of the state and, consequently, state institutions. State action is based on a hegemony that has a cultural and moral character (Gramsci, 1995: 1239). Apart from the repressive state, Gramsci sees the educational and ethical state that secures a certain cultural and moral level for the broader part of society, so that the modes of production, the demands for development and the general interests of the dominant class would be established. Carriers of these cultural and moral demands are not only schools and court rooms but also private initiatives and even activities that construct the apparatuses of cultural and political hegemony of the dominant classes (*Ibid*, 1043). The state gives orientation towards certain ways of thought and action as well as cultural, moral and intellectual habits on the level of everyday life. These ways enable the reproduction of hegemony and have the ability to lead ideologically a whole historical bloc (Priester, 1972: 522 in Ludwig, 2007:198)

Gramsci understands ideology as a form of cognition and perception according to which individuals find their position in the world (Ludwig, 2007:198). Hegemony is based upon the consensus on certain cultural and moral ways of thinking and their internalizations in the everyday understanding of individuals (*Ibid*, 199). According to Gramsci, every state is trying to create and preserve a certain type of civilization and a certain type of citizen (and accordingly is trying for certain ways of collective living and of interpersonal relations). Parallel to that, the state is trying to eliminate certain habits and ways of thinking and to establish others (Gramsci, 1995: 1548).

If we assume that gender is a fundamental characteristic of all social formations, then the procedures a state follows in order to establish certain gendered subjects and to integrate them into the everyday understanding of a whole society serves as a requirement for the formation of a socially and historically specific gender order (see Connell, 2005).

Respectively, 'feminine' and 'masculine' subjectivities are conceived as thinking, feeling and perceiving ways that result from certain material practices and, parallel to that, are structured accordingly. The reproduction of the economic relations (social division of labor and production relations) is linked to the formation of historical and social specific subjectivities, which are gendered according to the fundamental gender relations that are formed within the specific society (Ludwig, 2007:201). In Gramsci, formation of subjectivities (the active construction of the subject by social agents) is conceptualized as a resistance and, parallel, as a conscious adaptation to dominant and hegemonic ideologies in an attempt to make them livable for every individual (*Ibid*, 204).

Within the framework of the state, with these characteristics, the parliament, in which the political parties operate, is conceived as a field of reproduction of dominant ideology (Poulantzas, 1978:146-148). This dominant ideology is diffused in the political organization of the parties and the youth organizations attached to them and forms the perceptions and identities of their members. According to Gramsci, ideology is a very powerful domain, because it is in the best position to hide the real level of dominance and hegemony and is best placed to cement social relations, creating a consensus and a homogeneity on an imaginary level (Poulantzas, 1978). Within this analytical framework, we can view masculinity as a part of the dominant political ideologies developed within the framework of the state.

2.1 Ideology and Identity

One way to analyze the social organization of gendered differences and the ways that gender and social inequality is formed and reproduced is to see how class consciousness among men and women is reproduced and how the character of male and female experience differs according to political ideology, when the 'political' has a gender and a class dimension.

To connect gender to ideology using the analysis of Gramsci on ideology as a cultural construction that reflects the material economic, social and political conditions, while also having a representational character, it is important to underline that gender is more than a variable that affects people's behavior and determines social roles. Gender reflects a material as well as a symbolic reality and forms (and is formed by) organizational principles of society, structures that are translated into desires, habits and rituals (Hall; Steedman, 1986; Connell, 1987)

Gender consciousness, like class consciousness, is not only a matter of beliefs, opinions, ideologies about society as a whole, but it is also contained in the political view and theorization of society according to each one's position in the division of labor. It goes beyond that; it materializes within a structure of emotions, narratives from different stages of one's lives. Steedman talks about life histories that are contained in world history (Wetherell, 2005:415). As she argues, when we talk about gender, class, etc., we mean not only the results of material conditions of life but also memories, fantasies, decisions, dreams and the 'making of the selves'.

Gender is defined by structures but it is internalized through the process of the formation of gendered identity that varies according to cultural and historical context. The adoption of social identities is the process of constructing the self within a context of restrictions that are set by material and social conditions. Hall sees it as a 'binding narrative' (Steedman, 1986:6), as a narration of the self that makes sense at certain (historical) moments and in certain (social, economic, political and cultural) spaces. This is an ever-changing process, an eternal narration of stories, often set in a dialogue with others, as identity is formed through interaction. Connell (1987) suggests that we should not try to analyze the personality and society as static objects of analysis but as flows of actions and interactions. Post-structuralists underlined the fact that there are multiple stories and perspectives on personality that do not follow a linear narrative, so that in the end, we can only trace pieces of a fragmented identity (Barthes, 1994).

The formation of the self is affected not only by structures but also by the relations of power that are dominant in society and influence the ways identities are constructed. Wetherell (2005) links power primarily with violence and the right to use violence. Power and domination work within a framework of tolerance and consensus, and often power is seen as a property of a group of people resulting in their social position (Wetherell, 2005:427). As Gramsci (1971) explains, the justification for owning and using power is contained in major ideologies that work as networks of discourses and practices that explain and justify the actions of the powerful and dominating and appear logical and normal. In this normalizing process participate not only people or groups that directly profit but also the dominated in an orchestrated interaction of domination and suppression. Power means not only violence but also control of others, access to resources, fulfillment of wills and desires, independence, self-determination, autonomy from desires and interest of others (Wetherell, 2005:428). Very often, power takes forms that are invisible or not easily traceable through a normalization process or through a process of legitimization within laws, norms, morals, collective ideas. Foucault (1980) views identities as results of power, and power then becomes a constitutive parameter of subjects and society. The formation of society is based on complexes of power/knowledge that materialize and change through space and time: 'Power is a productive network that runs through the social body' (Foucault, 1980:119). Power is linked with social identity, as the position of people in a system of social organizations is related to the access to resources. To link back power with the process of identity formation, Foucault (1980) notes that power is a process of 'subjectification'. The moment people realize themselves as subjects of a certain kind, as active agents with certain identities, they are 'snarled' in the net of power.

Trying to connect gender and class at their intersections, we can look on the ways in which certain notions of gender and class are reproduced, spread and internalized and inserted in gendered and classed identities. Marxist thought perceives the collective class consciousness as deriving from the common experience of exploitations. Ideology comes out and reflects the production relations and is differentiated according to various categories, one of which is gender (Alexander in Avdela; Psarra, 1994:47). Class identities are not universal and static but are always connected to real gendered embodiments. As gendered identity is central to the development of class consciousness, and as masculinities and femininities are unstable and fluid categories, we have to trace class identities down to gender identities in order to understand them.

Consequently, research on class and how it affects gender constructions has shown that historically changing institutionalized social processes, such as capitalism and social divisions that come out of these processes, including class, race and ethnicity, play a major role in the constructions of male identities. Tolson and Seidler (1991) have shown that working class men, who usually have more power outside the job and for whom work is only a means to support the family rather than a career, tend to adopt more aggressive ways, but also based on comradeship and solidarity forms of collective and personal masculinities, sustain the image of the strong and authoritarian breadwinner and caretaker of the family. Middle class men, on the other hand, seem more concentrated on the self and their success in the job, seek and often gain acknowledgment outside the family and therefore tend to be more pro-equality and anti-authoritarian in the family. This stand depends also on the views of women on career, very much on their participation in the household and their identification with 'male' aims and aspirations (Brannen; Collard, 1982; Seidler, 1991, 1997). Feminist historiography has shown that, historically, skill has always been 'significant as a marker of social class, as a motor of worker mobilization, but also as a component of gender and work identity' (Chenut, 2005:78). The relation to work, the economic and social position that is related to it and consequently the role in the private sphere of the house and family, which is always in relation to one's position in the public sphere, has a major connection to the formation of gendered subjectivities. As Seidler (1991) notes, the experience between the private and the public, together with the institutionalization of antagonism (as the spirit of capitalist relation of production) create a 'depersonalization' that affects the general masculine psychology. Connell suggests that hegemonic types of masculinity are linked and backed by the competitive spirit, the aggressiveness and the distant emotional reactions, exactly because capitalist modes of production encourage these characteristics. Feminist critique has stressed that the social conflicts of capitalism are rooted in the bodies and actions of men producing certain experiences in the workplace and outside of it.

Despite all the changes, when looking at the working experiences of men and adding the variables of race, ethnicity, education, age, religion, etc., we can see that some groups of men are higher in the social pyramid than others. These different social positions affect differently the male identities, but adding women in different social groups, we get a totally different picture. In this picture, it becomes clear that the collective power of men is not absolute and is always relational. Connell (1995) suggests that men can be seen as a privileged group with common interests, who regularly get a share in the patriarchal system, the so-called 'patriarchal dividend'. Patriarchy has a strong material and economic dimension but also a phenomenology (Barkty, 1990), as it organizes people's consciousness, people's everyday experience and their sense of what is considered normal. This phenomenology, integrated in the existing capitalist system, creates contradictory masculine identities, identities that are multiple, relational, actively constructed and set within broader relations of power (Wetherell, 2005).

Here we should explain the relational character of masculinities. Men tend to define their identity first in relation and as reference to other men and then to women (Connell, 1995; Segal, 1990). Every definition of the self is a clarification of who gets in and who remains outside, creating a sense of otherness and marking what are the socially accepted limits. Relations of inclusion and exclusion are relations of power. Connell (1995) suggests that all men are involved in relations of power that create different types of masculinities, all defined in relation to their other.

In the framework of viewing gender as form of ideology or, rather, as an essential part of political ideologies and related gender consciousness, it is necessary to introduce at this point the notion of political ideology as a changing variable of gender construction. One of the main questions that this work poses is how political ideology forms a gender consciousness that affects the formation of gendered subjectivities, especially masculinities. In this direction, the work will concentrate on how political ideologies form relevant gender ideologies based on the example of political youth organizations in contemporary Greece.

2.2 Theorizing Ideology

Ideology is a parameter of reality, which is necessary for the existence and the formation of any society as a whole. Ideology refers to systems of ideas, values and beliefs about society, as well as referring to systems of social behaviors and attitudes. Usually these social attitudes include legal, political, moral, religious, philosophical and aesthetic ideas about the world and the role of the human in it. These ideas materialize on the level of how people behave socially, their habits, their practices, the ways they address issues. Ideology constitutes a crucial element of the social 'edifice'. According to Gramsci, ideology not only belongs to the overstructure, but it slides among all the parts of the social structure and, like cement, secures the stability and cohesion of it. In particular, ideology secures the integration and consistency of persons in their roles, their functions and their social relations. Ideology soaks through all actions and pervades the individual as active subject. It is inherited in the perceptions of individuals around economy and the organization of production. It exists within the political stands and beliefs of persons, in the cynicisms, individuality, complacency, expectation, demands, resistance and revolt. It shapes the personal and family life, the division of domestic labor, the role and position of women in the household and, most importantly, in reproduction. As Harnecker (1976) points out, we tend to view our perception of the world and things as an objective quality of the 'things themselves', because ideology is very much based on experience. Moreover, the systems of lifestyle and behavior are more difficult to change than ideas and beliefs (Harnecker, 1976:92-93).

Ideology helps people to adapt to social reality and to take over social roles and responsibilities within a certain social structural organization. It is often that people are conscious of the role they have to adopt, the compromises or the limits of action they have to consider in order to adjust to and find a place within certain social, political, economic and cultural frameworks.

When society is shaped by class divisions and other social inequalities, including a hierarchical political organization, the dominant ideology of a certain society at a certain historical moment (that is characterized by class, gender, race and other categories of social inequalities) serves to integrate people into this social reality. Dominant ideologies should legitimize the existing social structural organization and secure the social coherence. The explanation of inequality referring to accumulation of wealth and its connection to hard work and modesty, and when dealing with finances of the wealthy in contrast to the laziness and waste of the poor, plays this kind of ideological role. The same kind of argumentation is to be traced in talking about women's lack of interest in getting involved in politics in contrast to men's common political nature, which actually justifies the exclusion of women from the public domain. Dominant ideologies should therefore be in agreement with the social divisions, exclusions and inclusions and the offered social roles for people or groups of people, thus enabling the reproduction of the social system. Of course, certain ideologies refer to and are circulated among many different groups of people. It is rather impossible that every person has an another ideological orientation from the next, because personal ideologies and beliefs are often informed by dominant ideologies or are built as resistance to them, always having as a reference point the same dominant ideologies they aim to oppose. Dominant and hegemonic ideologies are generated within and between the most basic social institutions, such as family, school, church, state, military, university, etc. This shows that ideologies are analogous to the broader social divisions within which individuals are born and raised. The social positions of individuals give them a certain standpoint of viewing and understanding the world. Based on what Marx explicitly wrote, that the social being (society) defines the individual's consciousness, many philosophers of science, as well as gender and class theoreticians, developed the standpoint theory and methodology used for analysing individual views and beliefs in relation to their social positions and their place in society.

Standpoint epistemology, trying to distance from the methodological individualism and empiricist rationality that naturalized social divisions (man/woman, for example) and prioritized certain types of behaviors, beliefs, experiences, etc., draws on the Hegelian argument about the slave-master relationship and develops a Marxist proletarian standpoint (Hartschock, 1983). This epistemological attempt has a realist philosophical position that argues for the existence of an underlying material reality that structures the social world. Starting from experience, standpoint theorists argue that it is able to reveal the underlying interests that shape social life, by tracing experiences that are central organizing principles of social relations. Standpoint feminist theorists believe that distance from the experiences analysed gains an insight into the reality of society. Based on the argument that the social positions of individuals (and researchers) enable a viewing of the world from certain angles and through certain lenses, there are accordingly various standpoints from which someone can look at the world. The more distanced, the more objective, claims Sandra Harding (1992), arguing that women researchers ought not give up on reaching 'stronger objectivity'.

Feminist standpoint epistemology has been very influential in the field of research on men and masculinities (Connell, 1990), as it enables the critique of oppressive power relations and masculinist positions in the field and during the research process. As Hearn (1993) argues, men can consider the research situation as a political instrument that can enable men to acknowledge and identify the oppressive nature of their practices rather than distance themselves from research on masculinities and men, because this can reinforce a 'natural' oppressive order of gender relations (Mac an Ghail, 2003:109). B. Frank (1993:336-7 in Mac an Ghail 2003:111) suggests that finding out how gender is socially constructed within patriarchal relations does not ensure analysis of historicity and social construction of theories and methods themselves that produce knowledge. Drawing from Frank, it is absolutely necessary to avoid an endeavour that reproduces static notions of gender identity, that is, that masculinity per se is the dominant power in a patriarchal society. This would lead to talk about identity politics ensuring that homogeneity and cultural fixity mark the boundaries, instead of underlining the notion that gender identities vary as they are inflected with a diverse range of social categories, such as sexuality, class, ethnicity, and age, that shapes men's and women's social relations.More about feminist standpoint epistemology can be found in the methodology chapter.

Returning to the formation of gender, class, race ideologies, we can say that within the social reality, the social positions that different groups of people occupy have a strong material character and therefore are influenced by the dominant divisions of labor, the divisions of domestic labor, the gendered divisions in the public and the private domain, the exclusions of certain groups of people such as migrants, gay, lesbians and transgender, and undocumented people from the law and state institutions. Ideology is a rather autonomous terrain of society (Vlachou, 2005:69). However, within the domain of ideologies, there are many ideas, beliefs, presuppositions, stands and so on. What signifies an ideology as a social phenomenon is the way of combining ideological elements, their systemization in explaining the world, their structure (as an active process) that leads to the production of a 'central idea', of a 'meaning of what is this all about', where meaning defines simultaneously the meaning and the function of multiple ideas about the formation of social structure. Following this line, ideology cannot be restricted to the personal consciousness but goes over the images that individuals adopt and is structured as a social phenomenon. Ideology is a variable of social reality that can be analysed by analysing the parameters that define it as a social phenomenon and the relations between them (Vlachou, 2005:70)

Within the ideological terrain, there are many ideologies or ideological tendencies that are analogous to the broader social divisions. According to the Marxian perception, in capitalism, we can observe two main ideological streams, the bourgeois ideology and the workers' ideology. Bourgeois ideology expresses the beliefs and behaviors of the capitalist class and is the dominant ideology. The ideology of the working class is dominated by the bourgeois ideology, which it is opposed to. On one hand, according to Gramsci, integrated in the bourgeois ideology (even in a twisted form) are some desires and interests of the working class (which is the majority of the people), in order for the capitalist class to establish its hegemony over the working class. On the other hand, within the ideology of the working class there are some representations of bourgeois ideology that make the exploitation of the working class more systematic on a level of economic class struggle, as well as on the level of political demands. Inserting gender into the picture of class inequality, some Marxist feminists have tried to conceive women as an extra social class, being subject to a double exploitation by the capitalist class and the working men. However, this perception implies an unrealistic coherence within the category of 'women', where all women have the same interests and positions towards Capital and Patriarchy. This inconsistency can nevertheless be solved if we no longer refer to men and women as subjects but we perceive femininities and masculinities as ideologies that comply with or resist the dominant bourgeois ideology. Drawing from Poulantzas, in his references to the dominant ideology as a crucial parameter of bourgeois hegemony, we can say that masculinity as a part of the dominant ideology serves to sustain the hegemony of the dominant class, linking 'hegemonic masculinity' with dominant ideologies, as Connell has shown by drawing from Gramsci.

In contemporary capitalism, liberalism as a political philosophy and positivism as a theory of science seem to be elements of a *Weltanschauung* that is hegemonic. The positivist ideas, if they manage to convince the people that they are the objective laws of nature, as they are revealed and expressed by (neutral and objective) Science and as laws that determine the economic and social organization, will lead to the acceptance of this social organization as the best possible and, most importantly, as irreversible. Ideologies are usually not binding systems of thought, free from paradoxes, inconsistencies and mistakes (Fine, 1985 in Vlachou, 2005:71). The theoretical gaps are not always constructed on purpose in the form of propaganda in order to disorientate people. Whereas perceptions refer to elements of reality, they can be based partly on a theorization of society.

The ideological domain, even if it is influenced by the impact of the economy, does not constitute a simple reflection of the economic level. The ideological level has its own special content and laws of constitution, function and change. It is formed by various ideologies out of which one or a few are dominant and refer to various theoretical sectors (religion, morals, etc.). What is the dominant domain at a certain historical moment depends on the qualities of the ideological structure itself, in order for a more stable (hegemonic) relationship of the dominant class to the dominated classes to be achieved (Harnecker, 1976).

The variables and constitutive elements of the ideological structure are shaped by the traditions, values and morals of historical periods (like feudalism or the era of Ottoman Empire in Greece), the rituals, the habits, cultural elements of a certain society, etc. Important ideological material of the past is inherited by the dominant ideology. Not only ideological material but a whole institutionalized mechanism, including educational systems, schooling, libraries, archives, etc., is imported and inserted from past into present dominant ideologies, so that hegemonic ideologies do not create everything anew each time but use existing material within contemporary frameworks, imbued with another meaning.

In conclusion, we can say that the ideological structure preserves a relative autonomy. The ideological product is an outcome of an internal definition within the ideological structure itself and of an external definition (by political and economic facts) (Vlachou, 2005:72). All in all, there is no direct mechanical definition of the ideological structure but a multiple and context-related determination of it. Economic relations are presuppositions of a class consciousness. However, on their own, they cannot create a gain in this consciousness. As Harnecker (1976) writes, class consciousness as well as gender consciousness are presupposing a class theoretical analysis and political expression and organization. In the framework of the current analysis, it is obviously impossible delve deeper into the matter of the relevant construction of class and gender consciousness. The focus of this work is on the connection between political ideologies (that mostly reflect class interests) and gender perceptions of masculinity, which reflect the level of personal and collective consciousness. For this purpose, in this whole section I have tried to show how gender and class meet in theory and methodology. To set this theoretical analysis in the context of political youth organizations in Greece, we have to proceed with the analysis of political parties and forms of masculinities as well as an analysis of Greek political culture and related dominant forms of gender constructions.

2.2.1 Political Parties, Hegemony, Masculinities and Feminist Critique

Political parties are primarily constructed by class interests. As such, they defend the interests of the classes and social groups they represent and also constantly try to disorganize the demand and achievement of the interests of other classes and groups. Gramsci traced in this process the main purpose and function of the political parties, merely the securing of benefits and interests and the reproduction of the social classes they represent (Spourdalakis, 1990:94). However, the political parties often remain relatively autonomous from the social classes they come to represent[1]. This autonomy from the class interests, interests which the parties are supposed to represent, helps to understand the conflicts among groups within the parties and between power blocs in the parties and other groups, which belong to the dominant classes, or how labor or populist parties come to defend interests of the dominant class (bourgeoisie)[2]. This can explain accordingly certain similar practices or representations that appear within the power blocs or among dominant groups within very different parties. It becomes obvious that since parties are in the center of political antagonism, having as a major aim the achievement of (ideally absolute) political power, the

1 Poulantzas traced in the political scene a series of dislocations between the class interests and class political practices on the one hand and the political interests and the parties on the other (Poulantzas,1975: 96-97)

2 Here we have to note that capitalism creates two antagonistic social classes, the bourgeois and the working- that represent the amount of the existing modes of production in the certain historical and spatial framework of a country. Other groups, created by remaining or pre-existing modes of production, link their interests either with the aims of the bourgeois or sometimes those of the working class (Spourdalakis, 1990: 92).

groups that are closer to power or higher in the hierarchy or closer to a leading figure in the party share some common characteristics and attitudes towards power. This explains, first, the androcentric character of the parties (since men gain power over women, with the result being their isolation or exclusion from politics), and, second, the hegemonic forms of masculinity that suppress other forms of masculinity and femininity, as well as the 'patriarchal dividend'[3] and the share of power that all men enjoy, regardless of which form of masculinity they embody.

As for the dominant class, given the control over hegemony that it has, it is not necessary for it to create its own political party, and it can deliberately use the one or the other in order to achieve and secure its interest. The same argument is valid for the various forms of masculinities that appear in politics within the various political parties. Not one certain pattern is always dominant and hegemonic. The dynamics shift and promote one in relation to the others according to the political equilibrium between the parties, the power dynamics within a given party and the certain historical, social, and/or cultural context.

Masculinity becomes a part of dominant ideology that many within the context of political organizations that are active in the framework of liberal democracy are eager to deliberately share in order to achieve power, even if they have primarily different interests. Masculinity as ideology gets inserted in the whole political-ideological spectrum. Around a hegemonic form of masculinity are constructed other forms that are not always contradictory. On the contrary, they often express compliance towards the hegemonic forms, willing to get a share of power or to help sustain the existing gender regime that privileges the most masculine of patterns. There are certain parallels between political parties that express various ideologies and organize themselves in the system of liberal democracy within the framework of the capitalist state and the forms of masculinities that are organized around dominant patterns of gender construction within political gender regimes. The entire spectrum of ideologies is organized around the core character of the capitalist state, which expresses the ideas and interests of the dominant class. Parallel to that, all the forms of masculinity (that appear within the gender regime of political organizations) are organized around forms of hegemonic masculinities that express, in their turn, the dominant ideologies.

3 See Connell, 1990. The patriarchal dividend is mainly the share in patriarchy that privileges all men involved in the patriarchal system.

In the developed capitalist societies, central are not only problems and social, political, economic issues that have to do with the binary capital-labor but also a series of other issues that appear from 'post-materialistic' antitheses (Spourdalakis, 1990:198). Antithetical gender relations become a central issue. Nowadays, almost all political parties have introduced the gender issue in their agendas.

Around the crucial issues that belong to the political programmes of the parties, central political discourses that inform and get informed by social, economic and cultural discourses are usually developed. The political discourses are in turn informed by hegemonic discourses developed at local, regional, national and international levels. We can say that political discourses reflect the character of the whole political culture in a country or region and can tell something about the social, political and economic hegemonic relations developed within the different levels. To explain the connection between hegemonic relations that form whole political cultures, we have to provide some definitions. A sociological analysis of the political culture should involve an analysis of intersecting relations around the institutions that create them, the construction of the subjects within them and the dynamics of the relations between them (*Ibid*, 118). According to Demertzis (1989), political culture is the amount of schemata of perception, knowledge and practice, which in every society is set and realized in the political sphere (Spourdalakis, 1990:120). Within this context, hegemony surpasses the limits of political control and contains a more diffused notion of domination, expressed by the social perceptions of human nature and social relations as well as through the political and economic institutions that express a social group's sovereignty above the others and which is accepted by the dominated as a natural and logical aspect of reality. Hegemony has not merely the meaning of suppression but denotes the precedence that the dominant social group has upon the formation of a general social dynamic (Spourdalakis, 1990:122). In the same context and turning back to the parties that mostly represent the interests of different social groups, every party that is not in power or opposed to the power of the others is not necessarily anti-hegemonic. The anti-hegemonic character of a party would consist of its attempt to change the content of hegemony (Williams, 1980:42) and that does not fit within the framework of liberal parliamentarian democracy. The same is valid for the power blocs within the parties themselves. Not all groups that try to get power positions or to achieve privileged forms of power are opposed to power as such, and that explains the sustaining of hegemonic forms of masculinities and other dominant ideologies and practices within the very different parties.

Talking about 'political discourses', we mean the amount of spoken, unspoken, real and symbolic practices and speech acts that compose every human and social activity, as well as every institutional initiation, through which the social production of meaning is happening (Spourdalakis, 1990:123). Forty years after the second wave of feminism, it becomes clear that the division between public and private is not sustainable any more, and so the private becomes necessarily political, and, in this context, personal discourses get a clear political meaning. Subjects and the content of their political discourses are not a result of some transcendental, ahistorical relations but the result of very specific historical dynamics. This historical dynamic is constituted by the permanent referring of all discourses to the existing Political Discourse. This explains the relation between the ideological orientation of the different political parties and the political character of the 'personal' discourses that constitute the *Weltanschauung* of the members of the parties and the members of a whole society.

In the formation of the political culture, the political parties play a major role. From Neuman (1975), who defined the major role of the political parties as the education of the citizen towards political responsibility (Spourdalakis, 1998:124), to Gramsci, who underlined that political parties develop and distribute their perception of the world (Gramsci, 1971: 355), it becomes clear that political parties, through their ideological development and being in the center of the political discourses and practices, contribute actively to the formation of the political culture. Political discourses are also a constitutive part of the party ideologies. Ideologies within political organizations express the spoken, unspoken and symbolic crystallization of the Political Discourse, as formed by the class participation in it, the initiatives, activities, the structures and the personal relations among the members of the organizations (Spourdalakis, 1990:127). The political parties participate in the formation of the political culture through the promotion of symbolisms that develop in the context of their political practices. These symbolisms are created through the certain colours and symbols they use as well as through the organizational practices, the division of labor within the organization, the level of participation in the hierarchies and the different decision-making bodies, the political practices before and during elections, the lifestyles of the heads of the party as well as of the simple members and so on.

As becomes clear, political parties are living organisms. Their members live, act and interact in a broad social environment. Therefore, their ways of life, their cultural preferences and habits, and the patterns and models of personal and gender relations that they adopt constitute the cultural microcosm first of the party and second of the society as a whole. The symbolic contribution of the political parties in the cultural constitution of a society gets either the form of the preservation of the dominant cultural model or helps to develop alternative cultural expressions. Usually, however, as Gramsci already sharply noted, parties are hegemonic formations within the framework of the state (Poulantzas, 1994) and therefore try to sustain the existing social, economic, political and cultural order rather than change it. In the framework of society and in the certain historical gender order that exists, political parties as hegemonic structures are actively at work for preservation rather than abolition of the established order.

2.2.2 The Character of Modern Democracy, the Role of the Parties and the Demands for Broader Representation: a Feminist Challenge

Political organizations in Greece, including political parties, are operating in the framework of liberal democracy within a late capitalist state. Political parties, involved in the state of play around political power, are actively participating in the administration of state power. The development of state power throughout the last forty years has introduced challenges on the character of democracy, the role of the state and the importance of political parties in it. The state has basically developed to the point of being an element of the internal structural regulator of the accumulation of capital (Spourdalakis, 1998:81). The strong tendency towards a bureaucratic character of the modern state (a result of structural needs of the capitalist state, which actually have lead to the development of the welfare state) is broadening the chasm between politics and society, and that undermines democracy. Political parties are demoted to service providers and administration agencies well integrated in a homogeneous, closed political system (Spourdalakis, 1990:182). On the other hand, groups of organized corporate interests that influence a lot the processes of political decisions are undermining the responsible parliamentarian governance based on political parties (Offe, 1985:227).

The notion of democracy as it is nowadays seems to refer to the public sphere of human activities, and, as is often underlined in critical analyses, the dominant perception about the subjects that participate in it is very androcentric. The exclusion of women from politics has its roots in the material organizational principles of patriarchy and sexism (Eisenstein, 1979; Rowbotham, 1985; Perrigo, 1988). The liberal tradition defines politics very narrowly, as it restricts it to the state and governmental institutions, while the private sphere is considered not political; however, liberal political tradition does not exclude women or other social groups from demanding their inclusion in the political system. Liberalism gives the opportunity of a constant broadening of the whole value system based on the principle of political equality. This equality is theorized and practiced among persons (regardless gender, class, etc.) independently and far from conditions of social inequality (Pantelidou – Malouta, 1987:534).

The entrance of women into politics was based on the liberal idea of equality, resulting in the exclusion of the real conditions of formation and constitution of women's identity from politics and the public sphere. So, the achievement of the right to vote, for example, or partial representation of women in the parliament has changed the character of democracy only in name, bringing a quantitative rather than a qualitative change.

Feminist theory of the modern state has made clear that the character of the state is not gender neutral. The state interferes in the private sphere in order to give its own meaning to the political character of the private in such a way that the power equilibria, which define the content of the Political each time, will be reproduced in order to restrict the full acknowledgement of women's political identity in the framework of an 'asexual' political equality (Spourdalakis, 1998:104).

However, introducing the private to the sphere of the political, the character of the political is becoming broader, and this broadening opens opportunities to a more thorough democratization of the Political Discourse[4]. The political parties that are operating in the framework of the liberal perception of political equality, which does not acknowledge gender, are forced to consider this aspect, as well. Nevertheless, with so much attention surrounding the topic of women's equality on a social level (through the media, non-governmental organizations, associations, unions, etc.), political parties could not afford to lose the opportunity for the political representation of 'the half of the whole population' (Spourdalakis, 1990:206).

The adjustment of the political parties to this situation of a greater demand for women's representation was realized through intra-party women's

4 If these opportunities can be and are realized in the context of liberal democratic state is another interesting issue for further discussion.

groups or women's departments, changes in the programmes, which usually take the form of just adding the issue of gender and some of women's demands for broader participation to the existing programme, in changes in the political rhetoric, and, mostly, through the introduction of quota and equal representation systems of participation in the various political bodies.

Here, the issue of whether the demands of feminist movements can be really represented by the mainstream political parties[5] comes up, an issue which will not be further explored in this work.

However, as women as a category cannot be said to exist (Irigaray, 1979), meaning that they are not a homogenous part of society and that they have different needs, interests and demands according to their special material conditions, it is necessary for feminists to participate in the political parties and try to align with bigger political movements. Because only in the context of political parties are the different interests discussed and priorities negotiated (Perrigo, 1988), women and feminists' inclusion in the political parties, in the context of the introduction of the personal to politics, is directly connected with organizational practices and the programmatic theorizations of the parties. That means that in the existing socio-political framework, the structural and ideological limits that disable the equal participation, regardless of gender, of individuals in politics will continue to exist beyond measures of partial or equal representation, quota systems, etc. (Pantelidou – Malouta, 1989:28).

2.3 From Masculinities to the Political

If gender influences the political perception and behavior of people, the direction of the influence is not ahistorically given but is always determined by the type of gender relations that set the boundaries between the notions of man and woman. Only with the analytical category 'gender relations' as a reference point, which covers a complex net of social relations and refers to a historically changing network of social processes, can we grasp theoretically the changes that the 'man', 'woman' pattern of political perception and behavior have gone through the last years and to problematize the notion of 'womanhood' and 'manhood' within the political. In this

5 Poulantzas (1973) talking about the crisis of the political parties and a new revolutionary party has suggested that even when the ideal party exists, the parallel existence of a feminist movement is necessary, as even the most representative party cannot include all forms of social movements.

framework, political/ideological identity and gender consciousness are extra analytical parameters of the political physiognomy of subjects according to gender and can also be used to explain relative differentiations among women and men in this context.

In the Greek political context, men's dominant participation and the weak women's participation in accordance, seem less absolute and unifying phenomena and appear rather significant, containing various meanings and starting points for different categories of men and women. Although the notion of citizen has supposedly no gender marker, this is not expressed through the political behavior of the two major social categories of gender. Also, within the very categories there are very different behaviors and perceptions of the Political to follow. This has to do with the real living conditions of men and women that vary between generations and social positions, as vary the socializing messages that are addressed towards persons of different genders. The differentiated evaluation of 'male' and 'female' in all the domains of social life refers to power relations that determine the gender relations and make obvious that the political equality of men and women functions under conditions of gender inequality (Pantelidou – Malouta, 1992:10).

The androcentric character of politics (that has to be distinguished from the Political, although it is directly related) and of the political culture in Greece is undeniable, as well are the masculinized character of political organizations, practices, organizational structures and speech[6]. These phenomena cannot be traced down to the level of individual identities and issues of gender differentiation (types and stereotypes of political behavior of men and women), neither can masculine personalities lead to social structures that institutionalize women's subordination (or as a matter of fact, also certain groups' marginalization). However, as feminist theorists (N. Chodorow; S. Harding; N. Hartsock) have defended in their work, the hierarchical dualities in which masculinity is privileged over femininity establish a pattern of thought and action that is replicated in race, class, heterosexism, and other forms of social domination and subordination (Young, 1997:22ff).

For this work, the formation of masculine subjectivities through political ideology and the organized political life of young men in Greece serves as an empirical basis that enables analysis of the power relations,

6 The citation is characteristic of an interview with long time politician and head of government, K. Evert: 'In politics, manliness, guts and braveness are necessary.' Kathimerini, 26/2/91.

hierarchies, gendered practices and discourses that form the Greek political landscape.

The fact that 'gender' and, consequently, 'masculinity', is in the middle of constant historical and political changes reflects how politics and the political institutions, such as political youth organizations, constitute a strategic domain for the (re)construction and formation of multiple gendered subjectivities[7] of young men and women. Within the framework of political youth organizations, the limits of 'normal' and 'politically correct' are strictly controlled and under constant surveillance, so that patterns and models of 'accepted' ways of gendered behavior are established. Following the Marxist tradition, we can suggest that the masculine ideology that goes beyond patriarchy attempts to hide the hierarchical relations of power and subordination between general categories, such as 'men', 'women', 'citizen', 'the political', 'public/ private', presenting them as 'normal' and therefore 'normalized' and legitimized, as it runs through and is reproduced within all the state apparatuses (Althusser, 1971), such as family, church, education and which are sides of political socialization. Haywood and Mac an Ghail (1996), focusing on the role of education in the development of masculine subjectivities, perceive masculinity not as a monolithic notion but as a relational, local and dynamic one that is constructed in different sites in the framework of education, creating within schools gendered regimes that reveal a broad range of conflicting and contrasting masculinities and femininities. The gendered regimes[8] within political organizations are not an established and permanent situation, but a process of development and negotiation and are subject to many changes.

The case of political youth organizations as an institution is of special interest for gender analysis. The organizational character, the official political lines, the ideological, historical concepts that constitute their position in contemporary politics, the positions of their members inside the

[7] The term 'subjectivity' (a neologism out of subject and activity) is preferred in this work rather than identities, selves, patterns and other terms common in works on gender, as it pictures the process of the formation of the individual through structures and the parallel 'structuring' of structures through the individual's practices.

[8] Connell (1987:99) introduces in his theory of practice a structural inventory that aims to investigate more deeply the current interplay of gender relations at all its levels and dimensions. He borrows from Jill Matthews the concept of 'gender order' that describes systematically the patterns of power relations between men and women and the definitions of masculinity and femininity of an entire society (see 1st chapter). The concept of 'gender regime' focuses on the same kind of power relations within a particular institution.

organization, all these are sides where structures and representations are reflected in aspects of the individuals' identities, shaping in an intersecting process the political landscape of a society. The political institution of youth organizations plays a major role in the formation of various versions of 'masculinities' and 'femininities', intensifying and enforcing gender dichotomies through the adoption of certain discriminatory practices. However, the young men and women are not pathetic receivers of gendered socialization but active subjects who negotiate the political environment they are in and have a direct influence on the formation of their gendered identities, upon which they make complex social and psychological investments (Connell et al, 1982:77; Wetherell, 2005).

Political youth organizations are institutional sites within which a polymorphous variety of masculinities are developed. Members of political youth organizations negotiate their gendered identities through discourse, practice and in between structures of social, political, economic life, as masculinities appear to be subject to change, based on the political vision and political *Weltansschauung* of individuals and groups for new, utopian directions.

Clearly, looking at gender and political ideology and the intersection of these enables one to capture only some aspects of the Political and how it is reflected in the actual Greek political culture, as sexism, suppression, gender power relations and exclusion go far beyond ideologies and organizational structures and cannot be 'cured' through measures of women's quotas, equal representation systems in politics, anti-sexism committees and gender authorized representatives in political organizations and parties. Looking at the social causations, radical social change in the contemporary character of the Political, as well as the relations between the economic, social, political and ideological structures and related practices, with the aim of understanding and offering a way to (at least theoretically) abolish the categories of inequality such as class, gender, race, not only on the level of theory, language, and discourse but based on the very real material conditions of women, men and children around the world, is necessary in order to achieve social change with long-term impacts at all levels and in all aspects of life.

2.3.1 On Political Culture

The linkage between political identity, political culture and the formation of gendered subjectivities follows many directions. For one, we can say that the system of ideas and perceptions incorporated by individuals forms the political and social reality that they live in and simultaneously formulates their historical/social experience. On the other hand, the differentiated individual social experience contributes to the formation of a general system of political perceptions and ideas that map the political culture of a whole society (Pantelidou – Malouta, 1990:19; Tsaousis, 1983:15-25).

The term 'political culture' is very broad and differently defined by various theorists and always depends on the context of the analysis. Comparative Political Thought[9] has defined the 'political culture' as the amount of stands, beliefs and emotions that have to do with politics and exist in a certain society at a certain historical moment. Political culture, dominant within a certain socio-cultural framework, is formed throughout the history of a society, is situated in a certain national context and is determined by the social, economic and political reality (Pantelidou – Malouta, 1987:36). G. Patrick (1984) and B. Badie (1986) in their analysis focus on the aspect of individual political perceptions and their influence on the whole political culture of a certain society at a distinct historical moment. According to this analysis of political culture, the positions and perceptions of political subjects – formed historically and on the base of social experience – differentiate social groups from each other and give an insight into the political reality of a given society. These positions and perceptions that compose parts of a political culture, form variables of the political behavior of socio-political subjects, which in turn influence directly the physiognomy of the political system (Pantelidou – Malouta, 1993:19; 1987:31-39). The political culture of a certain society reflects the general social culture and borrows characteristics from the social reality.

Political perception, political behavior and political culture are not synonymous notions but are still directly related to each other. As referred to above, we can consider political subjectivities, which are based on the socially and politically differentiated experience of individuals and groups, as influential variables of political culture and the political system. The political system then is not a coherent, functional part of the national political culture, diffused throughout the different social groups and levels, but is a differentiated amount of positions and experiences of individuals and groups according to their class, gender, race, age, religion, etc., that form their social, political and economic reality. Following the relation between

---

[9] G.Almond, and S.Verba's definition. In contemporary political science, Almond has introduced a definition of political culture as an analytical category in 'Comparative political systems', *Journal of Politics*, 18, 1956.

subjectivities and political culture, we can use gender as a variable of differentiation and formation of social and political experience and trace its linkages to the political identities of individuals and groups and its relation to the political culture. This analytical view of a given political culture (Greek) enables an understanding of the formation of gendered subjectivities in the Political and the development of politics around gender within the political culture[10].

2.3.2 On Greek Political Culture

Talking about Greek political culture, we can trace some indicative characteristics of the particular political culture, even if the term is not expressing the 'political mind' of a whole society.

The influence of the dominant political culture on the ways in which individuals view and make sense of their realities as they experience them is quite substantial. There is a constant pressure diffused throughout all social, political and cultural levels to impose a common reality, valid for everyone and formed by a systemic symbolic violence, which hides the correlation of powers out of which it exists (Foucault, 1977). This reality forms the consciousness, ideas and beliefs of the majority of people and is reproduced through basic institutions of socialization such as family and schooling. These institutional environments are imposing a 'periscopic' view of individuals, offering a training in viewing the world through 'another's' eyes and from a certain perspective. Accordingly, the political culture is reproduced through processes of political socialization. Political socialization is a social process that links the micro level (individual) with the macro level (society), transgressing the domain of the political. Often, political socialization[11] reflects general socializing processes and differs according to the realities of certain social groups and generations. The process of political socialization changes through time, reflecting the changes of the political culture and the differentiation of the social messages that affect each social

[10] Attempts for more analytical views on the matter of political culture in the Greek context are made by M. Pantelidou-Malouta, 1987, where the political socialization of adolescents as a variable of formation and change of Greek political culture is introduced and ibid. 2000, where the issues of gender and democracy based on women's participation in Greek politics are discussed. Theoretical analyses of political culture are introduced by Terlexis, 1975-1976 and Ventouris, 1977.

[11] Political socialization is defined as the process through which the individual forms her/his beliefs, values, ideas around the political system to which she/he belongs and understands her/his own role as a political agent.

group differently. Nevertheless, political socialization is a process that takes place within a certain socio-political context, influencing its development in certain directions.

Political socialization differs according to the age group. Empirical research has shown that during childhood and adolescence some basic predispositions are created that form lifelong political behaviors of citizens. F. Greenstein (1965) suggests that the most influential political ideas and orientations of adults are formed during the process of 'political learning' during childhood (Pantelidou – Malouta, 1987:57). Children and teenagers are very sensitive to cultural transformations of a society and very adaptable to developing tendencies of socio-cultural phenomena, even if they have specificities as a social category[12].

In order to describe the political culture within the Greek context, I will consider two aspects that give an alternative picture rather than the classic political theory perspective on political processes.

Two variables that show the most about the morphology and development of a certain political culture are the involvement of young people (teenagers and young adults) and the participation of women in political processes.

2.3.3 On Political Socialization of Children and Young Adults

Teenagers and young adults are usually in a phase of 'searching for identity', which is often described as a 'phase of crisis', which is not linked to psychological factors but rather has to do with the position society attributes to the young persons (Pantelidou – Malouta, 1987:73). The attribution of general behavioral characteristics to young girls, for example, influences their political socialization and often explains their weak presence in the public sphere of politics (even if more recent analyses on the matter have indicated some changes in this direction). The preparation for entrance to institutions of higher education (which is mostly the case for teenagers in Greece) and the choice of occupation compel young adults to get involved within competitive procedures and force them to consider the chances for social development and the achievement of a higher social status. These processes bring young people mostly closer to centers of political decisions.

[12] Children and teenagers have an emotional connection with the family and make their first social experiences through school and peer groups and generally are viewed as passive receivers of social messages.

Political socialization is a continuous cultural process that is realized through intersecting variables and forms a system of political communication that sometimes sustains and other times destabilizes a certain political system (Metaxas, 1976:24). In this context, influential factors that can explain the socio-political phenomena of individual and collective behavior are not only the different levels of education but the possibility of early participation in decision making processes within school class, a factor that stabilizes the dominant form of political culture (Ventouris, 1978:123).

In the Greek context, the ways in which basic institutions within the context of liberal democracy have been founded have created ideological problems around the notion of democracy and participation of all social groups, such as children[13]. Basic carriers of socialization for young generations, such as family and school, have traditionally been carriers of authoritative and suppressive political socialization (Pantelidou – Malouta, 1987:61).

The contact with political youth organizations in the school and the university, as well as the changing relationship to mass media and sources of information, influences massively the political socialization of teenagers and young adults (Pantelidou – Malouta, 1987:74).

Political socialization is an interactive process. Young people receive political messages from various sites of the social world and bring them back to the peer group and the family[14]. Within families in which politics is a topic of interest, very often a site of conflict around this topic is created, if there are oppositions.

Focusing, however, on institutions as carriers of socialization for young people can lead to a functionalist view on politics that imposes an abstracted view of the person and does not consider personal and collective political practices and the importance of social structures.[15]

---

13 About exclusion of children, as legally not eligible for participation in democratic processes, see C. Delphy in DIOTIMA: To fulo ton dikaiwmaton. Athina: Nefeli, 1999.

14 As Pantelidou- Malouta mentions, this happens usually in the lower classes, among which the young person often informs parents and other members of the family of 'what is happening' and negotiates the family's political and electoral behavior (1987:74)

15 During the 1960s, studies in political socialization were focusing on questions around the transmission of political ideas from the parents to children and were offering explanations about the lack of working class political efficacy, among other issues. The political socialization research was focusing on formal politics, such as presidents, parties, elections, etc. Politics was not defined clearly through the struggle for state power, and political socialization was not seen as a series of consequences of state action or strategies of state controlling. Therefore, early analysis of political socialization was not

In the framework of a study about the socialization of teenagers and young adults in the context of political institutions, which actually entails talking about the political socialization processes, it is important to conceptualize the person as an agent, to consider patterns of resistance to socialization, and to bear in mind other collective practices. Human development is not an acquisition of norms, and political agents are not isolated individuals, but they learn to adjust to a social collectivity and develop new capacities for action. Especially when talking about political socialization within political institutions, we should consider an interplay between consciousness and practice at both the personal and the collective level.

For the individual's perception of the world, ideology plays also an important role. Ideology is not only formed through individual politicization but also through religious, cultural and social representations that exist in a society or that are circulated through institutional structures

Another site that offers socio-political values is the peer group, groups formed within school, sport clubs and various associations (Ventouris, 1977:124).[16]

It is important to understand that teenagers and young adults are growing in a field of social relations which is inherently political, even if we follow them into the families, the school, the peer groups, the sports clubs or student associations. In these frameworks, we are offered the opportunity to investigate how patterns of development are shaped by this politics (e.g. the construction of a particular form of femininity and masculinity) and the way the patterns of personality and practice which are shaped themselves constitute the political order in various ways[17]. Another way of looking into political socialization is the study of collective practice (e.g., the class practice of families or the institutional practice of schools) in which the person

---

able to explain phenomena typical for various political cultures such as chauvinism or nationalism (Connell, 1987:216-217). Political socialization is misleadingly theorized as a process that inducts inevitably the person into a certain political culture or as a process that inculcates on persons attitudes towards the political system (Metaxas: Politiki Koinwnikopoiisi. Athens: Olkos, 1976:17).

16 According to Lenski (1954), the increasing time of schooling (including higher education) in the last years and the integration into the educational system of members of lower classes, together with the industrialization and the development of urban centres, has as an effect on the increasing influence of the peer group among people of the same age and the restriction of the personal orientation through family (Ventouris, 1977:123).

17 In this framework, research on masculinities, violence and warfare and their implications for understanding the state, have been developed (Patton and Poole, 1985)

appears not as the object of socialization but as a participant in power relations, negotiations, ideology-formation, and so on (Connell, 1987:222).

All these different influences, in combination with further factors, form the orientation of a person towards authorities and the political system, generally. The consciousness of social and political responsibility, interest and the ability of participation in decision making constitute a personal system of values that refers always to the social context in which the person lives.

A series of influences that determine social and political attitudes have an impact upon society as a whole. Society is then something more than the sum of the parts and individuals that constitute it. These influences create the collective memory of a certain society and reflect the historical experiences that this society has concentrated on through time. Economic or political crises, revolutions, wars and terror attacks leave marks upon the consciousness of a society that can lead next generations towards certain forms of political behavior that cannot be explained otherwise (Ventouris, 1977:128)

Behavioral ways and attitudes typical for a social context, have been linked very early with factors of identity construction, a subject common for psychoanalytical methods. Erikson (1979) notes that socialization is a process that takes place within the person and in the cultural center of a certain community, which the person belongs to. The person learns to appreciate what is broadly appreciated and searches for acceptance by orientating towards values valid within the socio-cultural context it belongs to. At this point, the multiple structures of the personality intersect with the structures of the social context, so that the realization of the self comes through the relation and connection with the others.

2.3.4 Young People in Greek Political Culture

M. Pantelidou-Malouta (1987), in her analysis of the political socialization of teenagers within the Greek political context, has distinguished as a variable of the political culture the crucial role of the 'leader' within almost all parties and has described how that affects the political perception of young adults as well as older age groups. The 'customary system' that the major parties in power for the last 30 years have been cultivating and the poles left/right, central for the formation of political landscape are also some dominant characteristics of the Greek political culture (*Ibid*, 46).

Studies on Greek political culture were designed already in late 1980s. In 1988, 53.5% of Greeks admitted an interest in politics (45.5% of them were women and 61.5% men), a high percentage in comparison to other southern-European countries such as Italy, Spain and Portugal. As Pantelidou-Malouta (Pantelidou-Malouta, 1990) suggests, mere numbers do not exactly show who these Greeks are that are interested in politics and what exactly they mean by 'politics'. It becomes obvious that the central constituting element of Greek political culture is the notion of politics itself and the way it is perceived by the different groups of citizens. The interest in politics is based on personal experience and is rather determining for the whole political *Weltanschauung* of individuals and groups. There are various categories of perception of politics in Greek political culture. There is the perception of politics with a collective dimension, politics as matter of public interest, politics as an overarching element of all aspects of life, politics as show, politics as a means of solution for personal/family problems, politics as a random topic of general interest, politics as a process that refers to selected ones, negative perception of politics (*Ibid*, 48). Interestingly, a large number of people are positioned around the left/right axis. Gender as a differentiating factor affects the way individuals see politics as influential (or not) in their personal lives. The 'political' of the political culture, meaning the perception of politics as a controversial social procedure in which all issues refer to everyone and everyone is interested in them as part of a whole, is a minority perception on the level of general perceptions of politics in the Greek political context.

The two major perceptions of 'politics' are: first, that politics is not for all and about all; and second, that politics is a personal matter, and so political participation is a demand-supply relational process. Very few perceive the collective dimension of the political as a matter of public interest that has a major impact on all aspects of life. Therefore, the 'political' Greeks, an image that comes out of the high percentages of political interest and political involvement (any form of it), is shaken after an analysis of what is meant by politics, what is the motivation for political interest and who gets interested. There are several perceptions of politics in which the collective and the public get lost, and politics become a means of service for personal needs. The ephemeral, temporary and coincidental character of the political interest is also revealed.

On the level of organized politics, there is a high percentage of membership. According to the system of 'customer services' that has been in place the last 30 years by the two major mainstream parties in Greece, the political interest as a motivating factor for active involvement is set under question. Often party politics (usually parties of major power within the parliament) reflect the general direction of the political culture that is dominant at a certain historical moment.

In a democratic system, what counts are ideas about the common good and harmonious living within society and not physical persons often of a certain kind (white, middle class, high status occupation), persons who happen to represent peoples' will in the parliament. The carriers of these ideas that form and affect political, economic and social issues in the contemporary parliamentarian democratic system are usually considered to be the political parties. This notion of democracy that is described here is based on the idea of vaguely 'equal' individuals who have equal and valid rights to express their opinions, a notion that loses its validity more and more. The contemporary political culture in times of political, social and economic crisis is negatively loaded with scandals and corruption in the body of representatives, creating a bigger gap between the electoral body and the representatives of the will of the people. The homogeneity of most political programmes makes parties untrustworthy to a broader part of society (this is reflected in discourses such as 'all are the same, everybody says the same').

On top of that, the political dystopias around the 'death of ideologies' and 'end of history' are shaking the image of political processes and collective, organized political actions and therefore alienate many people from the Political. Moreover, the systematic isolation and exemption of many social groups (migrants, women, persons with disabilities) from the right to participate actively in the Political is bringing up debates and demands around equal representation systems and quota systems. However, these political demands that are welcomed by a broader spectrum of political groups and agents are not able to change and redefine the notion of democracy, nor are they able to add the issue of equal representation to the existing character of parliamentarian democracy and to reveal also other faces of the democratic system subordinated to the dominant and ever-present one (Varika, 1995:45).

Another special element that forms the character of Greek political culture is the co-existence of traditional and modernized participatory tendencies among the political perceptions and attitudes of young people. There are some traditional notions with long lasting effect, as the importance of self-sacrifice for the home country and others which are more popular among teenagers and young adults, such as the notion of unequal treatment of citizens by the state and the state as a figure of suppression. All these notions are integrated in a general system of democratic and representational perceptions of the political system (Pantelidou-Malouta, 1987:531). Generally, the main idea is that the citizen has obligations but also a wide spectrum for intervention. This perception of the notion of the suppressive state is not referring to the class nature of the state (that sustains class divisions, to the benefit of the people who fill in the structures, creating a division between state and citizen as two contradictory spheres (*Ibid*, 531)).

Greek political culture seems rather participatory and democratic, as the notion 'politics should interest everyone' is very popular, and political involvement is not perceived as a privilege of the few (despite the obvious under- representation of certain social groups such as women, migrants, people with disabilities, etc.) Citizen intervention is usually considered to 'bring something' and the reaction in a case of disagreement with a governmental decision is perceived positively, as 'people have a saying'. Research that was conducted with children and young teenagers in the end of the 1980s (Pantelidou-Malouta, 1987) has shown that children are informed about the political preferences of the parents (especially the father) and that they already have a concept of political processes such as elections and are able to make some clear distinctions between executive and legislative principles of the political system. This shows that Greek political culture does not exclude children from its framework, and a higher level of political inclusion of young people appears alongside the participation of teenagers and young adults in political organizations.

Some interesting findings from the research I have conducted are that, as expected, the system of perceptions between young people who position themselves towards the left or the right differs. Some of the people, however, do not identify with the party and claim a general political interest or will to somehow participate in political processes. These people do not have clear ideological positions (although they are interested in politics) and are to be found among the general category of the right or the conservative[18] (a description that they often give themselves). This tendency is an indication of the dominant Greek political culture. The left positioning of

[18] Conservativism refers to, according to Burke, a resistance to social and political change, the importance of traditional values and the disbelief on the ability of the people to change their fates on their personal or collective initiative. Adorno gave another definition to conservativism, connecting the notion with some expressions of everyday or political processes, as for example the attitude towards social welfare, underlining this way the political aspect of the notion (Ventouris, 1977:171). In my research characteristic was the definition a participant gave: 'Conservativism is the will to preserve rights and privileges that someone or a group already has. This is not a characteristic of the right but of the left in certain respect.'

the young informants of the research is connected often with more clearly formed ideological positions and tendencies, more clear identification with a certain political party or youth organization, bigger interest in political processes and issues of 'public interest'. Another interesting finding is that many members of political youth organizations positioned in the right have in earlier stages of political socialization passed through organizations of the left, some radical ones, also (often anarchist groups), in an attempt to orientate themselves politically. This phenomenon has to do with the radicalization of teenagers and young adults and especially women that seems to cease with older age (*Ibid*, 533).

Generally, the higher social position is translated into more participatory political attitude. The higher the level of information is, which is directly linked to higher educational levels, the more developed is the perception that individual or collective intervention in political processes can be successful. This is characteristic of the privileged classes and form the ways they perceive the political processes and the political system.

In the Greek political context, it becomes clear that better informed are the children and teenagers who belong to the middle class, who have achievable aspirations for social upgrading (through studying and specialized education) and that they are the groups that mostly criticize the traditional ideas about national and international politics and show more modern, participatory and radical elements in their systems of political ideas and perceptions (Pantelidou-Malouta, 1987: 535).

There are small differences in the range of political perceptions that have to do with gender differences, and that proves that the traditional patterns of differentiated political involvement according to sex/gender are becoming less actual. The differences in the political perceptions are becoming less clear as teenagers grow up, and already young adults share political perceptions regardless of gender differences. There is a tendency that girls form a clear ideological and political identity later than boys and that usually they adopt more mature and are therefore more resistant to changing political or party identities than are boys. Girls have the tendency to choose more compliant ways of political involvement, and they express more frequently ideas and perceptions of the dominant political culture. This has rather to do with the lower level of information that is typical for women (Pantelidou-Malouta, 1990: 31). The lower the class position, the larger is the differentiation among the perceptions, positions and political involvement according gender (*Ibid*, 33).

2.3.5 'Gender Equality': Participation of Women in Greek Politics

An indicative element of a political culture in respect to gender is the participation of women in the political structures and processes. In Greece, although women gained the right to vote in 1952, they had only token participation in the electoral processes. In the political era after dictatorship, a polymorphous movement of feminist groups and women's mass organizations actively developed. Their influential presence in the political scene led to the inclusion of the principle of 'gender equality' in the constitution of 1975. This typical acknowledgement of equality has been followed by a strong demand of feminist groups and women's associations for changes in the family law, the protection of maternity rights, the securing of gender equality in working relations, laws against rape, special rights for working parents, etc. Parallel to changes in legislation, there have been some significant changes on the level of social perceptions that refer to gender equality. First and most important was the issue of gender equality itself that started being discussed in different social and political debates and was very present in mainstream media. In research done in 1988, mostly young women (70%) had the opinion that often women do not have equal chances to access politics. In the same research in 2005 the percentage is 64.2% among women between 18-30 years old (less than in 1988) but it rises to 71.7% among women between 31-44 and reaches up to 74.5% among women between 45-59 years old (Pantelidou-Malouta, 2006: 90). From the 1980s until present, the social position of women, especially on the level of representations (equal chances in the job market or equal access to politics as a 'politically correct' social demand) has positively developed. What remains as a clear marker of the social marginalization of women is their under-representation within all political, economic and social decision-making structures. In this respect and under the general political climate within the EU for more 'gender mainstreaming', in the elections of 1989, for the first time, it was ensured that the quota system appears in the lists of the parties involved. Since then, there has been a constant political demand for a certain level of participation in the decision making processes within parties and women's organizations, regulated by a quota system that would ensure 35% participation in all bodies.

This measure was criticized a lot by various feminist circles and women's organizations as a modern legitimization of inequality (*Ibid*, 91) that seemed to constitute and establish the minor presence of women in the political scene. Since 1989, gradually all political parties have adopted various quota systems that regulate the participation of women and men in internal conferences and elections. Today, in all political parties[19] there are quotas (which usually secure around 35% of women's participation) for all organizational bodies and levels. In 2000, with the initiation of the General Secretary Office for Equality (N.2839/ 2000), an official quota system (one third female presence of the total number of participants) was enforced by law (N. 2839/ 2000) in all decision making bodies of the public sector, as well as in all companies and organizations that are state controlled. By law, in 2001 (N.2910, 75) the participation of women – one third of the total number of participants – in electoral lists on a local, national and European level was mandated.

As expected, the quota system has brought few changes in the morphology of politics in Greece the last years. Today, discussions about the next step, the equal representation in all public decision-making bodies, are open.

To map the situation of women's participation within the context of gender equality in politics, some recent facts should be presented. In the composition of the present government (composed after the parliamentarian elections in 2009), there are 9 women out of 37 politicians in the ministerial body.

In the national parliament, out of 157 seats of PASOK, 31 are occupied by women: out of 88 seats of Nea Dimokratia, 9 went to women; from the 21 seats of KKE, 5 belong to women; from the 9 seats of SYRIZA, 2 went to women. LAOS has 15 seats, 1 is occupied by a woman; 6 seats went to independent deputies, out of which 2 are occupied by women; and out of the 4 seats of Dimotiki Aristera, one went to a woman.

Looking at the organizational bodies within political youth organizations, at the top of the hierarchies (which is called either Secretary or President) no woman is to be found. Nevertheless, quota systems are in force among all political youth organizations, and they are reflected upon the composition of the central bodies of the political youth organizations. In the National Delegation of PASOK Youth there are 120 members, 48 of each sex. Within SYRIZA Youth there is a quota (1/3) for participation of women in all organizational bodies, and there is an open discussion for equal rep-

[19] The Communist Party (KKE) has been using quotas in its organizational bodies from 1991 until 1996, when the measure was dismissed. According to its constitution, however, the increased participation of women within the bodies of the party should be a major concern and nowadays it is the only party with a woman at the top of the hierarchy (in the case of KKE, in the position of the general secretary).

resentation measures. In the Coordinating Secreteriat of ONNED out of the 11 members, 4 are women, and in Administrative Board of NE.OS (LAOS) out of 10 members, 2 are women. In KNE (Communist Youth) there is no official quota system for women's participation, as is the case within the party, but special attempts to increase women's involvement in all organizational bodies are constantly being made (according to the constitution of the organization).[20]

These measures also have a negative influence on a symbolic and ideological level for women. In this research, it also becomes obvious that the majority of the active agents in politics are negative towards special measures that enforce gender equality.

In conclusion, we can still say that the minor presence of women in political leading groups is a structural characteristic of Greek political culture (Diamantouros 1983, 2000). The isolation and marginalization of women within power structures and power relations, which is a consequence of social marginalization, cannot be captured through notions of representation and participation of women. Based on the democratic principles and the ways the existing political system works, it cannot be considered that the women in the Parliament are representing women as a social category (Pantelidou-Malouta, 2006:100). As a matter of fact, the women who are in the Greek parliament right now represent only the interest of the voters of the certain party they belong to. The existing social, political and economic situation of women's inequality (as well as class, ethnicity, race, etc., inequalities) cannot be solved with more women's representation and participation but through political processes and positions that would change how gender is considered politically and socially. Here questions about the character of democracy arise. As Pantelidou-Malouta (Pantelidou-Malouta, 2006: 101) correctly suggests, the issue is not how the dichotomy women/men would be respected within politics, but how the gendered dimension of citizens will be respected in its multiplicity and multi-dimensionality and how gender will matter only as one of personal special characteristics that individuals have, without creating hierarchies and dichotomies among people and citizens.

What becomes obvious, when we look at the political culture with all its special characteristics as it is nowadays in Greece and talking to political agents within this context during this current research, is that sub-

[20] All the data are taken from the official websites of the youth organizations. http://onned.gr ßurlhttp://www.neolaia-pasok.gr, http://www.kne.gr, http://www.neolaiasyn.gr, http://www.neolaialaos.gr

jects (individual and collective) are lacking the ability to even imagine ways of expressing their gendered substance within the actual political context. There is a lack of perspective beyond the established categories of 'man' and 'woman', as there is a lack of political imagination of new social and political processes that can actually bring social change (a demand that is present in personal and collective political discourses). The true freedom from boundaries and binaries that a political culture should have as a goal cannot be realized through more women's participation. It should respect the individual and collective needs and aim for the realization of the demand of equality, but equality and democracy do not exhaust their meanings only in relation to women.

What the discourses of the informants of this research reveal is that gender continues to play a major role for the material conditions of life, the family histories, the work and working relations, the chances, aspirations and dreams of citizens. For this to become more obvious, we have to look to the collected information I gathered from the discussions.

3 Methodological Approaches-Epistemological Assumptions

Research is a way of knowledge production. In my opinion, there are three fundamental and interconnected questions that lead a research process: the first is what is there to be known; the second, how one is to know what is to be known; and the third is how the inquirer can go about finding out whatever can be known (according to her understanding). The theories about reality determine what there is to be known each time and how someone should go about it. What can be known is intertwined with the interaction between a particular investigator and a particular object of inquiry. Critical theory, which has its ontological roots in historical materialism, theorizes reality as shaped by a series of social, political, cultural, economic, gender and ethnic factors crystallized into a series of structures that are taken for real, natural and unchangeable (Denzin; Lincoln, 1994:110). Through a dialogue between the investigator and the subjects of inquiry, the historically mediated structures, taken as unchangeable, can be converted to an informed consciousness by uncovering the forms of historical and subjugated knowledges that reveal experiences of oppression, conflict and collective struggle, so that a historical understanding can lead to elements of critique and hope (Giroux, 1988:213 in Denzin et al, 1994:110). The aim of such a study is the critique first, and then comes the transformation of social, political, cultural, ethnic and gender structures that exploit humanity, by engagement in confrontation, even conflict. Feminist research has added to the ontological, epistemological and related methodological concepts of critical theory the fundamental question of who can be a knower (Code, 1991:xi), introducing women researchers as well as women as participants in an inquiry and women in general as contributors to a meaning-making process about social, economic, political, cultural and historical phenomena.

3.1 From Feminist Theory to Feminist Political Demands

The whole work is set in the framework of the feminist theory of science and follows the principles of 'feminist standpoint theory'. This theory of science, which introduces an epistemological line, has its roots, like critical theory, in the Marxist theory and draws on the demand of 2nd wave of feminism for a 'formation of women's consciousness' (Papageorgiou, 2010:93). On the methodological base of Marxism, feminist standpoint theory becomes an important epistemological tool for understanding and opposing all forms of domination (Hartsock, 1997:462), as it researches thoroughly the relations of knowledge and power. In this context, theorists believe that social knowledge cannot be distinguished from the political, which makes the relation between knowledge and power the main focus of feminist standpoint theory.

The concept of a standpoint can be understood if the epistemological significance of human activity, very central in Marx[1], is stressed. Marxist thought perceives the collective class consciousness, produced by the dominant relations of production, as an acknowledgement of a common and collective experience that comes out of the oppression of the working class. On the basis of this experience, a certain ideology that can be a motivating tool for resistance is shared by members of the working class and informs their views and understanding, as well as how they are experiencing the world. Feminist theory adds to and stresses this perception that the ideology, based on the certain viewpoint of the working class, differs among individuals belonging to the same class, in multiple ways and also according to gender. The feminist epistemology emphasizes the gendered differences and thus the subjectivities and subjective identities. That is why in this work there is constant reference to gendered subjectivities and gendered subjects.

Feminist standpoint theory takes off from the point that the division of labor, both by class and by gender, has consequences for knowledge. Class society as a whole produces a dual vision, a ruling class vision and 'the understanding available to the ruled' (Hartsock, 1997:465). On this duality, the feminist 'standpoint' structures a certain epistemology that refers

1 'As individuals express their life, so they are. What they are, therefore, coincides with their production both with what they produce and how they produce. The nature of individuals thus depends on the material conditions determining their production' (Marx, K (1970).The German Ideology, ed. C.J.Arthur .New York: International Publishers, p. 42)

rather to gender than class differences[2], offering an analytical tool for relations between both. It posits a duality of levels of reality, where on the surface, the vision of the ruling class (or gender) structures the material conditions for a whole society but, in a 'deeper level of essence', shows the ways that the appearance inverts the deeper reality (*Ibid*, 464). By offering the understanding of the oppressed, the standpoint lens reveals the real relations among people that are unequal in a certain historical moment, but 'points beyond the present, and carries a historical liberatory role (Hartsock, 1997:464). As Marxist epistemology explores, on the basis of an account of the division of labor, the oppositions between the activities of the dominant and the dominated, feminist standpoint epistemology explores the differences between women's and men's activity and what kind of consequences the sexual division of labor has for knowledge and knowledge production. This kind of epistemological analysis cannot focus on individual men and women but makes possible the exploration of institutionalized social practices, stressing that male domination concerns institutions that determine social relations between women and men.

The differentiated male and female activities in class society lead to a construction of identity that is formed, first, always in opposition to the Other, and, second, by a world view that is masculinized and formulated by the dichotomy (dominant and dominated) of class society that leads to hierarchical dualisms. The views on social reality differ from where each one stands (standpoint) and from which angle someone sees the world. The victims of hierarchies and categorizations experience the world differently from those who force their view on the whole society. The disadvantaged experience the marginalization in every aspect of social, political and economic life in which they participate or set their activities in. The dominant see the world as they think and construct it to be a continuously advantageous situation that inverts the deeper unequal reality to a fake appearance of normality. The 'social truth' is not obvious in the eyes of the people who set the rules, but most forms of knowledge about the social truth are informed by the dominant view. However, the consciousness of the different stands people belong to enables them to realise a broader part of the 'essence' of social reality. 'Social truth' is more reflected upon the eyes of the dominated rather than upon the eyes of the dominant. However, only few realise that, and the research process where individuals are asked to

2 In comparison to the proletarian standpoint that Marx introduces, which is formed by class divisions

re-construct their realities can be an informative and liberating way to gain consciousness about the experienced realities.

There are some central criteria that set the epistemological map of standpoint theory. The first and crucial assumption is that women's material conditions of life, what N. Hartsock (2004) calls life 'activity', constructed on the basis of class, or C. McKinnon (1982) names 'sexuality', based on the structure of sex/gender, is the main source of ontological and epistemological knowledge for a standpoint theory that aims to understand social relations. Based on the personal experience of women, the knowledge that is revealed through the feminist standpoints is always partial and never absolute or totally 'objective'. S. Harding (1992) talks about a 'strong objectivity' of the knowledge, as the knower is also the object of the knowledge and connected in real relations (based on experience) with the things that they know. D. Haraway (1997) stressed that knowledge is partial, meaning that it is always biased (being produced by very personal experience made upon the different gendered, economic, national, religious, local, and cultural stands within the map of social reality).

3.2 Knowledge and Power

Women's voices and truths are positioned in relation to the social power that forms their lives (Mies, 1993). Their view is formed by the patriarchal order, but their social reality reveals more from the true essence of the rules of human relations than that of men and becomes a source of a better standpoint from which an observer can have access to a 'better' understanding of the world. As J. Scott writes, what we know has a direct connection to how we look at the things: 'knowledge is gained through vision; vision is a direct, unmediated apprehension of a world of transparent objects' (Scott in Butler, 1997:23).

Therefore, in contrast to traditional social sciences, which tend to take identities as self-evident and ignore the differences between them, thus naturalizing them, feminist standpoint methodology poses the question about how the conceptions of the self are produced by the subjects. As Scott underlines, by giving authenticity to different experiences, feminist research takes women (or other marginalized people) as individuals with agency into consideration, and by mobilising a consciousness raising method to extract knowledge from experience, the research is activating a means for resistance to oppression (Scott, 1997:31). Not only by focusing on experience but by placing a point of view in a certain social, political, economic and historical stand, by 'historizing' experience, they reveal and give a chance to analysis of certain relations of power that lead to oppression.

Feminists who follow the standpoint theory are interested in producing 'more' and 'better' knowledge from different 'standpoints' or perspectives than the established, hegemonic and androcentric theories that overlook the social positions of women (and often of marginalized men), their views and their experiences. Therefore, feminist standpoint theorists are interested in collecting information examining the experiences of women within the various androcentric cultures. Difference is important to feminist standpoint theorists, difference of experience that is based on the different material, social, political and economic situations that influence women's lives. Standpoint theorists introduce into their works the differences among gender subjects that appear in regard to sexuality, class, race, ethnicity, etc. (Harding, 1993). Often theorists insist that the exploitation and suppression of women differs according to the different categories that women are put in. In this context, standpoint theorists insist that the researcher should share the same race or ethnicity in order to develop a better understanding and communications with the subjects under research. Taking into consideration the different realities and positions of women and men, standpoint theorists should consider not only the differences but also the power relations that link and relate each experience and standpoint with each other. Standpoint theory searches for heterogeneity, as relations (between humans, power relations, etc.) are about differences. The different social locations and standpoints make it possible to contextualize and give meaning to experience, and this moves away from the trend to categorize according to the similar characteristics and qualities that dominant, universalistic and androcentric categories offer. The deconstruction of major categories is done by the feminist standpoint theorists by revealing the differences between standpoints and experiences of women who are not part of the same, big group.

The social standpoint of each subject requires a process and a series of discourses to be achieved and realised. Gendered subjects gain consciousness of their social position as soon as they realise the process of their social construction. For both the knower and the object of knowledge, it should become clear that this social construction happens within a certain system of domination and unequal social, political, and economic relations. The knowledge of the personal standpoint and of the world comes from the very society that forms them and from their own experiences, which reflect the same society that influences their formation. Therefore, standpoint theorists focus on the social standpoint that becomes a standpoint for producing social experience-based knowledge. A standpoint forms the basis from which unequal relations are revealed and offers the opportunity to get distance from them. Therefore, it is 'an achievement of both analysis and political struggle occurring in a particular historical space' (Hartsock, 1997:476).

What standpoint theory and epistemology offer to research is the ability to go beyond the surface deep to the real social relations informed by the experience of the dominant gender and class. This moving beyond requires both theoretical and political activity. The feminist standpoint formed about and around women's life offers material (or materialism) with which critique can be used against phallocratic ideology and institutions (*Ibid*, 478)[3].

As feminist standpoint theory investigates thoroughly the relations between knowledge and power, the social experience and knowledge it produces cannot be distinguishable from the political, because the power relations that influence the formation of social reality, as sources of knowledge, have a very political character directly connected with the social character of the standpoint. Feminist standpoint theorists are not only looking for knowledge production that reflects more aptly the different experiences of women but are also looking for better, clearer and more knowledge, knowledge that is less distorted than that which andorcentric theories of science produce. By combining more standpoints, more experiences and being closer to the source of real knowledge, which is everyday experience of social reality, standpoint theorists aim to a relationism (and avoid relativism, because not all standpoints are equal and show as clearly as others reality) that leads to revealing interrelations and intersections of different categories and aspects that affect women's experiences, such as sexuality, class, race etc. (Harding, 1993; Moya; Alcoff, 2000).The focus of standpoint methodologies is on revealing the differences of the subjects under analysis, aiming to show a complex heterogeneity rather than creating homogenous categories in which each individual should fit.

Another important contribution of standpoint theory on epistemological methods of research is the inclusion of the researcher in the process of analysis. Traditional methods of research place women in a common category and describe their experience without taking into consideration the different roles of the researcher and the researched, their commonalities and their

---

3 'Only at the last culmination of the development of class society (that) this, its secret, appears again, namely that on the one hand it is the product of the oppression of women, and that on the other it is the means by which women, participate in and create their own oppression' (Marx, K. Economic & Philosophic Manuscripts of 1844 in www.marxists.org)

'points of touch' and how this affects the process of knowledge production. This crucial point, which influences the epistemological and methodological procedures of scientific analysis and which has been underlined by feminists of colour, stresses the fact that not only are there different categories of women, but the suppression of each woman differs according to her class, race, ethnicity, religion, etc., and that oppression happens under very real material conditions that differ according to time and place. They underline the fact that the researcher and the researched group should have some common points, common experiences upon which better communication and less distorted and disturbed production of knowledge will be possible. Among the different stands of feminist standpoint theory, there is consensus on the fact that women are suppressed by male domination and androcentirc institutions, and that the best way to collect information about the topic of gender suppression is to research as many different groups of women and their experience as possible, so that a combination of as many standpoints as possible will present a well informed picture of subordination and exploitation based not only on gender but on class, race, ethnicity etc. (Papageorgiou, 2010:98)

3.3 Feminist Standpoint Epistemology for a Study on Masculinities

What can feminist standpoint epistemology offer to a study on masculinities? Masculinity studies, in the light of feminist theory and gender studies, which put the natural and homogeneous category of 'woman' under strong criticism, declared 'man' also as a gendered construction with many analytical, epistemological and methodological consequences. The implications that the women's liberation movement have for 'men' in theoretical discourses are multiple, with the most important aspect being the turn to the understanding of the historical, political, social and economic construction of all gender categories. Sociological analysis of masculinities can introduce to gender studies a turn of epistemological focus on economic relations, patterns of social organizations, forms of political authority and ideology (Adams; Savran, 2002:77). Going beyond the fact that men represent the dominant class in many cultural contexts, social sciences have already demonstrated that forms of male domination are linked to economic and political institutions, ideologies and class formations. The political meaning of writing about masculinity turns towards an analysis of power. At this point feminist standpoint epistemology offers a view on power and power relations that combines gender formation with social, political and economic stands within an institution or society as a whole. For an analysis of masculinities within political youth organizations in contemporary Greece, masculinities become a form of political organization, part of material political practices, an aspect of patriarchal society, a metaphor that authorizes the renegotiation of masculinity discourses in an institutional context, an act of political socialization, all set under the light of ideology that informs the personal discourses of gendered subjects. The ideological view on society forms the individual and collective ways of making sense of the world and, parallel to that, offers various standpoints for looking analytically, epistemologically and methodologically at a phenomenon as masculinity constructions in the particular social, political, cultural and ideological institutional framework of political youth organizations. This work investigates the masculinized character of a whole political culture as reflected in the organizational and related practices, as well as in the political identities of the members of political youth organizations and, parallel to that, tries to connect these organizational practices and discourses with the broader political, economic and social power relations.

By using these stands, standpoint methodology can make many things possible in an analysis of masculinities. It can reveal the power relations that form gender subjectivities looking from different economic, social, political, ideological stands, offering then these very standpoints as tools for social and ideological struggle, which – at the very least – can aim towards social change by revealing the power of individual and collective agency. Feminist standpoint epistemology as well as masculinity studies have in common the pluralizing and problematizing of notions and views of masculinity: first, by denaturalizing gender, linking forms of masculinities and femininities to economic and social structures; and second, using personal and collective experience offers a key methodology for collecting valid and actual information that can become a source of knowledge.

Through feminist standpoint methodology, we can focus on various patriarchal institutions uncovering the social structures that produce admittedly diverse masculinities. This means to go beyond masculinity as seen as 'unrelieved villainy' and men as seen as 'agents of patriarchy' (Carrigan et al, 2002:100), but rather to view masculinity as anchored in ideologies, political discourses and organizational practices and as shaped by political, economic and social structures of power. This presupposes to relate different forms of masculinity to each other and to the relative structures. It also presupposes to talk about hegemonic forms of masculinity that shape the

Political (in the case of political youth organizations) and which are – in turn – shaped by various forms of contemporary politics.

Following the line of feminist standpoint epistemology and trying to analyse the social organization of gender inequality, we can see how political consciousness is produced among men and women and how the character of women's and men's experience differs according to certain political ideologies, as the political has a class and a gender dimension. The intersection of gender and class can be traced in the ways in which the definitions of gender and class are constructed, communicated and transformed culturally, as class consciousness is not universal but is connected to a gendered subject (Alexander in Avdela; Psarra, 1994:47). For this work, a central hypothesis is that if identity is gendered, then class is gendered, too. The gendered identity is central to the gaining of class consciousness, as masculinity and femininity are not stable categories but are formed and changed according to the class and other culturally and historically given categories. The importance of gender, sexuality, family, and the division of domestic labor is becoming central through feminist standpoint epistemology in order to realize and analyse the political aspects of class struggle in contemporary societies.

Under the light of standpoint epistemology the class and gender aspect of knowledge production becomes a central issue for this work. By focusing on gendered identities formed within political youth organizations through the influence of political ideologies that contribute to the construction of personal and collective discourses around issues such as politics, gender relations, women's and men's activities in political organized life, views of utopian society etc., the research tries to answer the question of if and how class and gender forms the perspectives of individuals and groups within institutionalized organizations. The work cannot and should not aim to attribute certain behavioral and organizational patterns and strategies to individual men and women who are responsible for the character of political organizations and the political culture, without meaning to initiate an undervaluation of the personal and collective agency upon structures. The differentiations among masculinities as well as the various subjected forms of masculinities are psychological as they are equally institutional and reflect an aspect of collective practice. In Greek contemporary politics, there are various forms of hegemonic masculinity, which have in common the marginalization not only of women but also men who do not share certain characteristics and are mostly young, unskilled, inexperienced in the organizations, unable or unwilling to join 'rituals' of organized political life, etc.

Hegemonic notions of masculinity that are popular in politics are usually social definitions of masculinity embedded in the dynamic of institutions, in the political organization as well as being rooted in the personality of individuals. The 'masculinization' of Greek political culture, followed by sexism, homophobia, nepotism and the generalization of compulsory heterosexual norm within political organizations cannot be blamed on the gendered subjectivities of individual members nor on the personal views and perspectives that are parts of broader discourses. By focusing on the organizational, political, social and economic structures that form the character and the role of political youth organizations within the framework of liberal democracy, we can actually see how the power relations that form the knowledge of individuals reflect the power relations within broader social, political and economic structures of the late capitalist state.

As the personal discourses are parts of the broader structures, they bear, however, the view of the personal standpoint that reveals different aspects of social reality, in the work on masculinities within political organization we can navigate through contemporary discourses of the notion of the Political, the State and Citizenship, revealing their gendered dimension and the impact they have upon different experiences and subjectivities. By re-constructing the ways and the processes through which people experience and understand the public and the private and related binaries, such as equality/difference, and by placing them in the certain historical, social, economic and political context of contemporary Greek parliamentarian democracy, feminist standpoint epistemology and methodology allows critical view(s) upon the central paradoxes of modern democracy.

3.4 Focus Groups Discussions

In the two phases of the field work I have done in order to collect the empirical data, which this work uses, I have chosen to employ the method of focus groups discussions.

A focus group is 'an informal discussion among selected individuals about specific topic' (Beck et al, 1986:73).

Focus groups research is especially used in feminist research (Wilkinson, 1998a, 1999) to contact research on people's own views and understandings. As method is helpful to detect and follow individuals' attitudes, opinions, knowledge or beliefs (Wilkinson, 1998:16). During focus group discussions, a collective meaning-making process is taking place, where reconstructions and negotiations of individual or collective understanding in a certain social context are revealed.

In the case of this particular research, the group discussions were supposed to reflect the character of politics as a public space (group discussion as a public discussion), where opinions about public and private matters are expressed. The whole method is based on interaction and offers 'a strong mechanism for placing the control over this interaction in the hands of the participants rather than to the researcher' (Morgan, 1988:18).

For the purpose of this research, the focus groups were small (2-3 persons). Although the method depends a lot on how actively and easily participants would discuss the topic of interest, which is my case was not a problem since most of the people participate in open discussions, panels and meetings on a daily basis, smaller groups appear to have a different dynamic that larger groups and the discussions in a smaller group are more in depth and intensive.

An advantage that the method of group discussions offered in my case was that I was able to collect many opinions from different people in a shorter period of time, testing the questions and re-adjusting them for the next discussion faster. Because the gender variable is central issue for the research and an influencing factor during the process of discussion, I created homogenous groups of informants according to their sex and their area of political engagement. In the first phase of the research, which lasted for two months, I participated in discussions with male informants from the same youth organization each time. From each organization I took at least two different groups of informants. Accordingly, in the second phase I organized groups of female informants, again divided by political group. The homogeneity of the group gives a secure and known feeling to the informants since they are always among colleagues or even friends. That increases the willingness of the informants to explain, discuss and express opinions in a casual manner.

On the other hand, two major problems appeared that have to do with the homogeneous character of the group: first, often people tend to agree or meet very fast a consensus on various matters disrupting the process of re-construction of individual and collective ideas. Second, the group was sometimes easily disrupted by 'experts' or higher in the hierarchy informants and uncooperative participants. Since the groups were small, this was a very disturbing factor, although it did not happen very often.

After the completion of the group discussions the collective material was set under discursive analysis of content, the results of which are presented, systematized, analysed and set into connection with the theoretical analysis in the fourth chapter.

3.5 The Role of the Researcher in the Research Process

Research methods, as well as 'do's and don'ts' in the field are described and explained in many various handbooks. Generally, the guidelines are helpful but in my opinion refer often to ideal conditions of research. The personal experience of the researcher during the research defines her role in the research process and this role is developed as the researcher explores and finds her way in the field. For this particular work, it was from the beginning of significance that I was about to enter a field that was familiar to me, where I was personally involved already in the past, I was informed about it and the on-goings inside it from various people, who I was and still am in touch with. This would not only enable the access, but would save me time with mapping and exploring the field, as I had already some pieces of the puzzle figured out. Nevertheless, it was more difficult than I expected due to time restrictions and incidents such as shortly announced national elections during the period of the first field work, which made the meetings with members of political youth organizations fully engaged in campaigning actions, impossible. In this occasion, I became suddenly – as a person who wants contact with the organization – a possible voter, and as such, people were eager to talk to me but not about the issues of my research. On the other hand, this gave me an interesting insight into political practices and provided a possibility for observation.

Despite the fact that I was familiar with the field, the role of the so-called 'gatekeeper' was very important, and without such persons, who could make the effort to find telephone numbers of possible research participants or bring me in contact with certain people, the research process would have lasted longer and would have been more tiring and disappointing, in the beginning at least.

Although I had the gatekeepers, it was not that easy to arrange meetings in the original places, where political youth groups meet and the spaces in which they operate. In most of the cases, the gatekeepers were men and were usually members with more responsibility in the organization. They made sure that the discussion was arranged and were interested in what was said (without actually controlling the content). For me, the process of arranging discussions was a process of breaking through the organizational structures of hierarchy, bureaucracy and administration of political organizations that reflect the masculinized, androcentric and centralistic character of political organizations.

To some organizations the access was easier than to others, but this does not reveal a more open to discussion character or more democratic atmosphere among the structures, but rather an acquaintance with a 'service offering' and 'customary system' character that usually big political parties have. It seemed that people often turn to the bigger political organizations 'wanting a favour' and the attitude 'we are here to please you' from the side of the members of the organizations applied to my situation, as well. For many of the participants it was just another obligation or a suggestion that came from someone higher up or more experienced in the organization, although most of the participants took an interest in the whole project and often were eager to know more about it.

As I am going through the notes, personal comments and discussions I had back then with various people about the research process, I realise that one of the central issues I was concerned with as a researcher and that definitely has influenced the research process was the relationship between myself and the research participants, who in their majority were men. One of the first questions I asked myself was how the others, my discussion partners, were seeing me, receiving my role, and how this affected the communication and the whole fieldwork. I guess for most of the participants, I was a young woman (only few years older than most of the research participants) who is studying (a student rather than a researcher) at a foreign university. Many of the participants asked me how long I lived abroad and if I was familiar with the political and social situation in Greece. A fair question, since they had to decide how much they had to explain and how to structure their answers. It seemed that my own knowledge was influential for the process of knowledge production, and besides pointing questions, I was involved constantly in the discussions even if I was not commenting or even talking. The informants were testing my reactions and often asked for clarifications or my opinion on the matter. I usually avoided answering by stressing the fact that it was interesting what they understood about the question and so they could freely express themselves. Generally, I avoided explaining much about the topic and the questions, and I was often surprised by interpretations that I would not have thought myself.

Coming to talk about masculinity, inevitably the issue of what it is to be a man came up. Interestingly enough, in some discussions the issue of 'Greekness' and the 'men in Greece' appeared. Usually, people who belong typically to the same cultural and national context thematicize their own cultural identity in comparison to another. It seemed that the informants could only talk about 'Greekness', if they were about to refer to, compare with or distinguish this notion from another. As such discussions were taking their course, I realised that the fact that I was living in Germany (and also the fact that probably the notions of man and woman there are different, because they belong to a different cultural context, at least in the understanding of most informants) brought the issue of ethnicity to a discussion about politics and gender. Suddenly, in the discourses about masculinity, people stopped using 'I', 'personally' or 'mine' and introduced the 'we' and 'us' in comparison to 'the others'.

In the course of such kinds of discussion, I found myself in the sudden position of being the informant about another cultural context, with all the implications this contains. Not only was I representing something or someone that triggered discussions about us and the Others, but I was directly asked how men/women are in politics in Germany.

In the framework of contemporary politics, some participants were interested in how German politics refer to and engage with their own history and past, basically referring to the Nazis, the Cold War Era and the GDR. This development showed also that world or European politics is a reference point for the local or national political context, and that national or local political discourses are informed in relation to more general and global political, social and historical discourses. The comparison with other national or European political structures and late developments was not always in favour of the Greek political context. Especially in the discourses about gender relations within political organizations, some people assumed or had the experience that sexist and patriarchal structures are not as obvious and present in other political contexts as in the Greek (reproducing partly stereotypes and partly their own experiences). On the other hand, some participants seemed to adopt or accept the role of the 'Other' referring to gender mainstreaming on an European level. On some occasions, people mentioned that 'we are not as European in this case' (meaning, gender equality in politics), commenting that this phenomenon has to do with remains of past historical periods and with the local, historical, political and economic structures that form social structures in different parts of the country. As a reflection about this side of the discussions, I find it interesting that this aspect of masculinities discourse was revealed only by the fact that I, the interviewer, was in touch with another political, social and cultural context.

Without trying to attribute behavioral patterns to any of the participants, I could not help but mention that talking to the majority of my informants, who were men, I sometimes felt a little patronized by the way they went on about the discussion issues. This tendency to dominate and manipulate the discussion process, in my opinion, except of being a personal characteristic that many people share, can also be linked to the general aggressive atmosphere that affects the communication among the political groups. Members tend to internalize the masculinized and often aggressive character of the Greek political culture that is reflected in the organizational structures and practices of the political youth organizations. In the framework of liberal parliamentarian democracy, politics are practiced on the basis of competition and struggle between organizations that represent different interests of various social, economic and political groups.

In the political youth organizations, the general aggressive atmosphere is rather reflected in the acts of physical and verbal violations that often take place among the groups. Another aggressive tendency that was revealed in the narratives is the 'trashing' of the members of other organizations, about 'their' politics, 'their' attitudes, distinguishing it always from the 'own'. In some cases, members of opposing groups were 'sissies', 'cowards', 'dirty bastards' or just untrustworthy and not serious enough. These kinds of characterizations were accepted by the rest of the discussion group with enthusiasm, and people were eager to elaborate even if I was not consciously encouraging them to continue talking in this direction, by not asking them further or by changing the topic. These characterizations came almost always from male members of various organizations. Female members were also disapproving of other organizations for their politics and for the attitudes of their members, even though this did not come up that often and was not expressed with aggressive or insulting words. Female members also happen to complain about the macho attitude of male members of other organizations and also of their own, in a context of mutual understanding between me (as woman and interviewer) and them (women and informants). Both male and female participants talked negatively about the response of female members to sexualized clichés and sexualized attitudes in the framework of the political organizations.

During the whole process of the fieldwork, which entailed mostly observation and conducting group interviews with members of political youth organizations, I reflected a lot not only on the perspective of the informants but also on my own. According to the standpoint methodological lines that I was trying to follow during the research process, I had to take into consideration the standpoint and views of the informants who were revealing their experiences, as well as my own. Definitely, the way I was and I am seeing the experienced world of the people, while they try to re-construct it in their narratives, affects a lot the discourses as such. Through my eyes, the content takes a certain form and shape, and everything makes sense according to my own experience and understanding of the narratives. 'There is no reading that does not bring to bear a certain context, interpret from a certain angle or set of interests, and thus throw one set of questions into relief while leaving others unasked' (Graff, 1989 in Pathak, 1992:426). As I am not pretending to be objective and reveal the 'true knowledge' about the topic I am working on, I simply engage in a discussion with the theoretical discourses, the personal discourses, my thoughts and try to make sense of the relations between gender constructions, political structures and political identities in contemporary Greece.

In order for the narratives and discourses of the members of political youth organizations to make sense, they have to be placed in the broader political, social and economic structures that shape the character of the political culture in Greece. The histories of the political parties and the youth organizations play a major role for the analysis of gendered subjectivities inside certain political youth organizations, as 'to know something, it is to know its story in context' (Barad, 1996). There is the need for the researcher to constantly develop a relation between the subject of research and the (formal, legal, collective or personal) narratives developed around it. As I mentioned above, this analysis is set under the light of subjective viewpoints (not only mine but those of the various informants), following the methodological suggestions of standpoint epistemology and against positivist principles that claim to reveal value-free facts. The findings are basically value mediated meanings. Moving consciously from the model of the generic knower, who does not seem to have gender, class, ethnicity, the researcher with her gender, class, ethnicity experience (in this case myself) is as involved in the research process as the participants with their narratives, as the theorists who offer theoretical 'backing' of the researcher's reading. Of course, the political identity of the participants, shaped by their political ideology and the political practices they participate in, as well as the political identity of the researcher, serves as a viewing apparatus, and the narratives that are re-constructed during the research serve as a source of knowledge. My role in the analysis is to place these narratives within broader discourses in order to reveal a clearer picture.

4 Let's talk politics: Discourses on Utopia, Ideology, Active Political Participation, Gender Equality and Difference

In this chapter, the focus will be on the group discussions. In the course of the analysis of the empirical data, there would be a constant attempt to go beyond the simple presentation of what people said on the various issues and try to trace linkages between discourses on politics and on gender. Therefore, by analysing the different references to the issues of utopia, political ideology, political traditions, citizenship, active political involvement and violence, I will try to draw the connections to references to gender relations and link the 'doing of politics' with the 'doing of gender', as re-constructed in the narratives of the political members. Furthermore, all through this chapter, there will be a constant attempt to address the links between theory and practice, between the political order and organizational analysis, between personal and collective action and narration.

4.1 Talking about the Art of Politics

Dealing with political ideology, which forms perceptions, ideas and beliefs about almost all sides of social, economic, cultural and personal life, we can focus on the topics of utopia, ideology, political identity and equality/difference, and try to trace how ideas surrounding these issues are crucial elements of political discourses and constitutive parts of distinctive political ideologies and form different kinds of gender ideas and different levels of gender consciousness. Furthermore, attention will be on how political ideas contribute to the construction of gendered subjectivities. In this way it may be possible to give an answer to one of the central questions that have guided the whole research, which is how political ideologies form gender ideologies, whereby ideologies is meant the whole range of perceptions, ideas, imaginations and practices.

The issues of *political involvement* and active *political participation* within a political system have a lot to do with the notion of citizenship, the notion of equality and differences of individuals and citizens among themselves and towards the law and the state. Political agency gets a different content according to the different perceptions of the public/private character of social life. The ways individuals and groups are categorized according to class, gender, ethnicity, religion and age, define their economic, social and political reality and influence the constructions of their political identity and the grade of their political involvement. Accordingly shaped are the various political ideologies that support the positions of individuals and groups in social reality and the ways in which they sustain, oppose and negotiate this position.

Research on a renegotiation and reconsideration of democratic practices and values can lead to a very central theoretical domain, that of political socialization and agency within political organizations. Very important is to investigate the ways in which the younger generation of political agents understands and reanimates the representations of gender relations linked to the notions of citizenship, political participation, equality and difference and the role of men and women in contemporary society and politics. Furthermore, it is important to consider how the perceptions on these matters are internalized and contribute consciously and unconsciously to the formation and construction of the gendered subjectivities.

Focusing on masculinities and their relations to femininities as formed in the context of political youth organizations, we can follow the discourses around the issues of social and political utopias, equality/difference, violence, power and ideology and their connection to gender constructions and gender relations. These notions describe the state of the Political in contemporary Greek political culture and have a direct link to gender representations, structures and identities.

In addition, the discourses around masculinities, femininities and gender relations in political youth organizations reveal the gendered character of these kinds of organizations. Through the unravelling of the power structures – hierarchy, authority, control, nepotism, family-cratism, as well as (hetero)sexism, homophobia and misogyny – which form the character of political youth organizations and define the relations between the members, we can draw conclusions on the dominant gender regime that rules in socio-political institutions. According to J. Acker (Acker, 1990:46 in Britton, 2000:419), 'an organization is gendered when advantage and disadvantage, exploitation and control, action and emotion, meaning and identity are patterned through and in terms of a distinction between male and female, masculine and feminine'.

As we will see in the discussions with the informants, the clear and constant distinction between the public sphere – where politics are situated – and private sphere, as well as the strong classed and male dominated character of the organizations that is taken for granted, represent discourses that draw on hegemonic ideologies and representations, which define masculinities and femininities in the political domain. These divisions are reproducing unequal gender patterns and sustain a gendered regime, which together with a classed regime defines the character of the Political in contemporary Greece. Within the gender regimes in political youth organizations, gendered discourses and practices reproduce inequalities and make it impossible for the young political agents to 'do one gender without second-sexing the other' (Gherardi, 1995:128 in Britton, 2000:430).

In the discussions, one major topic which came up was the nature of political identity and its implications for the notion of citizenship and the agency that members of political youth organizations have. Accordingly, pairs of relevant issues such as these of equality and difference, gender relations and politics, appear. These themes partly emerge in the course of the conversation and partly are taken up in an exploratory manner, when trying to observe ways in which young members describe how they define the character of politics and of active political engagement, whether they could identify a role for themselves or the impact on their identity and how gender relations might be shaped by such definitions. Attention is paid also to what constitutes the positive image of a 'good politician'.

The result of the analysis suggests ways in which the new generation of members of political organizations in Greece understands the relationship between individuals, the collective, the role of the state and the character of the Political. Certain discourses on politics are sustained by traditions, by government strategies and the ways in which they are being restructured, particularly by women and feminist ideas. Implications are traced between views on women's position and participation in production and reproduction in contemporary society. The parallel focus on gender relations in politics and society is an attempt to introduce a 'gendering-through-discourse' perspective in order to reveal the ways in which young political agents themselves perceive and construct the culture of political organizations and how they are involved in the reproduction of gender inequality.

4.2 The Men and Women of the Research: Talking in Groups about Politics

The following presentation and analysis is based on empirical data collected through group interviews with homogeneous – according to sex and political membership – focus groups in which participated a limited (often 2 or 3) number of members of every political youth organization. Apart from the group discussions and due to limited time and lack of bigger number of informants in certain sites of the research field, I conducted a few personal interviews also.

The group discussions were conducted first with 8 groups of men in September 2009 in Athens, Greece, followed by 7 groups of women and 2 groups of men in March 2010, again in Athens. In total participated 33 people, 20 men and 13 women, all members of different youth organizations attached to 5 parties that have seats in the Greek parliament. For the purposes of the analysis I will use the categorizations right/ conservative (referring mostly to representatives of the youth organizations DAP and ONNED which belong to the party Nea Demokratia), social-democrats (representatives of PASP and Neolaia Pasok, youth organizations of the party PASOK), communists (representatives of KNE and PKS, youth organizations of party KKE), leftists (members of Neolaia Synaspismou, youth organization of the party SYRIZA) and ultra-right (members of the youth organization FOS of the party LAOS). These are categorizations coming from the informants themselves and describe more concretely the ideological landscape of Greek political culture. However, references to the left/right divisions are also useful for the analysis not only because the informants themselves refer to it but because it is central within the Greek political culture. At this point, it is necessary to mention that the two poles left/right and the distinctions they represent on a political, ideological and social level still have considerable value as a notion. People orientate and differentiate themselves from each other according to this axon when it comes to the formation of political identity and the construction of various systems of perception about social, political, economic and cultural life. In Greek society, given the special history, the role of the left and the right in the Resistance movement during German occupation, the Civil War, the formation of various political coalitions in the post-civil war era, the role of the left in the Resistance during the military putsch 1967-1974, the position of the left and right towards the Cyprus issue, the Israel/Palestine conflict, the EU membership, the relations between Greece and USA and the relation of Greece with the Arab world as well as the rest of the Balkan area, all these historical-political developments make the distinction between left and right very emotionally loaded, and although historical changes and broader restructuring at global and national levels have happened, the reference to the left/right political position and political culture of Greece is still current within the political discourses.

As mentioned in the previous chapter, the youth organizations are to be found at a local level, divided in neighbourhoods or regions and within institutions of education, and are divided according the university faculties and relevant institutions of higher education. As the access to university organizations was easier (due to my previous experience as a student in Athens), I contacted student members of political youth organizations in various faculties and at different universities in Athens.

4.3 Reading Modern Political Narratives

The critical analysis of the narratives and discourses will follow the thematic structure of the interviews. Generally, the discussions followed a similar order, where the course was shifted between three groups of questions. In the first part, the focus is on active political engagement and citizenship, where discourses on utopia, political participation, ideology are intersecting with notions of gender and gender relations issues. The second part focused on the organizational structures and practices and the character of political culture. The third part focused further on the organization of political life around the binary public and private sphere, inclusion and exclusion, gender equality and difference. The intersection between structures, identity and representation levels within the discourses that appear in the framework of political youth organizations set the theoretical map in which the relations between gender and politics develop. Due to the fact that the issues are linked with each other, it is not always easy to separate the three thematic areas, and so the references to the various topics will not always follow the above order.

The starting point for all discussions is the topic of utopia, which reveals personal and collective representations of ideals and ideas around the form of society and what politics can do about it. The issue of utopia opens the course for discussions around the impact of economic and social structures on social and gender relations and gives some hints about the ideological and political background traditions to which individuals refer to. These traditions inform the political identity of the participants, as becomes obvious during the discussions.

The next issue is the character and role of politics in the everyday, meaning social, economic and political life of the informants. The discussions present discourses around politics. There are moral discourses developed around the notions of duty and responsibility as major characteristics of political involvement and agency. Political discourses underline the character of politics as being rather representational and participatory. Emancipatory discourses stress the resisting character of politics that aims for social and political change.

After the analysis of the political discourses on utopia, ideology and political participation, the discussion will focus more on the organizational structures and practices, as well as on the masculinities that appear from these. The discourses on violence, power and hierarchy will be discussed further and will be linked to the relevant practices of political organized life. The issue of the relations of political masculinities and femininities, parallel to a theoretical discussion on gender hierarchy, gender equality and difference in politics, will be presented in a further section.

4.3.1 About Utopias

Utopia is usually what its name expresses, no-place (greek: u-topos). It is the place that it is not there, at least not yet, and utopian ideas, ideologies and societies are the places of political imagination. Not all of the existing political ideologies can afford utopia in their discourses. Yet it is common that people do think about the future, the possible, the wish-to-be, projecting their hopes and desires on another place, space, idea for better life, society and political system. Almost all politically interested and involved people have an opinion and image of a collective utopia that often includes hints of their personal utopias. There are some common ideals of society (that could be characterized as utopias), as analysed and reflected in different philosophical streams, political traditions and ontological discourses. Not all utopias refer to freedom as the ultimate aim of human life. Emancipation can be reached through various ways. Sometimes the harmonious social life or the best integration in the society seems more desirable than absolute personal freedom and expression of needs. That these issues appear central in political discourses is expected, since politics is the expression of the public and private matters.

Political utopias also express ideals and patterns of citizenship, which are linked with active political involvement, in the case of organized politics. In the discourses, citizenship and utopia get another meaning according to the political tradition, theory and practice each organization applies. According to Heater (Heater, 1990 in Arnot, 2009:65), citizenship, which in our particular case is clearly related to organized political engagement, is portrayed as characterized by three major political doctrines.

Citizenship in the ideological framework of socialism gets the meaning of a chance to destabilize the dominant class and capitalist establishment:

S: '... generally speaking, people that get involved in organizations of the left, let's say with a socialist orientation, they do so because they want to change some things they do not like, but these are not only things that someone does not like personally or that are of their own interest. They do so, because they believe that this is right for the majority of the people, for society as a whole.' (b, syriza, Department of Social Policy, Panteio University, male)

Communist and Marxist ideologies are based on the demand of another, better, fairer society which of course includes issues of abolition of primarily class distinctions, and, additionally, gender, race and other categories of inequality. In their discourses it becomes clear that the class issue is central and that gender follows consequently, therefore it is not very current to talk about the gender issue explicitly. However, the issue of double exploitation of women and the unequal division of labor and housework is becoming a central issue:

G: 'Regarding the gender relations, in a future society, women will lose this subordinate role that they have in this present capitalist system. They are the victims of a double exploitation nowadays. They are exploited at work and then traditionally have to do the housework. This housework is not paid and it is work like any other, cleaning, cooking, raising the children. The modern woman is a mother and simultaneously has to work, she is pregnant and has to hide her belly, so that she won't get fired, so that the firm she is working for does not have to pay extra insurance, all these are real situations nowadays. These are situations that no man, just because he is a man, any man, does not have to face... In the ideal society, the differences of women will be fully acknowledged and supported and women will be primarily financially supported and motherhood would be considered a social issue and not a personal problem. Because today it's like, you want children? Then find the solution to this complicated situation on your own! But these are rather class issues and not really gender issues or let's say, they have to do with gender of course but will be solved only if class inequalities are abolished' (e, kne, Athens University of Economics & Business, male)

In discourses on utopia, gender equality and the possibility of true love outside of the framework of a capitalist system of exploitation appear in the context of class abolition by both men and women:

An: 'I really believe that it is not possible to find true love in this kind of society that is constructed according the demands of the capitalist system, based on exploitation of people by other people. We need another social, political and economic framework in order to cover our true needs and express our true feelings.' (e, kne, University of Economics, male)

In the context of Marxist and communist political discourses, common is the sensibility around issues of inequality, concentrating rather on structural causalities. Often women on the Left show higher levels of gender consciousness than men on the Left and men and women on the Right (Pantelidou-Malouta, 1992):

M: 'The social divisions are primarily based on class, but have to do with gender, too. We as women, we have a reason more to point to this unfair situation... There are problems that men don't have, but which are sides of the same coin.' (l, neol.syn, Faculty of Biology, University of Athens, female)

Liberal democracy, the second doctrine, requires a citizenry to 'cast its vote with understanding' (Heater, 1990 in Arnot, 2009:65):

K: 'For me (organized political action) is the only democratic way to understand how things are and do something about what I believe, to make them happen.' (c, pasp, Athens Technological Institute, male)

Young social democrats mention in their discourses on utopia the equality and abolition of exploitation issues in a rather vague way, and this idea commonly occurs as the glorification of past forms of pre-historic societies, where apparently the division of labor was fairer and the social organization more linear, a phenomenon that appears also among the young conservatives

T: 'Personally I find that when we talk about the ideal society we should talk about a society based on equality, a society with characteristics very similar to the characteristics of a primitive society and which is based on a social organization that can be found in the antiquity and even earlier' (a, pasp, University of Economics, male)

The issue of gender is current in discourses surrounding the equal representation system and women in politics, rather than the division of labor in production, reproductive issues, etc.

K: 'Regarding the gender issue, in our times and even earlier, there is equality between men and women. Look in politics, there are so many women in our organization. So, we cannot imagine something else than that for the future.' (c, pasp, Athens Technological Institute, male)

A characteristic that appears both among the social democrats to a certain certain and often among the conservatives is self-censorship and the limitation of personal utopias by the informants, as we see above. They seem unable or unwilling to recognize the power of utopia and the necessity for change on a representational level, which is possibly followed by a feeling of powerlessness towards the change of structures and representations:

S: 'To start with, there is no such thing as ideal, this is for sure. A society that would be ideal, this is utopian, something unreal, something that cannot happen. Now as for the gender relations, equality and support to each other are two necessary qualities of a modern democratic society, as this we live in.' (a, pasp, University of Economics, male)

Generally, the sharing of utopian or no-utopian ideals of a future society reflects, on the one hand, some common basis of political socialization and development, which is a major part of a mass political youth organization, and on the other hand, shows a certain level of homogenization of individual perceptions and ideas. Someone could be sceptical about the originality of political ideas within groups of young people. However, this 'periscopic view'[1] on things and relations is typical of an institutional framework such as political organizations. As Hearn; Parkin (2001) note, an important aspect of the character of organizations is that they are not collectives formed simply by individuals and are constituted only by actions of their members. 'Organizations occur in the context of pre-existing organizational social relations' (Hearn; Parkin, 2001:2), so that members are involved in struc-

[1] Periscopion (greek) is the lens in a submarine through which it is possible for someone to see above the surface of the water. In this context, the metaphorical use of the term is based on the position of the viewer underneath the water and the access to the "real" world through a lens. It is impossible for the viewer to see the world above the water surface without using the lens, and the individual gets informed about the world only by the picture the lens enables him/her to see. By using the metaphor of the periscopion, I intend to stress this dependency of the viewer on the lens, in order to gain knowledge about the world outside the water. This is parallel to the constructed dependency of the members of society on the institutional apparatuses that control and shape the general perceptions of social reality.

tures and processes within organizations and to those of the public domains, where organizations are placed.

Nevertheless, all references to utopia show how current is for the members of political organizations the relation between the recognition of inequalities and the understanding of social change through political discourse and practice with perceptions of existing gender relations and the role of gender at the personal, social, economic and political level. It seems that utopia and gender have a strong relation, not to mention the central role of utopia as an analytical tool for feminist theories. Analyses of utopias show the tendency towards change on all levels and structures, something that influences the perception of how to deal with gender inequalities and unequal gender relations on a social and personal level.

4.3.2 History and Tradition

At this point, of interest become the references to characteristics of other historical societies that in discourse served as examples for ideal models of social organization. Especially among the right, liberal and in some occasions social-democratic groups, references to the ideal society as described in the philosophy of Plato, where everyone had a place in society according to his inclination and skills, to the Golden Age of Ancient Greece, referring to women's central role in society, and even further back to pre-historic communities, where the division of labor was clearly distributed according to the sex roles and where equality among the members of the community and absence of exploitation were apparent, were developed:

K: 'Plato has said that in an ideal society there are the philosophers, the kings, the workers, etc. It is not possible that all are the same. I agree on this. This social chaos nowadays is impossible. It is ok to have freedom of speech and freedom to express ourselves but either the kings will become philosophers or the philosophers kings...

Everyone will find his speciality, some in intellectual jobs, some in practical, some in sports, arts, etc., and I believe this is how people will be happier and society will become more productive.' (d, Dap-apox., Law School Athens, male)

On some occasions, nostalgic references to childhood and a society on a 'young stage' were used to describe social and political utopias:

N: 'Ideally all people in a society should be peaceful. Something like I know from the elementary school, at least in my time... All children back then were friends, there was no competition, no privileged groups, no boys against girls. Nowadays there is a constant antagonism between the two genders that has passed in the collective unconscious.' (f, dap, Faculty of Chemistry, Athens University, male)

Following liberal and right political traditions, references to ideal society concentrate on free access to opportunities given by the economy and the market:

I: 'In the ideal society, all people will have equal opportunities and this is the most important. This and the absence of discrimination based on gender, ethnicity, disability. A society of equal chances. I do not agree of course that everyone gets the same salary, but it is important that there is the opportunity for everyone theoretically to get better money. If someone grasps this opportunity or not, it is a matter of personal choice... ' (h, dap, Marine Engineering, Metsoveio University, female)

Among the leftist and communist groups, discourses around the ideal society focus on the future. The notions of change and freedom from past and present ideas, social structures and practices are emerging in this context. On the other hand, references to the Soviet Union bring examples from the past and from another political tradition.

An: 'The ideal society is based on the ideal economy, for us Marxists. If the economic base has quality, then social relations will follow, the moral, legal and political framework will advance... Phenomena of inequality, suppression and exploitation between the people, among the gender relations, racism and other forms of marginalization will disappear. Also dogmas, stereotypes and other relevant issues will disappear very fast when this new economic base will be established.' (e, kne, University of Economics, male)

Ag: 'The ideal society is a big issue. I would rather say that the ideal society is the classless society, where no exploitation of human beings by other human beings exists.' (g, pks, University of Economics, female)

Another doctrine around political participation and active citizenship is nationalism, which requires a citizenry 'schooled to display enthusiastic loyalty' (Heater, 1990 in Arnot, 2009:65):

K: 'You cannot force someone into it (political involvement). It all starts from the education one gets. Someone has to learn at a young age to love politics, to love the fatherland, the nation and the state which someone belongs to, in order to commit and engage actively' (d, dap/apox, Law School Athens, male)

Conservatives follow a similar line of fair and equal society, similar to the political traditions that generate libertarian and egalitarian discourses in the case of social democrats. However, they do so by using different concepts, such as the right for access to opportunities for everyone, which usually means that individuals bear the responsibility to grab the given opportunities:

I: 'In the ideal society, everyone would have the same opportunities as all the others, not in the sense that all people will be equal, but at least they will have some equal opportunities. I do not agree that everyone should earn the same but at least should have the same opportunities, and then if one can manage to take advantage of the given opportunity or not is a personal choice.' (h, dap, Marine Engineering Institute, Metsoveio University, female)

Characteristic is the pragmatism and often critical view on the necessity of utopias and the narrowing down of utopias to certain frameworks. Interesting is the reference not only to past forms of social organization, defined by a simplicity and primitivism, but also a longing for the glorious times of the golden age of Ancient Athens. This system of selective democracy seems for many people nowadays the best-functioning and is informed by elitist and aristocratic philosophical views on society, such as Plato's society and Aristotle's perception of the Political. Especially, the pattern of 'every one finds its own place in society' is repeated and linked with Plato's theory of ideas and ideal society. Very interestingly, among the right there is some acknowledgement of other types of political regimes (references to Soviet societies), where the social positions were more clearly distributed and the social organization tighter. This reveals the central role of persisting references to the Other, often the antithetical in order to define the local position, also in the framework of political representations:

K: 'For example, in the totalitarian regimes there is a certain central planning. There (in the Soviet Union) were certain clear categories, there were the professional politicians, the proletarians, the workers and through these categorizations many of the people were finding their social inclination towards certain roles. Plato said that in an ideal society some will be philosophers and some kings. It is not possible for everyone to be both or to be all the same (for example kings). I agree on this. It is impossible, this modern confusion. It is all right to have our freedom, to be free to say whatever we think, but either the kings will become philosophers or the philosophers, kings, and that's about it. In such an ideal society people will become truly happy.' (d, dap, Law School Athens, male)

As we will see as we proceed with the analysis of the narrations, the constant reference to formal political theses and lines is not concentrated only when the discussion is around the ideal society or the best possible way of organizing social relations, but extends to perceptions of the gendered division of labor, the notion of the public and the private sphere, as well as when talking about organizational structures and practices of political life. The reflection of formal political and often party lines in discourse is the reflection of more general structures in the micro level of political organizational relations.

4.3.3 On Active Political Participation

Discourses around political participation and active citizenship are identified by the informants as influential for the relationship between the individual and society. Referring more to participation within a political system that constitutes an entity represented by the state rather than defining citizenship in cultural terms (Araujo et al. in Arnot, 2009:71), members of political organizations see political engagement as a way to be part of a framework that sets and secures benefits for individuals.

On the other hand, political participation is a chance to protect individual freedom and rights against the organized state that is often represented to follow interests and directions that are against the simple citizen. The state is represented as an overarching system that grows above the institutions and the people and has its own functions and will. From the discourses appear two sites of 'being political'. One site is concentrated around having respect for the state, its institutions and the laws, and the other, perceived as contradictory, focuses on the need for political actions and political reform. The first site shows or demands a certain degree of conformity, respect for core values, community-based volunteer work and limited political engagement. This attitude is compatible with the politics of representation and politics of duty that the bigger political youth organizations in Greece represent.

Talking to the young members of organizations, it becomes clear that in the role as citizen most informants see themselves as members of a living community within a shared democratic culture. This legitimizes their involvement and active engagement. Striking is the fact that many of the informants do not have a shared sense of a common good, the achievement of which requires the rule of law and certain obligations and rights for everyone based on consensus. However, there is an understanding of democratic principles, values and processes, and there is an agreement that individuals should have the necessary dispositions and capacities for democratic participation – the lack of which causes critique and is viewed as a reason for concern about crisis of democracy –:

S: 'Our organization is big, 90% of the people are in because of their family's political tradition. Or another big part of the members are here because their friends are here. Then we throw parties and organize excursions, collect and distribute past papers or notes for the lessons. Islands, girls, that's the organized life for most of the people. Nobody cares if the programme says something for or against the privatization of universities or other topics. Is this now democratic participation? How can something good for the future of this country come out of it?' (d, dap/apox., Law School Athens, male)

Here appear issues of political orientation based on family tradition and a generational linearity. Also, the influence of the peer group on political socialization is an issue. The organization functions more like a cultural club rather than a political institution. Lack of common imaginations and representations of what active political engagement means initiates a problem for democracy.

Critical engagement and participation in political and social life, although required and asked, is not translated to membership in a political organization. Rather, the latter often translates to conformity. What comes through from the above discourse on political involvement is that the representational ideal of active participation as a member of the state concentrates on the public sphere, so that the public political identity defines the role of the citizen. This is an exclusive character of the political, as it separates the private from the notion of politics and attributes the Political to the public, a very male dominated and therefore masculinized domain.

Political discourses of representation and participation that often have a strong egalitarian character signify a tight relationship between the individual and society and between the state and the individual. The right to make political choices, the right to be informed and not be left out of political processes, and the right to have access to opportunities, with all the obligations and responsibilities that follow, is the picture that the politics of representation, participation and duty in the discourses of the informants get. In the Greek context, however, participation in the political sphere translates to participation in the financial, cultural and social spheres. The notion of participation concentrates more on the sphere of social/human rights towards a social equality. An ideal characteristic of the politics of the left, participatory politics is often presented as a way of cooperating with the existing system without approving of it.

A: 'This is the notion of politics for me. I cannot comprehend the meaning of politics otherwise, politics can only be participatory...

Many people just observe reality and have an opinion about it, which can be critical, positive, respectable, but they reproduce it at home while sitting on the couch. But this means you are not interested in influencing others or in having a political result that might make the things you don't like better. These people are only interested in being consequent against themselves. This I have never liked. I am not a utopian, I don't say here we are going to turn the world upside down, we create everything new. I believe that you can mobilise small things in this system, you can do things in your personal environment first as well as in the broader level of society, and politics is one road to this.' (b, syriza, Social Policy, Panteio University, male)

Around the politics of resistance, more interventionist and critical political discourses are circulated. The notion of active political engagement goes beyond representation in the public sphere and influences every aspect of private, personal and professional life:

F: 'Looking around, seeing my parents going through difficult times year after year, although they have always been and still are working hard, seeing kids that cannot finish school and have to go and work in the gas station and the supermarket, seeing kids in the so-called third world starving to death while others live in total decadence somewhere else, all these are reasons for me to get politically organized, because I have decided that this society doesn't suit me, I don't want it and I want to do something to change it now. I want a society where the dreams of every single one can become true one way or the other. And I am not organized to just sit around, be cool, meet new people and go to parties.' (g, pks, University of Economics, female)

N: 'What is characteristic of our political action is the attempts to convince more and more people of the necessity to overthrow the existing system, through a polymorphous intervention. It is more than talking, it is going on the street, participating in occupations, strikes and other sides of organized struggle.' (g, pks, University of Economics, female)

A: 'You cannot support something politically, something that forms your whole consciousness and then not try to live it in your home' (g, pks, University of Economics, female)

On the other hand, informants, especially women, stress the difficulties of combining political involvement with family life:

A: 'The bourgeois ideologisms, or let's say the ideas that liberal democ-

racy circulates, present the woman as wife, mother, housewife and working professional. There are many demands and pressures on women, more than on men, and this often can be an obstacle for women to develop political activity as men do.' (g, pks, University of Economics, female)

Especially for women, leisure and free time is an important precondition for politics. The issue of time and the division of labor and housework according to the time represents an actual problem for women:

I: 'When I have a family, I want to have free time and to be able to do politics. I am not sure if this is possible, though. Somehow it is good to support these things in the public, but in the private, there are so many factors a woman is depending on. If the man is supportive, if the children understand and share responsibilities. It seems that nobody wants to face the situation at home, and women feel responsible for it automatically.' (h, dap, Marine Engineering, Metsoveio University, female)

In contrast, politics of representation or of duty generate a division between politics in the public and personal life in the private:

D: 'To have an ideology, this is yours. You can talk it over with other people, even with people that have different political opinions, but you cannot let this define your whole life. Like losing friends because of politics. A friend of mine from school, he is a leftist, he doesn't talk to me. That shows you cannot accept different opinions, and you are not able to separate what is politics and what is personal life. It is an issue of political culture every organization or political site has. . . ' (o, dap, Department of Theology, Athens University male).

The politics of duty are promoting the service to community rather than political principles. At the centre of the moral discourse is 'the good person':

R: 'Our role here is to help. We offer help to the students in this faculty, something that they don't get from the state or elsewhere. And we prove to the others that look, we are doing something good and we are good at it, so you can trust us and we are not going to disappoint you. That is nice and gives a good feeling.' (k, dap, Theology, University of Athens, female)

In the discourses, the 'good politician' is often represented either as someone who does his duty of helping for the common good or presents a leading personality. The both representations appear within the same political site:

K: 'What counts for a good politician is to be able to listen to the problems and be able to help, to give solutions. People do not care if the other is man, woman or black, we have seen it in the U.S with Obama. They want a good, helpful person . . .

S: Now our prime minister is a good speaker, he is smart, serious, well-educated and knows the tactics, he is not ignorant or obnoxious. He can give good interviews, seems like the guy that has a solution but you walk downtown Athens and see if he has done anything to help the people. In Peiraios (a central street in the centre of Athens) you see drug selling, migrants, prostitution, crime, you have to be careful for your mobile or wallet.' (d, dap/apox, Law School, Athens, males)

The similarity of the necessary characteristics of a good politician and the masculine characteristics of a 'man' appears strongly within relevant discourses:

D: 'Man is not only the person who can keep his word, is trustworthy and serious and you can count on him, he is the one who has correct behavior towards the others and towards women' (o, dap, Theology, University of Athens, male)

Ag: 'Many men are not behaving like a true man. A man gives his word and he holds steady. The one that has the pants on, should respect them and should not change his mind, whenever there is a difficult situation, behaving like a chicken, like a little woman. This is not a man, because he doesn't respect the others and himself.' (o, dap, Theology, University of Athens, male).

These metaphoric connections between the notion of 'man' (trustworthy, caring, someone you can count on) with conceptions of the political man, who has to be a 'good politician' (who listens, cares, helps) reveal some aspects of the masculine character of active participation in politics.

Other political youth organizations reflect a political culture that does not have in its centre a single person and avoids personification, promoting a more linear organizational structure:

S: 'The left generally has a more advanced notion of collectiveness and of the collective subject and it (the left) never had good relations with persons and leaders, who were expressing personal views and were imposing personal situations. Obviously there are always leaders whom nobody doubts, but for us that does not count, because we have ideas that focus on collectivities. To get involved in a process of choosing a person, a central figure is a bourgeois ideal.

A: This is established since decades now in the space of the traditional Right and among the social-democrats. In those parties the role of the leader is very central. Everything evolves around the president, the central figure.' (b, syriza, Social Policy, Panteio University, males)

Through the issue of leadership, the relation of the role and the importance of the individual within the collective and within the group becomes an issue:

G: 'We are not viewing leadership as the aim of political involvement. Of course, we value a charismatic personality but the collective has a greater importance.

A: The relation between the person and the group is a very misunderstood notion within political organizations. If you ask others, they are going to say Karamanlis or they are going to name someone else

G: They are going to talk about leaders and important personalities. But, between the person and the collective, there is dialectic relation.

A: The collective brings changes...

G: Never the person alone. And in the last instance, political action comes from collectivity.' (e, kne, University of Economics, males)

Interestingly, women are less enthusiastic about leadership, and they avoid mentioning leading personalities or find it difficult to identify with any political figure, even if they are situated in organizations that have an individualistic political character:

E: 'Well, there are some politicians who have made a name in politics the last years. They are respected and have their followers and cronies, but I cannot really go crazy about supporting a leader. Maybe because they are old men, if it was a young charismatic woman... I don't know. But maybe it is not in the nature of women to have a leader or so, women are not that competitive, they don't want to stick out. They are more loyal to a group.' (u, dap, Theology, Athens University, female)

The characteristics of a good politician, the centrality of its role, the ability to gather a group around them, to provide solutions, secure trust, and establish respect, are attributed in discourse to the father or the son in the family, even if often this does not reflect the reality:

A: 'I have grown up in a very traditional society in Crete, where men have incredible privileges. Even if you are living excessively in Crete, people would not see it as false, they will admire you even. If a woman does the same, she would be stigmatized... I see it in my family. I am the only man in the family, and I get respect from everyone. Respect that I do not deserve or that I have not yet gained.' (e, kne, University of Economics, male)

The politics of duty reproduce the ideas of common good, social integration and harmony. However, the dominant political culture is perceived as class dominated and oppressive, and so the model of the caring and thus conforming citizen is less positive.

It becomes obvious that, because of the strong class and gender biases, the common good is difficult to define. Within various ideological sites, the good citizen that also makes a good political agent is often portrayed as the 'productive citizen', somebody who works for the good of society by contributing to the wealth of the nation. Although this includes women's contributions to economic progress, in this discursive framework, domestic labor is made invisible, damaging in a way women's status.

Trying to systematize the discourses on politics and link them with those on utopias and further on, with the discourses on gender relations, I have drawn a table that shows the connections between the individual and collective ideas around politics with those on gender and gender relations:

	REPRESENTATION	PARTICIPATION	RESISTANCE	DUTY
On politics	• Stress political participation as a member of state • Focus on public sphere	• Focus on human, social rights • Demand of social equality	• Focus on abolition of political, social, economic inequality	• Focus on common good • Social integration, harmony
On utopias	• Athenean democracy • Plato`s society	• Minimization of power relations • Abolition of inequalities	• Classless society	• Primitive societies • "childhood" of humantiy
On gender relations/ women`s issues	• Focus on the presence of women in public sphere through law enforcement	• Focus on the role of women in family • participation in public sphere through women's initiatives	• Division of labour • Focus on „double exploitation"	• Enforcement of the role of women in the family/ communities

Table 4.1 Discourses on politics, utopias, gender relations

4.3.4 Building Up a Political Identity-The Role of Ideology

As mentioned in the previous chapter, political identity is constructed by elements of the political and, more generally, the *Weltanschauung* of the subjects. That includes not only the perceptions around the social, economic and cultural aspects of life but also perceptions of gender relations. Regarding the political/ideological identity, just how far and in which direction is gender a differentiating variable of the latter, is a crucial question about the relationship between gender and political identity. A central point of reference will be the axis left/right as long as this dichotomy seems to be central in the construction of ideological identities. The left/right distinction codes different perceptional systems around the notions of democracy, state, social equality, gender equality and, on a personal level, the perception of the political agents around power, violence, utopia and subjectivity.

These notions are directly connected with the perception of the social position of women, the 'naturalness' of their inferior political position or the rejection of the social suppression of women, the division of labor and the dichotomy public/ private, the role of the state in the regulation of production and reproductive issues, as well as the role of the laws and regulations towards social equality. The positioning around these tendencies informs the political identity of women and men, with the reference point the being left and the right, and reflects the level of gender consciousness that characterizes the different political identities.

The hypothesis that a left political identity equals a developed gender consciousness (Pantelidou-Malouta, 1992:222) can be tested and can be useful for linking political identities with certain perceptions of gender.

Connected to the above, we will examine in how far the left and right political identities influence differently men and women in the ways they perceive gender relation systems and the social roles that are attached to the genders.

The party identity of the gendered subjects is also a hint towards the ways that the party system mobilizes in the same directions and with the same intensity 'left' and 'right', 'men' and 'women'.

Especially for the relationship between masculine subjectivities and political identity, it is interesting to follow the discourses around power, violence and political utopias, gender relations and gendered subjectivities and how they change according to the political context and the party positioning. As the notions of masculinity and femininity do not refer directly and strictly to men and women accordingly, they do not exhaust their meaning within certain cultural, as well as social, economic and political frameworks. Focusing on masculinities is an analytical way to look at gender relations and not at men per se. In a political context, ideas of what is masculine/feminine and what is normal/accepted/possible for men and women in relation to ideas of the role of the individual in society, the political, the role of the state in the regulations of reproduction and gender mainstreaming, their positioning in the production and their perceptions of the division of labor (in the labor market and at home) and the perception of the dichotomy public/private and how it is related to the gender relations, are connecting points between the political and gender formations (masculinities, for example).

4.3.5 The Gender Variable in Discourse

Focusing on the discourses around political involvement and its impact on individuals, there was an attempt to trace linkages between different political ideologies and ideas around gender and gender relations that shape gendered subjectivities.

Interestingly, discourses around these issues were differently expressed and analysed by men and women. For some of them, there was a consensus among people sharing similar political ideologies and/or among belonging to the same organizations. For others, there were differences among people of the same organization and among different ones. From the discussions about the notions of politics and gender relations, there was a revealing of representations of masculinity and femininity within the public and the private sphere, as well as in paid labor.

S: 'I believe that the role of the women in the society is determined or let's say directly influenced by the role that she has in the family' (d, syriza, Social Policy, male)

A: 'The position of women in the family and by extension to it, in the society, has its roots and origins in the role of women in the paid labor. When a woman as a member of a family is responsible for the child care, and often this role is given and not chosen and she is dependent financially on the man, the man has clearly then the role of the breadwinner. This was typical in Greece 100 years ago but nowadays the ideas remain and often we see their reproductions in our reality. This is a great example, one which shows that the Economic determines the ways someone functions and forms relations to other people and the economic relations influence deeply the whole society.' (d, syriza, Social Policy, Panteio University, male)

Furthermore, evaluations of gender differences and critiques of inequality, as being created through structural measures such as quota systems or electoral processes based on equal gender participation, were formed. Imaginations of political and social changes in the future were expressed in relation to that.

Discourses around politics, political involvement as a matter of representation and political participation were popular among egalitarian and social democratic organizations. Political involvement as a matter of duty, as a contribution to the common good and to common social values that should be respected in a society in order for it to work, were popular among conservative groups. Doing politics as a way to achieve a better state of life within an organized society and to have access to opportunities for self-determination were popular among liberal groups. Discourses on political participation as a social right and political involvement as a way to demand social and humanitarian rights were promoted as a model of the resisting political agent that is more popular among left organizations. These discourses on citizenship and political involvement were revealed through group discussions, parallel to discourses on gender equality and gender relations.

Although feminist ideas have been rather influential the last decades, in the discussions references to feminist political demands and movement were silenced or rarely mentioned and many members, especially women, stressed the fact that although they care about women's issues, they are not 'feminists'. However, members of political youth organizations, especially women, are constantly touching classical feminist issues, focusing mostly on various aspects of gender inequality.

There were discourses focusing on women's inequality suggesting a legal securing of equality through laws and measures (such as quota systems or female representation in the work places and decision-making bodies). Women who stressed the inequality issue were suggesting inequality in the work place and in politics – mostly right, liberal and social democrats – or in the work place and family ('double exploitation') – the majority view within leftist and communist groups. There were discourses on gender differences that ignored the existence of inequality as characteristic of the past and emphasized gender differences that logically put people in different (but not unequal) places in the society – mostly popular among conservative groups. Among the groups of the Left, there was a critique on real women exploitation in the workplace and in the family that contradict popular representations of women's emancipation. They trace exploitation also to the domain of ideologies and representations. Among the left, critiques of the internalization of sexist and masculinized norms by women and the unconscious self-victimization of women were central.

The discourses on men's inequality in politics and the workplace were sustained by arguments of men as victims of measures that promote gender equality and place women in positions where they do not belong (because they do not have the skills, knowledge, experience, etc). These discourses often indirectly pointed to biological differences or sex role socialization that reproduced stereotypes which were shared by some women, too. These discourses also concentrated on the image of the powerful woman, the eternal mother that suppresses and dominates the family. Although these discourses were more common among conservative groups, some variations of them appeared in various political contexts.

	POLITICAL MEMBERS ♂	♀
DISCOURCES ON PRO-DIFFERENCE	• No inequality in public sphere • Focus on differences	• No inequality in public sphere
DISCOURCES ON PRO-EQUALITY Inequality against women	• Acceptance of a partial equality • Equality through law enforcements (quotas)	• inequality in all aspects of life • Patriarchical relations in work and family
Inequality against men	• Discrimination in public through quotas • Suppressive female figur in politics/ family	
Reasons of unequal gender relations	• Biological differences • Women`s fault	• Stereotypes • Women`s fault
	• Systemic inequality	• Systemic inequality

Table 4.2 Discourses on equality and difference in politics

4.3.6 The 'Common Good': Further Discussions around Citizenship, Politics and Society

Talking about political participation in combination with citizenship, two major issues run through the discourses. First appears the relationship between citizenship, the economy and the use of participation and of organized action as a means of control, resistance and administration on a political (and economic, social) level. The second topic connects politics to patriarchal relations, which underlie liberal democratic Western European political traditions and the systemic character of liberal democracy.

Citizenship, which in most discourses appears as a combination of rights, obligations and active interest in a broader 'common good' for the society and the nation, becomes an issue when the informants are asked to describe the(ir) ideal society. This question aims to reveal the ideological representations and individual ideas surrounding the relations between the individual and the society as well as the notion of political agency. Discussions around the influence of personal ideals, ideas and morals on social relations, in comparison to the impact of social norms and economic structures, were developed following different ideological and analytical paths in discourse. Great consensus appeared on the fact that the economic structures are very determining for social and especially gender relations. Here, the informants were referring to issues of productive politics as well as the division of labor and the public/private division of social life:

T: 'Imagine something similar to ancient Greece. There, the women enjoyed a high social status and so on and we could take some lessons from it and apply them in the future. Definitely, this has to do with the economy, we cannot oversee the fact that in all these, the economy plays an important role. Either in capitalism, or socialism, or communism, or liberalism, or whatever system, economy plays the biggest role. For example, if S. works and his wife doesn't work and she has to stay at home then, consequently their personal relations are structured accordingly.' (a, pasp, University of Economics, male)

In the discussions around the ideal society, the necessity of political agency and involvement towards 'a better society' is thematicized. Informants from various sides of the ideological spectrum (right/left) underline the issue of class and its impact on the formation of political identity:

M: 'I believe that the economic conditions are playing a major role, for example if in a country all people were rich, I don't believe they were going to get involved in political parties. Economy plays also a major role in the lives of the people. Let's take two married couples, one is rich, the other poor, among the married couple there would appear bigger problems, which are not easy to get solved. Because nowadays a lot of things are necessary, when a child is born, it has to get extra lessons at home for example and there appear problems. In contrast, a rich couple has more economic advantages, therefore an easier life and there are not many conflicts within the gender relations.' (c, pasp, Athens Technological Institute, male)

G: 'The ideal society is the one where the social relations and nature will be above profit. And that will affect the gender relations, the genders will become equal but not the same.' (l, neol.syn, Faculty of Biology, Athens University, female)

M: 'In the ideal society all the inequalities will be abolished on the basis that the means of production that are owned in the capitalist system by few, will then belong to the workers. The capitalist system is based also on patriarchy, the major reason of women's oppression. When all inequalities that nowadays exist will be abolished, the notion of the father as the owner of property will be abolished, so patriarchy will not exist and the inequality between the genders will disappear.' (l, neol.syn, Biology, Athens University, female)

In the Greek framework, the good society appears to be a well-functioning, steadily developing, productive society. This representation is reflected in discourses that stress the determining role of economic structures in the formation of the social and political character of a country. Consequently, the good citizen is the productive citizen, a pattern that appears in conservative as well as egalitarian and resisting discourses:

K: 'Everyone has his/her special role in the society, none can do everything. Not that one cannot try to reach everything, but in Greece everyone wants to become a doctor or a lawyer. Some people should however work in agriculture, some have to deal with intellectual work, some others to be active in sports, arts, etc. Only in this way can people be truly happy, and the society will become more and more productive. But now that everyone believes to want to be and do everything, there is no programme and no systematic organization of the society. This is chaos. In the ancient times, when the Greeks were literally producing culture, everyone was finding, somehow, his role. But in an ideal society and at some certain historical point (this requires a depth of time) people having the right socialization will be able to reach the point were they will know what is best for them and will choose their position and role within society.' (d, dap, Law School Athens, male)

The citizen that works for the good of the society by contributing to the wealth of the nation shifts to the citizen that has to work to secure benefits that the state cannot provide. In this process women's contribution in the production is valued; however, her major role in domestic labor and reproduction remains invisible:

M: 'Nowadays it is common and rather necessary for women to go out of the house and be active in the production. Their place is not any more the home, and they are not seen as belonging there. Whoever says I don't want my wife to work, she has to raise the children and cook all day, he is out of social context, I think.' (c, pasp, Athens Technological Institute, male)

Although liberal democracy is promoting an agenda in which all citizens are encouraged to develop their talents and interests, and the general idea is that everyone has a vote and a chance for a balanced political socialization, there is a strong tendency towards political ignorance or passivity, which is rather popular among young people, something that in the narratives is linked with the lack of political socialization:

K: 'This tendency nowadays of 'what do I care?' is very dominant. Earlier, 20-30 years ago, this was a strongly politicized historical period for the Greek society, as we all know. Poor people were participating in demonstrations and very bad incidents were happening, violent stuff, but people were still participating. Today, if you care who gets to govern, who is implementing taxes, you are considered démodé. Everything is a matter of political socialization and schooling. If you see the education that our parents got, even 30 years ago, they are now much more educated than me and you. But this is the state's fault and its politics.' (d, dap/apox, Law School Athens, male)

Striking is the linkage of political socialization influenced by age and history. The memory and knowledge of civil war and dictatorship in Greece appears central in the constructions of a politicized citizenry, even in the younger generations (Arnot, 2009:75).

Regarding early political participation, two discursive tendencies appear, one being that young people do not care about politics, and so the old generation remains established in this domain. Although the official discourses as reflected in formal party lines promote an ongoing and joint process between generations and between adults and youth, the young members are sceptical about this attitude of 're-shaping democracy' through early political socialization. In the discussions, there are references to organized youth politics as a matter of involvement in a process of establishing order:

K: 'Within the youth organizations of big parties, there is a central committee with a small number of people and they elect the president, the leader. All the energy is put into who is going to become the head of the organization, and there are alliances around certain people. These 5 people, let's say, are guided by the older in the party. These young people will get the positions of the old members within the party when they retire. These 5 people will have their networks, know a lot of people in the party and the 200 rest have no relation or access to it, whatsoever.' (d, dap/apox, Law School Athens, male)

It seems that young political activists have to navigate adult power and what Westman (1991) terms 'juvenile ageism', or, 'institutional, interactional and individual-level discrimination against young people perpetuated by a variety of adult social factors' (Gordon, 2008:33). However, the link to the adult political world also gets a positive meaning of mutuality and support. It seems that parties with strong hierarchical organization sustain tighter links to the youth organizations than parties that have a more lineal organizational character. The ideological linkage between the parties and the youth organization, as well as the relation of dependency, is a common topos in the discourses, often expressed through symbolic representations of the family or the relation between children and parents[2]:

Ag: 'Our organization is according to its constitution guided ideologically and politically by the party. It is however a youth organization and has other expectations and demands. The young members have an authenticity that the members of the party do not have. Our relation with the party is like this between children and parents, not in the patriarchal sense, of course. The party needs the youth organization, it listens to us, because we are the future of the party, but the party should make sure that our positions and programme is in accordance with real life. Our relation is superior to this of a family, because it is a conscious choice. It is a relation of love, dependence and trust.' (j, kne, University of Economics, female)

A: 'I do not know how it is in other organizations, because internal structure is an ideological issue, as we know. We try to be open to the different, and this is reflected in the organizational structures. There are some typical structures and some informal structures. Even if we try to have open structures, and that translates to an openness in the relations among the members and with the party, there would always be the issue of

---

2 The binary children-parents is imposing a certain dependency from the side of the weaker and younger, the children in this case, and it is very expressive of where young activists see themselves and their organizations in the political landscape.

hierarchy. This is an issue that is connected with leadership, which is not institutionalized but rather ideological. There would always be some people that hold the ideological leadership. So, there would always be atypical power structures, which would be constantly transformed. In our case, as a youth organization, we try to change and develop so that we can avoid the arteriosclerosis of the traditionally big, I mean size and also power-wise, parties.' (b, syriza, Social Policy, Panteio University, male)

In other discursive frameworks, organized politics are presented as a matter of structural strategies based on age, gender or class divisions. Politics of change refer to dichotomies in their discourses, in order to stress their character based on difference. Divisions form the character of organizational structures and are reflected in the age, gender and class profile of the youth organizations and the parties:

Ag: 'The orientation of our organization is clearly classed. It is about who is going to get the power, the working class or the bourgeois. I think nowadays there is a continuous division between men and women, or young and old and many organizations use them. For example the young/old division that exists in many political organizations: Young means progressive, old translates as fossilized. Other organizations play with dichotomies, such as men/women. They draw the line there. So they are organizations with a lot of women, and people think this translates automatically to political equality.' (p, kne, School of Architecture, Metsoveio University, male)

Clearly, class, gender and age are structures that influence the character of political organizations and are used differently according to the political/ideological framework the organizations are operating in.

Regarding the orientation of modern political youth organizations, there is a turn from the political to the technical. The new emphasis on efficiency, surveillance, control and service-providing organizes political socialization within youth organizations far from the Greek ideal of educating the citizen 'for intelligent and active participation in the civic community' (Giroux, 1980:329). The modern social narrative on democracy, as Lyotard (1984) argues, has more to do with social control than freedom (Arnot, 2009:66):

K: 'I find it unacceptable when someone has no political criteria and votes only based on superficial preferences. In this way my future and the future of the whole society is determined. If you ask anyone nowadays with what kind of criteria he decides to vote, you receive answers like it depends on how the candidate looks, what kind of people he knows, what is the grandfather or the father voting for and so a situation that some people take advantage of is formed. And the people that do not know anything about politics, they are responsible for this misery, and then no wonder they get manipulated. Like Nixon said, the bad ones got to govern, because the good ones didn't go to vote.' (d, dap/ apox, Athens Law School, male)

The criteria of getting involved in a political youth organization are not always ideological and have to do with involvement in administration or access to hierarchies within institutional frameworks, such as the university or associations in the workplace:

A: 'I am in this organization not out of ideological reasons. If it was because of ideology, I would go directly to the party or the local organization of the party where I live. But in this (university) faculty, this organization gets a high percentage of votes in the elections. That means people before us established a high profile, and these people cannot lie. And the rest trusts them. So, it feels good to be part of this. And we are here to do ideological work. We are here to help people with notes, books, past papers, in order to pass the exams, we cannot of course give them free degrees or find them a job, and it does not mean that people that support us have to become directly members of the party.' (o, dap, Theology, Athens University, male)

For women, citizenship takes another dimension of dichotomous character. There is a distinction between motherhood and citizenship, as well as a clear division of agency in the public and in the private sphere. This is, of course, opposed by many younger women but is often supported by men:

D: 'I think when women work, there are more problems in the family and more fights. I see it in my own family. My father does not like that my mom works, he just tolerates it, because it is financially necessary. Let alone she will be out doing politics! But mostly, all of the fights in most families are about work or lack of work.

A: But even if your mom had the option to stay home, maybe she would still go to work.

D: I am not sure what she would.

A: Maybe she would continue working, because she would like to contribute to the family.

D: The mother contributes in other ways than working. She contributes by being with her children, taking care of the family, nurturing it. Family means to raise first your husband and then your children. That is a hell of a job. Sometimes she has to pay more attention to the man. Especially in the beginning of the marriage, men are so immature, and so women have to support them and show the way, and then men go to work and support the wives and the children.' (o, dap, Theology, University of Athens, males)

R: 'I guess when I am done with my studies, I would like to work on something related to what I have studied. And investing in your job and later in your family is something much more safe and meaningful than running around doing politics. As soon as someone becomes a mother, she has very little time to do anything except taking care of the children and the little time someone has, she wants to spend it only for herself.' (k, dap, Theology, University of Athens, female)

Given the different positions women in comparison to men have in society, they have a different orientation and character of participation in political organizations. Even if youth organizations help to facilitate women's participation, youth groups are clearly structured by gender groups. That appears evident when talking about political participation. As seen above, continuous political involvement looks impossible or aimless for many women, and it seems as if they are viewing their involvement as an interesting experience before real life begins. In the interviews, no man has expressed a time limit for political participation, and the youth movement seems to be only the beginning for long political involvement.

Critical voices oppose the traditional roles attributed to women that restrict their action in the public domain, such as those of motherhood or house-holding. Nevertheless, the difficulty of combining roles comes up in discourse, even if people negate the idea that the major role of women is concentrated in the private sphere, something that proves the importance and actuality of the public/private division as a modern social and political problem:

A: 'Time is restricted for everyone, especially when you work and have a family. This is a general problem. Everybody is making sacrifices out of lack of time. I prefer to make sacrifices that will have a long-lasting impact. That is why political action is priority number one, even when I have two jobs and later maybe a family.' (j, kne, University of Economics, female)

In discourses on citizenship and active political participation, political representation is presented as a key symbol of the duty and freedom enjoyed by all citizens. Political participation is also linked to participation in economic, social and cultural aspects of life. These discourses fit well into the framework of liberal representational democracy. On the other hand, there are sceptical voices about freedom of speech, freedom of opinion and freedom of action, especially on the left spectrum of political organizations. The concept of the 'good citizen' varies a lot from political site to political site, as it appears in the discourses. In the Greek context, the good citizen is someone who has a duty to act, the responsibility to change the established order, to mobilise and fight for rights, or the one who cares for the common good. Mobilization and participation in decision making in political life present an image of the citizen fighting to keep control of a potentially dangerous state (Araujo; Deliyanni; Invinson; Tome in Arnot, 2009:74). As we have seen above, history plays an important role in the formation of political identity during the process of political socialization.

From the different discourses it also became obvious that, except from gender representations, issues from national tradition, from certain historical periods and specific political phases of Greek history affect people's values in relation to politics, political involvement, state and citizenship, as well as gender relations. As Deliyanni et al (*Ibid*, 75) suggests, the collective memory of dictatorship in Greece seems to be present in these constructions of a politicized citizenry. When talking about citizenship, participants are mostly referring to the relationship between individual and society, and the state represents a political entity (Deliyanni et al, 2009: 71), something that reveals again the political character of the relationship between state and citizens. However, this political relationship has its own contradictions, being perceived as a relationship between a protective state and an unprotected citizen. This perception of an unequal relationship in the Greek political context produces tensions among the citizens, who acknowledge the need for respect of and to the state and, parallel to that, the need for civic activism and political reform (Deliyanni et al, 2009:72).

S: 'There are two roads in doing politics. One is to sit at home and reproduce popular political ideas, without being interested in influencing others or producing a positive result with your actions. The other is to get active and try to change even the small things in your personal environment even.' (b, syriza, Social policy, Panteio University, male)

Taking a closer look at the discourses about the relationship between citizens and the state, interesting points come out. First, the relationship between the state, as a political entity, and citizen is strongly political, which gives the notion of citizenship a politicized side. Furthermore, there is a gendering of different spheres (private and public) in relation to notions of citizenship, what Connell (1990) referred to as the European equation between authority and a dominating masculinity. The image and the language of the discourses associated with political agency are largely male. Even concepts of community were associated more with male notions of responsibilities rather than female contributions within the family and neighbourhood. Political and egalitarian discourses, especially, appeared to apply to public spheres, and to assume both a relevance to men and role for men in terms of civic action (Deliyanni et al. 2009: 88). However, the gendered nature of the concept of the individual and the gendered basis of the state (Connell, 1990) are not realized. It becomes clear what Walby (Walby, 1994 in Deliyanni et al:88) underlines about the new forms of patriarchy that create new ways of inclusion that are parallel ways of exclusion for women in the public sphere. Although there is broader inclusion of women in the public sphere, the major shifts in private and domestic spheres appear to focus on the weakness of men to participate rather to recognize the forms of patriarchal control which affect women's lives (Deliyanni et al, 2009:91).

4.3.7 Talking about Quotas

The discussions around measures for larger women's participation in political organizations (parties and youth organizations), the so called quota, have as expected triggered discussions about the issues of gender equality and difference in organized politics. As I have mentioned in the previous section, the quota system has been active for years now in Greece and has been adopted by almost all of the political youth organizations attached to political parties that have seats in the parliament.

Male and female participants from organizations that cover all the ideological spectrum have clearly opposed the system, stressing the 'unfair' character of the measure that causes discrimination against male and female members of groups. Some voices have underlined the positive effect of the quotas in embracing difference. However, in their majority, female and male informants have expressed criticisms doubting the effectiveness of the measure to change the women's unequal situation in politics, following, however, different lines of argumentation.

Once again, the views on the quota system were informed by the ideological framework of the organization which the members belong to. Informants gave answers in the context of representational and participatory politics and politics of change and resistance:

M: 'Rules and measures alone cannot change anything and cannot bring political equality. What is needed is a change of consciousness. And a quota system cannot change an unequal situation for women that has a deep class character and is based on years of patriarchal suppression, so that it has become an undistinguishable element of capitalism.' (l, neol. Syn., Biology, Athens University, female)

S: 'There is a huge ongoing discussion in our organization about the quotas. It is difficult to force women to participate. The idea behind the quotas is: They (women) have to be set under pressure in order to par-

ticipate, or they have to realise this themselves and take the situation into their hands and say, here we are, we want also to do something. I do not agree with that. I don't believe that motivation has to have a forced character. I believe that this is the job of women and men in any political area and cannot be achieved through quotas, because this system reproduces the same dichotomies over and over again.' (b, neol. Syn., Social policy, Athens University, male)

S: 'I tell you clearly. It is all women's fault that they don't participate in politics. Even if they belong to a group, they are mostly part of the decoration or are looking for a husband. It is a matter of personality. Women are not interested in politics. So, the quotas are not necessary. On the contrary, it might come to a situation, where a good candidate cannot participate somewhere, in an assembly, a conference, in elections, even if he is clearly better informed, a better speaker and so on, because it has to be a woman in this position. Is this democratic?' (d, dap, Law School Athens, male)

A: 'In our organization, there is no quota system. And this is so out of practical reasons. What to do in some areas, even universities, but also regions or trade union associations where there are no women around? You cannot have a list or a committee then? The quota system is restrictive. But, there is a constitutional decision to help women to become crucial members of our groups and take positions. The burdens of their double exploitation and the loads of extra work at home, with husband, children, etc., we can realise them in a way in the organization.' (e, kne, University of Economics, male)

Interestingly, quotas are also seen as a formal interference of the state on the inner affairs of an organization:

Ag: 'The quota is pure hypocrisy. Besides this is an issue that has to do with the organizational structure each party or youth organization wants to have. Also, it is not an issue of numbers: I have so many women, how many do you have? These women that participate or are promoted to participate and go to the parliament and all this stuff, what kind of politics do they reproduce? We see now (name), a popular actor, she is the minister of cultural affairs. And so? Or do you think because she is a woman, she is doing better politics? She is reproducing the bourgeois ideology, exactly like her male colleagues and everybody else in her party.

And I do not believe in women's solidarity, because (same name) and me, we do not have anything in common. She wants me subordinated and so she is my class enemy, regardless of gender.' (j, kne, University of Economics, female)

M: 'I don't agree with the quota system. Women's participation in politics should be normal and obvious. It proves the stereotypes against women that are central in our society.

E: But at least quota is the first step in another direction, a better situation for women. Should we try always to prove our selves?

M: Women do not have to prove something. Or at least they have to prove the same amount of skills and capacities like men. This is an issue that has to do with knowledge, communicational skills. Women even can attract attention easier that men.

R: Right, women can attract attention by their looks. There should be more female presence in politics. Who needs quota? (laughs)' (k, dap, Theology, University of Athens, females)

K: 'I think this (quota system) is very good, because sometimes in certain issues you need a female mind. Women tend to think differently and have other opinions on things that sometimes is more correct than the views we, men, have.' (c, pasp, Athens Technological Institute, male)

The above parts of the discussion about the quota system, besides giving some insights into the ongoing political and social dialogue around gender equality and difference, underline some critical points regarding the ways and directions the contemporary democratic system follows, as realised in Greece and many other European countries (not to forget that the quota system is a regulation enforced by E.U. laws).

The fact that the opinions are informed by ideology and formal party lines, as well as the fact that they refer to notions of gender equality and difference and express views on general gender relations, shows once again the gendered and classed characters of political involvement.

4.4 A Brief Note on Equality and Difference

Departing from the discussions around quotas in political youth organizations, as well as political bodies at European, regional and local levels, we should have a look at the theoretical debates and discussions around the issue that measures, such as quotas or equal representation systems, the issue of equality and difference based on gender but having intersections with categories such as class, race, ethnicity, age, bodily ability, religion, etc. The binary equality and difference has a special theoretical and analytical use for this work, as it touches once again on the relation between masculinities and femininities in the context of organized politics.

It should not be considered as a repetition if I note at this point that in order for an analytical work to be complete, one which has as its object the knowledge of 'masculinities', the notion of masculinity should be theorized and analyzed as masculinity in a relational context (to other forms of masculinities and femininities). Connell stresses this suggestion explicitly in *Masculinities* (Connell, 2005:43): 'Masculinity and femininity are inherently relational concepts, which have meaning in relation to each other, as a social demarcation and a cultural opposition. Masculinity as an object of knowledge is always masculinity in relation.'

Many of the theorizations about gender and constructions of gendered identities stress the so-called 'gender difference', which is meant to be the assertion of two qualitatively different natures, the feminine and the masculine, to women and men accordingly (Kimmel, 2000:xi). Through the analyses, it is implied that the differences between the genders are the cause of inequality and domination. However, what is characterized in these theorizations as biological or cultural difference is very often difference resulting from different historical, social, economic and political positioning. In this way, the fact that domination and suppression, through categorization and classification, causes difference, is overlooked. By focusing on gender as a component of one's identity, theories that focus on gender differences view differentiations between genders as the source of discrimination, reversing the argument that discrimination and dominance are the cause of difference.

Theories that focus on power and domination have pointed to this inversion of the relation between difference and dominance and have shed light on the structural character of gender inequality as reflected in basic social and political institutions.

The focus on difference, however, implies involvement with discourses about sameness and equality. On this point, the relation between sameness and equality, as well as between difference and inequality, appears distorted. Taking as an example the political youth organizations, we can say that this institutional structure is organized around demonstrating and reproducing masculinity, as it depends upon the separation of the public and the private sphere, the separate allocation of tasks, the different involvement of women and men, on hierarchy and authority. The assumed and broadly represented in discourse idea of institutional gender neutrality actually serves to maintain the gender politics of this institution (Kimmel, 2000:16) that sustains masculine domination and gender inequality. Regarding this phenomenon, social theories and political practices suggest that the best way to eliminate gender inequality in these kinds of institutions, such as political organizations, is to promote sameness, as if 'we are only unequal because we are different' (*Ibid*).

Against this notion of the antithetical genders, there are theories that promote the relational and complementary character of gender relations. Nevertheless, the issue of (in)equality, difference and sameness remains central to theoretical discourses and political debates and, as shown above, influences the character of organizations.

4.4.1 Equality-Difference, Theories and Political Scenarios

All through the history of the feminist movement, the issue of the oppression and subordination of women by men, patriarchy, capitalism and normative heterosexuality have all brought demands for equality. Since various theoretical stands have had various views on the cause(s) of women's suppression, they have adopted different positions around the issue of equality. On the basis of the discussion of if and how women can become equal to men in a society that is structured and developed based on inequalities, many theorists and activists pose the question of whether it is possible and even desirable to become equal to men, considering that women have different interests and needs. Equality feminism, which represents as a theoretical stand the earlier feminist thinking, stresses as a crucial source of women's oppression their exclusion from the male-dominated social, economic and political system. On the basis of the exclusion based on gender, gender differentiation is viewed as negative, and equality is perceived as inclusion in all the male-dominated systems. Therefore, demands for equal participation in all structures that organize social and political life are thought of as promoting the way to equality. The radical feminists uniting all women under one category argued for the superiority of women, the positive, caring and mothering Woman who cannot comply with the negative side of the Male. They accuse the equality feminists of opportunism and stress a positive view on gender differences. They suggest that the basis for gender equality is the recognition of gender difference and the distance from negative notions attributed to women. Socialist feminists stressed the fact that women are double exploited within two parallel and intersecting systems, capitalism and patriarchy. In order to fight against exploitation by capital and the dominant classes that serve it, women have to cooperate with men who belong to the same working class, as they share the same class status and same economic, social and political interests. However, out of the workplace and in the household, women as victims of patriarchal exploitation clearly had different interests from both men and women of the dominant classes. In this spectrum, equality is based on stressing the difference from men and also among women based on class, race and other categories, and, on the other hand, on going beyond difference against the patriarchal order that suppresses all women, even if not with the same intensity and with the same material consequences. Difference among women is stressed also by lesbians and women of color. In their critiques, they assume that notions of equality include notions of normative heterosexuality, gender identity constructions and reproduction. By stressing the demand for equality, women automatically reproduce heterosexism, racisms, classisms and ethnic biases. Liberal feminists are more concerned with the public sphere, where they demand equal rights and the same treatment as men, stressing similarities and equality rather than difference. Marxist feminists theorize women as a class, while they often distinguish between working class and bourgeois women, with the first being both exploited by capital and the patriarchal system that goes with it. Multiculturalist feminists highlight group identity and cultural difference and are heavily criticized by those who support multiple, intersecting difference and view identity as negative. The last group argues on the basis that all identities are inherently repressive (Grant, 1993).

As N. Fraser (1997) has criticized, most of these points fail to take into account the social politics of equality, because they elaborate upon the cultural politics of difference in the abstract (Gouws, 1999:56). The demand for equal or different rights is in itself misleading, because it is directed to the public or mainly political domain, leaving unarticulated the social and economic disparities between the social groups, without touching the issue of access to economic and social rights focusing partially on political and civil rights. The general rights claims coming from different feminist stands and inserted in right and leftist political programmes (often very undifferentiated, since they remain general) oversimplify complex power relations (*Ibid*, 56).

Nevertheless, the equality-difference debate became – and still is – one of the most crucial political debates within the feminist movement, as well as outside of it. Based on personal experience of exploitation and talking-fighting-resisting against it in personal and public discourses, feminists make the personal political, and this has become one of the central demands of the second wave of feminism.

What constitutes the political character of this demand is not its inclusion in political programmes, laws and discussions within the parties and the parliaments. The political character is based on its openness, inclusive character and universal dimension. Experience of every form of personal, collective, institutionalized violence, exploitation and subordination of women that reproduces inequalities that shape the Social and the Political is becoming an issue relevant and important to every single member of the society and, therefore, is political. Personal experience of inequality is an issue that concerns society as a whole, and has to be thematicized in public discourse and so gets a political dimension.

Sexuality and sexual politics belong also to the issues that are still considered private and therefore not to be mentioned in public discourse, which, if they were mentioned, would be considered feminism 'made political'. Many people then and now have often said, 'I don't care what others do in their privacy. Everyone should be allowed to do whatever he/she prefers'. On the basis of this fake tolerance and security of the private, the private sphere becomes invisible. But if even a single woman gets sexually harassed by her husband, this issue is of general concern and therefore becomes political. Equally political is if the company owner underpays the employees, and as equally political is that certain countries of the 'first' world operate imperialistic wars in countries of the 'third' world. Feminists, through their critique on gender inequality, turn the focus of the Political, the Social and the Economic to personal experience of exploitation. So, in a critical analysis of gender, the politicization of a matter as important as equality-difference cannot be dismissed.

4.4.2 From Feminist Theories to Politics: Linking Equality and Difference to Citizenship and Political Involvement

The 'equality-difference' debate transgresses the borders of a 'women's issue' and becomes an issue for social and political theory. It refers directly to the categorization of individuals according to their gender first and second to their access to public and institutional sites, as well as their position in the private sphere.

Concentrating on politics and political involvement, we have to make clear the connection between the equality of social, political and economic rights and the notion of citizenship. Furthermore, the issue of equality-difference and the notion of citizenship are connected to the public/private dichotomy. Dichotomies between special groups of 'citizens' with special rights (Delphy, 1995), as 'women' for example, reproduce essentialist ideas that naturalize and legitimize ideas that sustain rather than eliminate the differentiations and categorizations among 'citizens'. The public character of the legislative exceptions, in which the private is reflected, reveals the existence of a meta-law, in which contradictions are a constitutive element (Delphy, 1995:426). Delphy criticizes the binary public/private, which is reproduced through laws and legislations, as underlying the fact that every category of knowledge is not simply reflecting the nature of things but is socially constructed and used according to the historical time as well as to the economic, social and political organization of a society.

Gender is a basic organizing principle of society and an institutional form of hierarchy. Therefore, its deconstruction is required in order to disconnect the notion of citizenship from it. It is doubtful, however, that the problems reflected in the connection between democracy and gender can be solved if and only when the gender differences are typically accepted (through the quota system or the system of equal representation in politics). The question is whether the distinction between women and men creates two different universalities, something that is theoretically enforced through the system of equal representation. Following these trends, we can see that democracy, in its liberal version, continues to oversee the universal perception of the human as a constitutive factor of society, of which variety is a crucial part. Pateman shows in *The Sexual Contract* (1988) how all concepts derived from the liberal tradition privilege the ontology of maleness and the 'epistemic' dominance of masculinity in liberal political thought (Arnot, 2009:31). Rights for participation and representation within the liberal democratic tradition include women as symbols of morality and femininity (Yuval-Davis, 1997 in Arnot, 2009:31), but its greatest weakness is the principle upon which women's citizenship has been constructed: the gendered nature of public/private. According to this 'arrangement', gender inequality is embedded in the political principles and social relations which are legitimated by a theory of liberal democracy (*Ibid*). Pateman (1970) underlines that since the 1970s, social equality has become a great requirement for democratic participation, which in turn promotes the development of social equality. The principle 'political equality through and with social equality' is a constant democratic demand, which at the political level persistently re-emerges through debates about quotas and equal representation. These political demands seem alienated from the social reality that most people, women and men, are experiencing. The fight against inequalities is no longer a socialist demand or a major concern of pro-rights social movements, but becomes established as a part of the liberal tradition (Young, I.M., 1998:481-482). The question is whether this demand for equality within liberal democracy is a real demand for social change.

As a highly political issue, the debate is discussed within different strands of political thought, having a different meaning according to the political tradition it is referring to. The politicization of a traditionally 'feminist' concern passed unattended for many decades as feminist theory, although it introduced a critical perspective to political modernity, did not re-theorize political theory through a gender lens, and so missed connecting the 'political' with politics and political power. Talking about the gender struggle, feminism failed to view the struggle as a constituting element of the Political. However, the first and, moreover, the second waves of feminism have been able to show the structural character of power that is reflected in relations of everyday life. The political nature of these power relations was not recognized clearly; however, it became apparent to what extent power is a constitutive element of all institutions, like school, family, heterosexuality, gender division of labor, the androcentric structure of work and politics (Varika, 1995:44). During the 1970s the feminist movement in the USA, by introducing the issue of racial discrimination that was an outcome of systematically unequal power relations, for the most part brought a new notion of the political into the public domain without, however, connecting directly the notion of power with political power.

As it seems nowadays, many political traditions have taken into consideration the issue of equality and difference, each one perceiving it according to its political lines, ideas and histories. Some political streams – especially on the left – have embraced feminist ideas and critiques on the issue, and as mentioned above, even liberal and political streams on the right have engaged with the issue. That becomes obvious when we follow the major discourses that appear around equality on a political and social level, which developed during the research with members of political youth organizations.

4.4.3 Talking about Difference

Categorizations, such as woman, migrant, gay, etc., place individuals into minority groups that are politically, socially and economically underrepresented and marginalized. This differentiation and distinction from other groups of people gives a certain social meaning to them that tends to become 'natural'. Ontological meanings are attributed to socially and politically constructed categories on which the isolation and discrimination of certain groups of people, e.g. women, is based. On a political level, a paradox appears then by the 'naturalization of difference': pro-difference positions and politics are to be met in the essentialist strands of political thought, as well as those of liberal and 'progressive', which embrace difference for different reasons. The inscription of difference of gender on political institutions is more relevant to the above political orientations than to those that focus on the inequalities and view gender as being a result of power relations.

The notion of difference is apparently difficult to connect with that of democracy. Pro-difference feminist strands try to embrace the (different) but valuable qualities of the female. Irigaray suggests a constitution of 'positive rights for female citizens' (Varika, 1995:53), by stressing that democracy means civil adulthood, as long as we do not forget that the universal has two sides, masculine and feminine (Irigaray, 1989). This line of argumentation suggests that in this ideal democratic model would exist rights for male citizens, too, in contrast to the contemporary western political culture where the special case of women and their different characteristics are becoming an issue, while the whole role of the citizen as well as the whole political domain have a clear masculine character. No matter what, the presence of women in politics will have different meaning than the presence of men (who are supposed to be elected because of their abilities rather than their gender) (*Ibid*, 43). As M. Sineau underlines, the female representation in politics tends to be followed by an unstable legitimacy (*Ibid*, 54). The pro-difference feminist streams are often in favour of equal representation parliamentarian systems based on the idea of embracing women from different and various political strands and thus avoiding the political sectarianism of traditional feminist sites in cooperation with the organized Left and off-parliament leftist groups. They often encourage women of all political stipes to get mobilized on a common basis. Nevertheless, the common basis is a blurring notion, as it hides or blatantly ignores differences in class, race, age, ability, etc.

The fact that gender domination runs through all social classes does not make feminism a movement without political inscriptions and does not solve the problem of contradictory and antagonistic social interests. At almost all sites of the political spectrum there is nowadays a consensus on the necessity for a broader representation of women as long as women have managed to find ways to combine the gendered division of labor and the division of public and private sphere. Facts show that not all women have managed to bridge this gap. A high percentage of female representatives in the parliament does not necessarily mean a better gender coalition nor a more open political culture. Most of the time, female members of the parliament represent the interests of the party they belong to and not the interests of women in general.

The equality-difference debate is connected to and affects theoretical and political ideas surrounding the notion of citizenship, which in turn affects gender structures, relations and representations within the Political. In the case of Western European countries especially, the issues of gender and democracy include discussions on the role and character of the welfare state. Analysing the relation between class, gender and citizenship (a triad that affects – together with the ethnicity/race category – the character of the Political the most), we can see that in the most theoretical spheres, the development towards broader social equality has been theorized as the latest step of the evolution of the notion of citizenship, going from securing individual rights to political rights and finally to the achievement of securing social rights.

The consideration of women as citizens challenges evolutionary theories of the development of rights. As Yuval-Davis (1992) argues, processes of inclusion and exclusion are contained within national political histories (Arnot, 2009:67). The 'community' is a term broadly used nowadays and which refers to a whole social entity, drawing from ancient Greek philosophy. T.H. Marshall (1965) has used this concept of community – in the context of United Kingdom – as a social construct, where boundaries are natural and internal divisions are rarely recognized (Arnot, 2009:67).

As Marshall (Marshall; Bottomore, 1977:128) showed in his analysis of the relation between class and citizenship, within a system such as the welfare state the differences between the social positions (and I add to that gender, ethnicity, race differences) are legitimized, as accepted in the framework of the democratic quality of the citizen, as long as they exist in a culturally homogeneous society and as long as they do not rely on essentialist and purely elitist ideas of inherited privileges or privileged groups (as in feudalism or fascism, for example). The path to equality, which in the framework of the welfare state has been designed (even if not realized fully) with broader acknowledgement of social rights in the sectors of health, education, work and broader and more collective control of productive sources, could be viewed as an outcome of direct progress towards democracy (Webb, 1989 in Bottomore, 1995:130). Through this perspective, the attribution of more social rights is viewed as an outcome of achievement of more political rights by the working class and other marginalized social groups. However, in the framework of the welfare state, the economic growth was an even greater concern than the attribution of individual, social and political rights, so that the economic and social politics become a result of negotiations and agreements between the state, big capitalist consortia and trade unions that, with the common aim of preserving stability, would reach a 'class compromise' (Offe, 1980 in Bottomore, 1995:133). The welfare state, as another form of a capitalistic state, was an attempt to introduce a unifying, central principle for a new social reality in the post-war period and also after 1989 in Europe, something that expressed a mentality or a general spirit rather than a structure. It was restricted to the spheres of public affairs and social policies (*Ibid*, 134). As Marshall (Marshall, 1981:131-5) suggested in his class analysis of the welfare state, the democratic freedoms still depend on the economic freedom, and the antagonistic markets are more important for efficacy and economic growth. On the other hand, the capitalistic economy of the market has caused high levels of social injustice (Bottomore, 1995:135). This contradictory relationship between economy and democracy shows a rate of conflict between the notion of citizenship and the class system and other systems of social inequalities within capitalism, a conflict between the coverage of needs by social services and the market. In capitalistic societies, the broader distribution of social rights in the framework of the social welfare state has not modified the class system (or the gender, race or ethnicity systems of social inequalities).

Around the issue of citizenship, a political dynamic of contradicting political lines and traditions that try to embrace the quality of citizenship and insert it into policies and measures has been created the last years. Very dominant are the ideas of the New Right that rail against the 'culture of dependencies' that the character of the social welfare state creates in the society and the support the development of a 'business culture', in which the individuals secure prosperity on their own, and the role of the state is restricted to offering help to those who are not able to take care of themselves (Lister 1990 in Bottomore, 1995:154). The marginalized, poor and isolated groups are treated as second rate citizens and receivers of charity who often live on others' costs and account. Lister (Lister, 1990: 41-46) shows the ways in which the tendencies towards isolation and political marginalization of the weak and poor, which are directly linked with economic and social factors, are involved in this process.

Although feminist thought did not introduce an alternative nature of the state and democracy, it had an impact on the concept of citizenship. As

H. Araujo, K. Deliyanni, G. Ivinson (2009) have shown in their research about young teachers and their changing concepts of citizenship in public and private spheres, popular in the Greek socio-political context are political discourses of duty that promote a model of the 'critical' or 'sceptical' citizen based on Greco-Roman traditions of active citizens as political beings (Aristotelian tradition). Present also are egalitarian discourses and discourses on social rights that promote the 'protesting citizen' based on the political tradition of civil rights and welfare. In my fieldwork with members of political youth organizations, similar political discourses on citizenship and the relation between the state and the political subject were developed.

4.5 Masculinities and Femininities in Political Youth Organizations

Within an analytical framework that is defined by the notion of power and its influence on gender relations, it is very important to question the terms we use, to avoid employing concepts that hide power relations, hierarchizations and categorizations. Talking about masculinities and femininities, it is important to ask how these meanings change from site to site (ideological, institutional, organizational, subjective) and how the process of defining masculinities and femininities in discourse reveals the mechanisms and operation of power. In the discussions with young members of political youth organizations, I explicitly avoided the use of the terms masculinities/femininities, male/female (although I had to refer a few times to 'men' and 'women'). That was partly an experiment to see if and how these notions would appear, in which context and how they would be used. As expected, individuals, while trying to define their political and gender identities within the relevant discourses, constantly referred to themselves in relation, opposition, rejection, or affection to the other, mostly dealing with two general gender categories, men and women that were differentiated (in this context) according to political identity, class, skills/education, age and always by the biology and culture inscribed on the body.

Even talking about organizational measures in contemporary politics such as the quota system brought up categories such as women/men, which people were negotiating, evaluating, trying to give meaning to. In the attempt to reconstruct their gendered, classed, organized realities people participate actively in a process of meaning-making that reveals how cultural practices are organized and how people define their identities according to how they understand the world around them. Social structures, as well as science, construct the ways according to which people experience themselves, and even by resisting them, people just establish whatever they try to overcome. It seems that the consequence (reproduction of structures) of a process (subjective reconstruction of the experienced self) is not easy to refrain from. We can go as far as to say that even resistance needs a certain level of compliance or at least the recognition and internalization of norms and structures, as a necessary first step.

How confident individuals are with the discourses around gender relations in politics was evident from the intensity of the use of ideas such as equality, political representation and respect of difference. By claiming knowledge of institutional aspects (legislations, organizational structures, political systemic structures), socio-political relationships ('politician', 'political representative', 'leader', 'ideological elite', 'political activist', 'parliamentarian'), they were moving in and out of discourses, very often reproducing established political ideas and cultural perceptions about gender relations.

The meanings of gender that individuals deliberately or systematically attribute to the others and themselves reveal the kinds of cultural representations that form and establish the ways in which relations between women and men are organized and understood (Scott, 1997:760).

The difficulties people had in explaining what they really meant by equal society, equal rights, and the fact that these terms were systematically repeated by various people with clearly very different notions of society and equality and rights, brought up the idea that the debate equality/difference is actually a vicious circle which does not offer really any solution to the very real problem of hegemonic gender order, gender inequality, oppression based on gender, etc. What does equality mean? Equal to what, who gets to define the term, and is difference really the opposite of equality? Can't there be equality and difference, or as S. Scott (1997) underlines, even equality because of difference?

Within a dominant gender hegemony, where the main orientation is towards the formation of a homogeneous desire (for certain ideals, representations, relations) that produces stable, controllable identities and ideological security, it is very problematic to talk about equality and difference. Difference is, if accepted, only tolerated as long as it remains within the known gendered patterns that sustain the dominant gender regimes within various social, economic and political institutional areas. Upon these pyramids of antagonistic social relations of capitalism and productive value is based the construction of the public man (and woman), and within these regimes the social roles attributed to the members of the society are formed.

What remains striking in the empirical data I was able to collect during the discussions was that even in talking about masculinities, people were referring more often to femininity, as a relational, antithetical, compatible term/idea/ structure/relation rather than to other forms of masculinity. Even the metaphors used and the representations they referred to showed the relevance or distance from the idea and ideals of the feminine, also when they were not explicitly talking about gender relations. For example, talking about the ideal type of a good politician or leader figure, the metaphor of the father or the son came up often. People attributed confidence, authority, strength and the ability to protect and control that these figures incorporate in the imaginations of the people, but they still referred to father and son, implying always (even without saying so) the contrast to the mother or the daughter:

T: 'Like the father or the son in a family, who enters the room and the floor is shaking, he (a good politician) can be saying hello, hypnotize the people, he can look the audience in the eyes and offer them a vision, something to dream about. This thing, very few politicians have it nowadays, not only politicians but people in general don't have it.' (a, pasp, University of Economics, male)

Metaphors and allegories always impose a moral dimension that includes and projects something as positive and excludes negative aspects. In addition, as was often the case, the image of the suppressive mother who controls life at home was, once again, underlying a negative notion of womanhood and motherhood, implying a comparison to the father or the son (or to men in general). The typical topos of the slightly hysterical and neurotic woman who can tyrannize the people around her proves to be either useful for politics or an attitude that proves the incompatibility of women with politics:

M: 'There are some women, they can sell you and buy you and you don't even realise. I know some families, there the mother is the commando, she is like a dragon and nobody, not even the husband or the son, can even say something different. Of course, this attitude, or let's say characteristic of some women, can be a useful skill in politics. You don't want to mess up with such women in a meeting or debate.' (f, dap, Athens Technological Institute, male)

A: 'Women tend to see things with more empathy, and this is not always good. Many times it is bad, because they cannot prioritize the things and identify the real important problems. Ok, you see 10 people that you want to help, but you can only help 5, so you have to set priorities. You have to learn to say no. Sympathy does not help you to keep a clear mind. One of the reasons that in my organization, especially the older members think that there cannot be women in higher positions is because they believe that when the president in a sitting has to shout to keep order – this happens all the time – women cannot be able to do this or if they do, there would be an escalation of a fight. If men shout to each other, after a while there is no problem, no harm done. It is funny that the more we grow in the organization and the older we get, we see this tendency, this generally accepted idea that women cannot leave their personal preferences or problems outside the room when it comes to politics. They can feel sympathy or hate or envy or even love, it does not necessarily have to be bad feelings. Let's say I am in a political youth group and you come in and I will start like who is she, who brought her here, what does she think she is doing? In the end the fights among women in political organizations or unions are clearly personal quarrels.' (n, onned, Law School Athens, female)

Individuals tend to generalize talking about 'women' or 'men', even if sometimes they acknowledge the fact that 'not all people are the same'.

As will become clear in the analysis, the equality versus difference debate has been central in the various theoretical discourses surrounding politics, democracy and the state. However, this binary has proved misleading and has inhibited feminist theory from offering real political choices. According to Scott (1997), difference does not entail inequality, nor does equality presuppose sameness.

What becomes evident from the whole analysis is that men construct their masculinities, having as a reference point women, the female and the ideals of femininity, something that does not remain in the domain of the imaginary but has a very real, material impact not only on the organization of household, work, leisure and politics, but on the economic, social and political identity of gendered individuals. The very same is true for women. Especially for women as socially, culturally, economically and politically constructed gendered subjects, who are concerned by their positions in the domains of housework, labor and reproduction, the reference to men/masculinities is more central and constant. *Important to underline is that notions of masculinity and femininity are not always antagonistic and antithetical, and the one does not imply the negative of the other but almost always the negation of and the limitation to the other.*

At least in the framework of the political youth organizations, the masculine and the feminine are formed within a masculinized culture, under the light of hegemonic masculinity patterns, so both male and female subjectivities are informed in their formation by these variables. Male subjectivities usually tend to find a way to position themselves in relation to hegemonic masculine patterns, mostly by 'doing' hegemonic masculinity or being compliant, and rarely resisting and being deviant. The notion of 'doing' is used here to stress the fact that the agency implies the gender construction, which is most of the time conscious. Accordingly, female subjects 'do' gender in relation to masculinities, which is also a conscious, active gender construction. However, male and female subjectivities are distinct from each other and take different positions within the matrix of power and domination in organized politics.

A revealing example of 'doing' gender in politics is the division of political activities and the areas of political involvement that the gender subjects choose, or are expected to choose. So usually, women tend to choose communications, family, gender and cultural and educational issues, and men obviously choose the rest, such as governance, finances, administration, foreign affairs, military, etc. Even in 'cross-gender' thematic areas such as environment and work, the division of activities is very gender specific.

4.5.1 Masculinities and Sexuality: Sexual 'Normativities' in Politics

The political youth organization, as a site of political socialization, mobilization and organized political action, functions as a mechanism for masculinity construction. The formation of gendered identities is a process of negotiation, acceptance and ambivalence. The organized members are not passive receivers but are participating actively in the formation of their own masculinities. The peer groups play an active role in the formation of gendered identities that stress heterosexual masculine behaviors and contribute to the construction of gender hierarchies.

In organized political settings, similar to institutional settings of education, there is a dynamic intersection of political processes, political youth cultures, culturally available discourses around masculinity and heterosexuality, broader social relations and 'a constant involvement of the unconscious that produces heterosexual forms of masculinity' (Mac an Ghail, 1996), which are experienced as 'natural' or 'normal' sides of given personalities.

Sexuality is a central point in the process of constructing masculinities. Heterosexuality, then, is not a balanced (or even unbalanced) institutionalization of masculinity and femininity, but rather of masculinity (Holland; Ramazanoglou; Thomson, 1996:145). Drawing from Butler (Butler, 1990), we can say that the landscape of sexuality among political organizations is organized within the framework of the heterosexual nexus. The obviousness of heterosexuality is coded within the language, institutional practices and within the personal relations on the everyday level. The sexual 'normality' or 'naturalness' of a dominant ideology makes it invisible – normal, a-political, commonsensical and broadly accepted, as Gramsci (1971) explained about the workings of ideology. In this framework, different forms of sexuality are stigmatized, isolated and discriminated (Politis, 2006:311). The notion of masculinity loses its meaning with the absence of the heterosexual framework, and the masculine in sexual relation to the feminine only has meaning inside it. Often, heterosexuality becomes heterosexism. Sexual identities are constituted by institutional and empirical practices, and the institutional sites (political organizations, universities, etc.) are places where an active construction of gendered and sexual identities takes place. Heterosexism derives themes and motives from the dominant and hegemonic heterosexual and homophobic discourses that are popular and spread throughout different social sites, discourses around marriage, family, heterosexual love, division of labor, household work, reproduction as presented in the public domain of mass culture, politics and state. In the gendered world of political youth organizations, heterosexuality is presented as social or moral law. Sexuality seems to belong somehow in the silenced domain of the private and is separated from politics, which belongs to the public domain and therefore becomes an issue for discussion.

The heterosexual ideology makes up a key factor of the construction, evaluation and hierarchy of masculinity. Young men as gendered subjects are involved in a 'race' for the construction of their masculine identities within the framework of political organizations through the adoption of various sexualities relevant and analogous to political ideology and referring to patterns and models that belong to a certain ideological space. The 'objectification' of women, the direct or indirect devaluation of political abilities and possibilities of the others, and the 'feminization' of the opponent assist the re-construction of masculinity through heterosexist practices in the context of organized political life. As an example, the so called 'hard-core' ideologists often construct an 'ultra-masculine' identity that is informed by heterosexuality, whereas the so called 'egalitarians' are viewed to have a more 'feminine' identity, a rather asexual sexuality, even 'homosexuality'.

The homophobic jokes can serve as ways of surveillance and control of masculine identity and reflect sexuality construction processes within youth groups (Nayak; Kehily, 1996 in Politis, 2006:320).

According to the culture of hegemonic heterosexual masculinity, the fact that a boy is in a relationship with a girl adds to his status and popularity among his peers.

G: 'When you are young, there is a constant social pressure, especially by your peers, around sex. All the discussions are like: 'I have been with so many (women), how many did you score?' and so on. For me, because I was maturing slowly, so to say, I didn't have experience with such things, I was late, but until I started having experiences I was feeling very weird, like something was wrong with me. But it was simply not the right time for me yet, and all these talks and stories were not helping.' (e, kne, University of Economics, male)

The narrations of 'heterosexual accomplishments' contribute to the sustaining of the strong heterosexual character of youth organizations. Young men who behave differently or alternatively are supposed to undermine openly one of the central principles of masculinity, the principle of the obviousness of heterosexuality (Anderson, 2002:875). Another point of masculine (hetero) sexuality is the emotional distance and isolation of boys/men from girls/women, the concealment of emotional need or dependency.

V. Seidler (1987) has suggested that masculine identity has so much lined up with rationality – a quality that most women apparently do not have – that rationality becomes the critical base for masculinity, associating women with a source of unoriginal knowledge, as emotions, intuitions and experiences (Politis, 2006:312).

Emotion is a female characteristic and belongs rather to the private domain, whereas rational thinking is a male characteristic, which places him in the public domain.

The heterosexual forms of masculinity that are constructed within political youth organizations are in a constant process of development and are always relational to other forms of masculinity developed in the same context. They are determined by the hierarchical relations between similarity and difference and always try to sustain a balance among social contradictions. In this framework, the different forms of hegemonic masculinities are organized around contradictory and even conflicting poles. Within political organizations, practices that promote antagonism inside and outside the organization promote different kinds of antagonistic masculinities. For example, usually men from lower classes focus on activism, which demands skills other than good educational or theoretical political levels, thus 'devaluing' good theoretical skills. According to antithetical and antagonistic forms of masculinities, we have different subject positions within a group. It is important to stress that the creation of hegemonic and other antagonistic masculinities that sustain the androcentric character of a political organization should not be transferred to the boys and young men, but to consider, rather, that hegemonic masculinity is to be traced among the structures, the representations and the individual practices within political youth organizations.

4.5.2 The 'Sexualization' of Political Life

Political power is interdependent with broader structures of gender and class inequalities as they take form within organizational structures and political practices. The constructions of hegemonic and subordinated masculinities provide some men with interpersonal power that, when exercised, reconstructs and reaffirms interclass male dominance (Pyke, 1996:527). Structures of gender and class inequalities form the power dynamics within political youth organizations and construct ideological hegemonies that legitimate and mystify the power of privileged men over lower-status men and women (*Ibid*).

Hegemonic forms of masculinity seem to sustain not only dominant political ideologies but also the established status of big – in size and political power – youth organizations. On a symbolic level, masculine traits such as size, power, status, as well as male heterosexuality, form the sex-appeal of political youth organizations. Sexuality and power construct the political profile of organizations from the inside and the outside.

Every youth organization, according to the ideology and political organizational form it has, reflects and represents different forms of ideological hegemonies around the notion and the practices of masculinity. The different dominant patterns of masculinities construct the gender relations within each organization differently. However, in opposition to each other, the pattern that intersects with the dominant political ideology in the given political system and political culture remains hegemonic. The general structures of power affect the dominant cultural ideology that backs up the legitimization of existing power relations in every institutional domain (Connell, 1987; Foucault, 1980). The cultural ideologies tend to neutralize, symbolically at least, the structural inequalities and form a kind of acceptance and consensus on a broader social level. Cultural ideologies are becoming parts of other dominant ideologies, such as political ones. As Gramsci (1971) underlined, the consensus that ideological hegemonies construct works to legitimize inequalities such as women's subordination, which happens constantly with regard to both men's and women's acceptance.

The ways men oppose one another, among the antagonistic relations of hegemonic and subordinate masculinities, affect the ways that they oppose women (Rissuew, 1991 in Pyke, 1996:532). Especially through everyday practices of organized political life within political youth organizations, misogyny and the sexualization of women become strategies that sustain the masculinized character of politics.

The sexualization and objectification of women are accepted by both men and women in organizations:

I: 'How women are sometimes used for various purposes, it is very devaluing. But there are so many women that go with it and many of them know why they do it. They know that somehow, metaphorically speaking, you have to become a whore in there. You know that as a girl you are the window to gather attention. They represent the status of the organization in a way, they say look, if you come to our gathering, these kind of hot chicks will be there.' (h, dap, Marine Egineering, Metsoveio University, female).

This misogynous attitude towards women is criticized by male political members, who indirectly criticize hegemonic masculinity and represent alternative forms of masculinity:

S: 'There is one big organization that every year prints posters with sexist pictures of semi-naked women as advertising for parties or events. And we are totally freaked out, because this thing reproduces patterns that we resist and not only women but men are criticizing them. And we go and tell them so, especially to the girls of this organization, you know, this is sexist, this turns women's flesh into a product and the girls themselves are attacking us and saying things, what do you want? She is sexy and she is nice on the poster! This shows how women themselves have internalized patterns, that they are oppressing them, and now I might try to convince this girl, but if she doesn't understand that she has the right to fight this kind of discrimination, nothing will change and this sexist culture will remain among political youth organizations.' (b, syriza, Social Policy, Panteio University male)

On the level of micro-politics (organizational life) as well as on the macro-level of the whole political culture, there is a common pattern that repeatedly appears, namely the men in opposition are pictured as the undersexed Other, while the women are the promiscuous Other (Nagel, 2005:338). While conflicting masculinities are sizing up one another, women are restricted to minor, often symbolic roles to be defended (Nagel, 2005:400).

The internalization of masculine ideologies by women in politics shows once more the direct relation of masculinities and femininities within political youth organizations. In the established gender regime with a dominant masculine character, femininities tend to show a certain compliant compatibility with hegemonic forms of masculinity.

How sexist and misogynous practices affect the political socialization of women becomes clear when female informants underline the 'dirty' character of politics, describing a tendency to immorality, antagonism and aggressiveness that only men can deal with, underlining once more the masculine character of politics:

X: 'Sometimes I don't understand why women keep getting involved in politics. There are not so many of them anyway, the majority of women have better things to do than getting in this dirty game. Women cannot deal with dirtiness. They are somehow more moral, although morality is a strange notion. There are so few that they do not care, and I am one of them, but the majority cannot stand it, and I understand somehow the reason.' (i, pasp, Communications, Panteio University, female)

This kind of symbolic victimization is connected with the notion of passive femininity and refers to sexual availability.

For radical feminist thought, any form of sexual harassment is an everyday female experience and reflects the way men objectify women and, parallel to that, composes sexual violence and the masculine mechanism of control over women (MacKinnon, 1979). It is a phenomenon of 'heterosexism'[3] that certifies the character of 'heteropatriarchy' (MacKinnon, 1979). The fact that many women are not able to acknowledge that they, at certain moments, are sexually harassed in any way shows how much heterosexism has pervaded the practice of everyday gender relations and has forced women to adjust their femininity to the desires of men or use masculine behavioral traits to adjust to everyday situations.

Connell (1995:230) has stressed that by the principles of psychoanaly-

3 The compulsory heterosexuality that enforces masculine domination and patriarchal law through the acceptance of the hegemonic position of heterosexuality and masculinity (Politis 2006: 342)

sis and social constructivism it becomes obvious that women are carriers of masculinity as much as men are (Halbestram, 1998).

Often, women react to heterosexist male views by using some of the masculine strategies themselves in order to undermine male power and negotiate a part of this for themselves (Politis, 2006:432):

X: 'When you are a woman among all the men, you somehow have to act accordingly. The moment you enter the room, you realise you are a woman now, besides being a member of a political organization or whatever else, because this is what they see in you. And if you want to be heard, you better use this attention, because it gives a certain privileged position. But you should be careful not to overdo it, not to be like a Barbie girl or something, because then you become a joke, but to do what men do, you know coalitions and networking.' (i, pasp, Communications, Panteio University, female)

4.5.3 Heteronormativity, Homophobia and Exclusion in Political Youth Organizations

In a gender regime, which has its character structured by heterosexism and a strong ideology of heteronormativity, homophobic reactions to homosexual masculinity patterns are usual. To come again to the relationship between masculinity and femininity, even in the discursive context of homosexuality, when the discussion is clearly around gay men, the distance from the feminine is again important. Talking about gay men, one guy expressed explicitly:

A: 'I have no problem with someone being gay. Just, he has to be serious and keep it for himself. Not acting like a woman with these feminine gestures and mimicking a woman's voice. Then he is not a man, not even a gay man, he is too much of a woman. It is very irritating.' (Group o, Theology, University of Athens, male)

As L. Ouzgane, D. Coleman (1998:78) suggest: 'The reason why homosexual practices have been so violently subordinated is that they are symbolically blurred with femininity, and thus those men associated with such practices are almost completely debarred from collecting patriarchal dividends'.

It seems that the 'formed on demand' – mainly on social demand according to established inclusions and exclusions – character of human relationships is not restricted to heterosexual relations but also is included in homosexual ones. Masculine traits in homosexual identities are perceived as superior to other homosexual patterns and as preserving some of the dominant masculine ideals:

D: ' To be straight does not mean to be straight in your sexual preferences, it means to be straight in your life, to keep your word, be correct. I know many straight people who are acting gay. They do not know how to behave like real men, to have a word and keep it... But then, there are men and men. There are some that are effeminate but straight and others, very masculine and gay. And among the gays, there are different kinds. There are some serious and some totally like women.' (o, dap, Theology, University of Athens, male)

Heterosexual relations follow the 'sacred' distinction between the public and the private, enforcing the Law and the Norm, in contrast to homosexual relations that are characterized by 'the undifferentiated desire for the known that has its source in the private' (DD aka Dr. Limit, 2010:18):

D: 'I do not care what any one does in his bedroom. This is a private matter and everyone has to keep it to himself. As long as he does not provoke with his attitude, I do not care. The thing is to respect the fact that you are born a man. If you respect what you are, nobody can blame you for anything. You are a man, wear your pants, go anywhere you want. You have to accept your nature. If you are born a man, you are man. Where is the point of turning to a woman? And if so, keep it to yourself, I don't have to see it.' (d, o, dap, Theology, University of Athens, male)

As it appears from the discourses on gender, there are two basic groups of gendered identities: heterosexuality that transforms the antithesis 'masculine vs. feminine' to love and the homosexual that loves the privately familiar. In addition to that, even though under-represented in mainstream discourses, there is also bisexuality, which experiences the plasticity of the body and the antitheses of the same and the different, the equal and the differentiated, celebrating an uncertain identity that suits the contemporary zeitgeist and inter-sexuality 'that wanders, as the science focusing on it, wanders' (DD aka Dr. Limit, 2010:18).

The previous comment about the preservation of clear categories of identity, both heterosexual and homosexual, could appear undifferentiated in various discursive contexts. In the framework of a political organization, the comment gets a strong political dimension. 'Keeping it to himself' distinguishes the personal from the political, the private from the public, respecting the clear borders between manhood and womanhood, accepting the symbolic or representational violence that organizational structures, the structures that define the political system as a whole, have upon gendered, classed, racial and ethnic objects. It seems that structures, in defining the relations between individuals, do not let any space for them to get out of the categories that objectify them, so that they eventually can become self-fulfilled Subjects. On the other hand, on a subjective level, individuals can choose compliance, cooperation, resistance or rejection of the given order. They can even try to escape it, if and when they can really think about utopias and realise them in one way or the other.

Homophobia and sexism expressed in everyday talking, acts, gestures and discursive practices in the framework of political youth organization have a distinct political/organizational colour. Describing negatively the political opponents (members of other political organizations), by expressing doubts regarding their 'manhood' or using descriptions as sissies, girlies, etc., is an indirect way of insulting them about their political strategies, ideas, motives. As the following incident reveals, young men mostly among themselves use coded words or gestures that have insulting, sexually diminishing meanings, meanings which are not always understood by outsiders but nevertheless belong to the everyday active vocabulary of organizational life:

(From my fieldwork notes) 5 male members of a political youth organization and I are sitting outside the cafeteria of the university faculty around a table. We are talking about modern life conditions for men and women, the pressure of the working load and its impact on everyday family life. The young men are very careful to stress the fact that women nowadays can and should work and with their spare free time they should share the housework with their male partners. Simultaneously, a group of 3 men runs by holding some posters and leaflets and then disappears up the stairway. This sudden appearance stirs some uneasiness in the group I am sitting with. One of them starts screaming in a low, fake, thin voice, another in a similar thin, fake voice is shouting the name of the organization, which the people running apparently belong to and they all burst into laughter. When I asked what caused the sudden uneasiness in the group, they replied that the people who passed by were members of an opposing organization, and they are not on good terms, because, as they said, "they don't play fair". Then, they explained that they are secretive and fishing for information, and they behave like little women (that explained the fake female voices). When I asked why they should think that this is typical women's behavior, they said that it is typical behavior of people who are not strong or brave enough to come straight to you and ask to your face what they want (implying that women adopt this kind of behavior because they are weak or at least weaker than men, so that makes it a typical female behavior and an object of contempt).

The most interesting part of this small incident hinges on the fact that the political opponent, the Other, is always in an antagonistic relationship to the own. The Us has to be defeated, diminished and devalued in every possible way, not only through usual political practices such as elections or organized debates but also through negative propaganda, where categories of class, sexuality, age and gender are used systematically to symbolically or discursively suppress and dominate the others, as different, lower, weak, dominated and excluded.

As Anderson (2002) has observed in his research on gay athletes, in institutions where collective practices and discourses are developed around a certain topic, in our case politics, there is an acceptance of homosexuality and homosexual members only under the condition that they meet 'the mandates of hegemonic masculinity' (Anderson, 2002:860), with the exception of their sexuality. In the case of political youth organizations, when talking about homosexuality in the youth group, there is an acceptance of gay people as political members, but not as homosexuals:

G: 'There is a matter of self-definition. A serious gay person, how should he define himself? He can wake up and say, 'I am the gay George' or, 'I am the political activist George'. He should define himself as a political person and he has to live it. What he does in his bedroom is not of interest and has nothing to do with the purposes of our organized political life. There is a general political disorientation caused by various movements, environmental, gay rights, animal protection, etc., that aims to split the movement and distance the people from the real purposes of political struggle.' (e, kne, University of Economics, male)

Heterosexual political members more closely conform to hegemonic masculinity, so their identities as heterosexuals and as political agents become nearly tautological in the context of a political youth group. The combined effect of the attempted silencing of gay identities within politics and the promotion of heterosexuality serves to elevate heterosexuality as broadly accepted, while marginalizing homosexuality (Butler, 1997; Connell, 1995 in Anderson, 2002). Homophobia and the silencing of homosexuality are practices that sustain the 'orthodox' hegemonic masculine character of the dominant gender regime within political organizations.

4.6 'Waving Their Testosterone as a Flag': Patterns of Masculinities

Referring to the public/private distinction, the notion of public or common good as an ultimate social ideal – in models of western liberal democracy – is connected with the philosophical stand of humanism[4], which stresses notions and qualities that could be linked to the 'masculine', acknowledging deliberately in it some 'feminine'[5] characteristics, whereas the notion of rupture, struggle, as a principle of politics of resistance and change focuses on notions that would be described as 'masculine'. Both of these political theoretical streams, still very present in contemporary political movements, are supporting the masculine character of the public, not doubting the androcentric regime of masculinity in politics but rather sustaining its stabilization.

Focusing now on the political culture of Greece and through the discussions with members of political organizations, we can conclude that the very centre of domination is an ideological construction, as well as a material condition that draws upon class as well as gender differences and as an element of both social and political culture is a defining structure of institutions, such as political youth organizations. In the mainstream culture of gender ideologies, male, successful and sexually aggressive forms constitute not only hegemonic patterns of masculinity but also hegemonic forms of masculinized political organizations. This organizational ideology, although it is based on a clear domination of men and hegemonic masculinity, blurs and legitimizes differences and inequalities within the political culture, so that the whole political culture of liberal democracy, in the Greek context, appears to be gender, as well as being class, age, race and ethnicity, neutral. At the site of political youth organizations, hegemonic masculinity influences the political attitudes and practices each organization applies.

---

4 This philosophical tradition can be traced back to Aristotle, who concentrates the political in the public sphere and separates it from the private: 'the polis gives each individual... besides his private life a sort of second life, his bios politicos' (in Cornell, 1997: 213). This tradition is followed by Arendt who distinguishes the realm of necessity (private sphere) from the realm of freedom (political sphere) (see Arendt, H.(1958).*The Human Condition*. Chicago: University of Chicago Press.

5 Derrida, imagines democracy as civic friendship and attributes to it 'feminine' virtues, such as care, gentleness, an appreciation of heterogeneity (see Derrida,J. (1988). The politics of friendship, *Journal of Philosophy*, 80: 2, 632-45.

4.6.1 Models of 'Political Hegemonic Masculinities'

Hegemonic masculinity as an ideology and practice sustains the formation of different forms of 'hypermasculinity' to be met in different organizations, formed according to their political tradition, ideology and the organizational content of the different groups. In the Greek context, various forms of hegemonic political masculinities appear, such as the masculinity of the 'radical', the 'ruling' kind of masculinity, as well as the 'egalitarian' masculinity.

The true masculinity of radicalism, as it aspires to be the one that suits the true character of politics, coexists in an antagonistic relationship to the true masculinity of the 'ruling'. The radicalism of the first, observed obviously in organizations that apply politics of resistance and change, is in opposition to the righteousness of the next, met in organizations that have a ruling dominant representation in the political culture and belong to big political parties. These two hegemonic forms of political masculinity are in contrast also to the more civilized gentility of the masculinity of egalitarianism, which appears in organizations that express participatory and egalitarian political demands and usually have more open organizational structures. The egalitarian masculinity is not in clear antagonism to the other two and represents a less aggressive and alternative form of masculinity. The 'doing' of egalitarian masculinities works sometimes as an indirect criticism on violence, misogyny, homophobia and masculine brutality in politics that the other two major patterns of political masculinity apparently perpetrate, although supposedly do not share.

The demonstration of male dominance of the two antagonistic models of radicalism and rule, models which expect female submission, aims also for the submission of political opponents.

In the given two party political system in Greece, the clear superior position of the political youth organizations that belong to these parties, also in the institutional framework of the university, makes clear that the hegemonic masculinity based on ruling[6] will define the others either as deviant or as subordinate. Even if sometimes they are respected as political identity forms, they are clearly not so as gender forms:

M: 'To tell you the truth, the real ideologists are these of the Left. But they are too extremist, they always cause problems and I don't like them.

---

6 Here 'rule' and 'ruling' is used in the sense of setting the rules of the political game, or in respect of gender, the rules and limits of the dominant gender regime.

S: It is a matter of taste. We do not like to wear black, be dirty, do not care how we look, have long hair…

M: It is not only about this. They are violent, they hit people.

S: They smashed the shops in the centre of Athens last December. The leftists and the 'out-parliamentarians'[7]

M: They are against property and then they smash the car of their neighbour. The most of them are rich kids, they have their own offices and money to print posters, leaflets. And they say we get money from the party, that' s why we are so big and successful in the elections. But, true, they are not corrupt, they do not care about taking positions and winning the elections, they are not dependent on those above, etc. But as persons, they are not nice.' (d, dap/apox, Law School Athens, males)

This dialogue animates the intersection between economic resources, political power, organizational size and networking with class (rich kids), political ideology (true idealists, not corrupt) and embodied masculinity (black clothes, dirty, long hair, not nice, violent) in the context of the political youth movement. Especially the issue of violence is clearly connected with hegemonic forms of political masculinities:

K: 'In demonstrations there are always problems because of the extremists – the anarchists. I have been in a fight with these people, more than once. Even if you try to stop them, they are clearly not in the right state of mind, they are on drugs, they come and hit you with stones, molotovs, sticks. If you are there, you do not understand what's going on, but you must react. They say they have political reasons and ideals, but they are just crazy.' (q, fos, Athens Technological Institute, male)

From the above dialogues, it becomes clear that the political opponent is always the Other and always embodies male characteristics that are despised as well as political ideas that are not approved. In this example, political opponents are rejected both as political subjects and as gender/masculine subjects. The general categorizations and attributions of vague characteristics that describe both the political and the gender attitude of the people such as anarchists, crazy, etc., initiate a process of self-definition through dismissal of the Other, a typical strategy of political rhetoric. In addition, the negation of the other as deviant or inappropriate describes vividly the culture of spoken, unspoken and symbolic discourses and practices that construct the institutional character of political youth or-

[7] Here, he is referring to the incidents of December 2008 after the killing of a 15 year old by a policeman in the centre of Athens.

ganizations, as well as the activities of the people inside them. Through these discourses the production of meaning about masculinity and politics, in our case, forms the gendered and political character of the youth organizations and influences the political culture. In this context the normal and the deviant are in antagonistic relation to each other, influencing the notions and construction of different forms of political and gender identity. The 'normal' or 'natural' are forms of power that regulate and control the process of sexual identity as well as political identity construction. As Bourdieu has stressed, social distinction is projected as natural within societies following the obviousness of the natural law (Bourdieu, 1999:40).

The informants repeatedly refer to a certain type of heterosexual masculine ethic that is also central in the capitalist managerial ideology that stresses rationality, success, disregard of moral, ideological and emotional concerns, networking and career, as the major pattern that political agents follow in most political organizations. The masculine ethic of management (Pyke, 1996:545) is – in the case of organized politics – associated with politics of control and order and evaluates negatively alternative forms of politics. As this managerial ethic is connected with status in an organization, age plays a big role, so that older political members enjoy statuses that younger men cannot have. Within the division between leaders and followers and the division between intellectuals and activists that are common in political youth organizations, the structural inequalities produced by class inequalities are also evident. As the managerial ideology presupposes higher class status, additional exclusions based on class are also formed within political organizations. The same ethical lines exclude homosexual men and women. As Messerschmidt (1993) has correctly analyzed, this exclusion reinforces the construction of 'compensatory' forms of masculinity such as hypermasculinity among male youths (Pyke, 1996:545).

The ideological hegemony of masculinity on a cultural and political level has a different impact on men and women according to the sexuality, age and social class in ways that reflect and (re)construct relational conceptions of masculinities and femininities. Within organizational sites, these different gender conceptions influence the power dynamics among the members and form accordingly the gender regime of the political institutions. Although political organizations are institutions in which masculine structures and practices operate, the ways according to which young men and women position themselves within discourses around gender relations, political ideology and political action differ from organization to organization.

As mentioned before, sexuality and gender are crucial featuring factors of the character of political organizations. The sexual profile or the 'sex appeal' of the various political organizations is a sustaining part of the grade of success they want to project to the outside. From the discourses, it becomes clear that sexuality can be understood as both a foundation of gender (McKinnon, 1982) and an aspect of gender relations. Sexuality is a fundamental material aspect of the production of patriarchal relations. As Hearn (Hearn, 1987: 101) notes, 'productive relations, including capitalist ones, are after all also forms and matters of sexuality, procreation, nurture and violence'. Most institutional sites, including political youth organizations, continue to sustain heterosexuality and relevant ideologies and practices:

A: 'I think that the man is defined by his sexuality, because what else can masculinity mean?

An: Sexuality and property.

A: And there are political organizations that are based on these two.

G: They wave their testosterone as their flag, and they are like 'I do not want to hear anything', they act as if the university is their territory and if you say something different, they are ready to punch you in the face. And if you are a little polite and want to discuss logically, they call you effeminate. Because you are normal. The tragic is that this ideology passes to women, too. I know girls who do not care about these things, but I know other girls, when they see someone behaving like a total macho, they immediately fall for it.

A: As I said, this is a whole culture in some organizations. They have of course a certain political ideology but they represent also this kind of lifestyle ideology. People go to these organizations to live this lifestyle and this is one of the reasons why certain big political youth organizations are established within the university and get even bigger and bigger with the years. They want to impose on you this kind of thinking: 'I am going to get in this youth group, to get to know people and to f... around' '(e, kne, University of Economics, males)

The relations between the members of political youth organizations are mostly determined by the internal organizational structures, the organizational practices that members reproduce on an everyday level in the organizational site and the division of political work within the political group. The division of political work on an everyday level facilitates further two production processes: the production of ideology and services and the production of gender. Similar to what S. Fenstermaker (2002) suggests in her analysis of household work and gender, members of political youth organizations do gender as they do their work in the particular context of the politics they belong to. Political members develop personal and collective discourses around how they do politics, which in turn gives insights into how they do their masculinities when they do their politics. The connection between political practices, relevant discourses and masculinities becomes clearer when we try to identify the structural imperatives as well as the normative expectations linked to how work and responsibility is allocated among members of political groups. Hierarchy and power as part of the structural imperatives influence the ways in which members do their politics and, in relation, the ways they do their masculinities and femininities. Around certain patterns of work allocation appear certain patterns of hegemonic masculinities. Although each political group has its own organizational structures, there are some certain common topos of doing politics and doing gender that can be identified.

In general, we can say that there are certain forms and models of masculinity according to the different characters of political organizations. In each different group, there is usually a dominant, hegemonic masculinity pattern and all the other related forms are antagonistic to each other, (re)positioning (themselves) hierarchically in relation or referring to the hegemonic pattern. Mac An Ghail (Mac an Ghail, 1996:55), in his research on masculinities in schools, underlined that schools, as institutional sites, are creating certain conditions which promote hegemonic masculinities, around which different notions of masculinity are competing to get established.

There are various factors and variables that influence the construction of hegemonic and alternative patterns of masculinity in the framework of political youth organizations. The influences of the local culture (when we refer to local youth groups), the interaction and relationships between members and instructors[8], between members of youth organization and the party organization, the access to decision-making bodies or regional, national bodies, the access to information, the different organizational or political practices each group uses and its acceptance or influence on the local or institutional context within which it is positioned, all these are parameters that form different models and patterns of masculinities. Even within the same political landscape, within the same political organization, not all members

8 Especially, the ideological, psychological and verbal violence that instructors and leaders are using on the members of political organizations, is an interesting issue that reveals valuable knowledge about gender and masculinities constructions. It remains, however, a topic to be analysed in a further work.

have the same opportunities to access certain positions and gain advantages from their political involvement.

4.6.2 Theorists vs. Activists: Structural Divisions within Political Youth Organizations

Tensions between various masculinity patterns are often created by the division of labor and information. Depending on the kind of obligations and duties the members have, they are often separated automatically between the 'theorists', those who are accepted as 'most read', or 'theoretically trained' and who get to do ideological and educational work, and those who are 'activists' and are mostly in touch with the broader audience, or 'the outside world', and are doing more practical organizational work. Even if both groups have their share in all organizational practices, they are often defined by the one or the other category.

Many members have stressed the fact that the structures, internal hierarchies and power relations within organizations have an alienating impact on the people involved, by creating a distance from ideals and personal ideas and forcing upon individuals practices and politics that they are not willing to follow. The real material conditions of politics in general and organizational politics in particular force many young members to view in a more pragmatic and less romantic way politics and their role in it. Especially in political sites, where power relations are reflected in strategic interpersonal networking, clever communication strategies and profiling are becoming crucial for the gain of political power within the organization. In this case, power translates into participation in decision-making bodies, election as representative or electoral candidate, representation of the political organization at the national and international level and, consequently, broader acceptance within the group and from other political groups. In this respect, most young members have a very realistic view of politics, a cynical view of the Political and a rather opportunistic view of personal relations, which affects their perception of gender relations in the group. In the context of alienation, members of youth organizations often have a distanced view towards the Party (which constitutes a different entity from the youth organization but usually has continuous and influential relations with it). Young members often do not identify with certain persons or practices, even with ideological or political lines. Many of them view the party as an entity or an institutionalized power structure from which they are excluded to participate (see Connell, 1989:160).

4.6.3 Skill: a Class and Gender Related Variable of Differentiation within Political Youth Groups

Especially among youth organizations within different educational institutions (such as those which I contacted during my field work), which are located within the institutional site of universities, there is a tension even among different groups of the same youth organization, which can vary organizationally and administratively due to the fact that they are located inside different faculties. The topic of studies seems to become another differentiating variable that affects the form of gender relations within political youth organizations. This has a lot to do with the fact that usually in the natural sciences, there is a strong majority of male students, whereas in the humanities and arts, there is a majority of female students. The gendered character of the institutional site influences directly the gendered character of the youth organizations inside it. In events (gatherings, conferences, assemblies, even protests and demonstrations), very often selected groups represent the political organizations of each school/faculty, which apparently most of the time are constituted by male participants.

In the same framework, there are categorizations according to the subject of studies which determine mostly future occupation. These categorizations according to occupation or scientific specialization are producing multiple and contradicting forms of masculinity. As H. Chenut has suggested, skill has always been a marker of social class, serving as a component of gender and work identity (in Frader; Rose, 1996:78). Considering that the current politically organized students will be after graduating – if they remain members of the same or any other party organization – organized in their work places (working associations or trade union sections are organized according to profession in Greece) or in local groups according to their place of residence, both two very 'classed' and gendered categorizations, it becomes obvious that skill matters even when it comes to political participation at the university.

Usually youth political organizations in Greece, except the few cases where they already exist in high schools, are placed either in universities or work places. The access to higher education identifies the character of the different political youth groups. The youth groups in the universities consist of people who get to study (achieve higher grades in school, which mostly means the families have invested money in preparation for the final exams that allow entrance in the universities), whereas the groups inside the work associations and those at the local level consist of people who recently began to work. This distinctive variable shapes the character of membership within most political youth organizations and often divides categories of 'achievers-educated' or 'sophisticated- intellectual' and the 'losers-uneducated' or 'unsophisticated- simple workers' that form of course different patterns of masculinity. Even if not mingling with each other, members of different types of groups often complain that they cannot communicate with each other or are not quite in the same line or political level. Skill and education enable the achievement of status among the peer group. Usually education or extra knowledge is appreciated by the so-called 'theorists', whereas among the activists, experience in practical and organizational matters is acknowledged to a greater extent.

Sometimes, education is not so much of a privilege as is experience, good rhetoric and communicational skills within politics. Then, obviously, other characteristics that sustain dominant forms of political masculinities are celebrated and valued rather than the 'well-educated' theorist. As Sewell (1997) has stressed, the nature of middle class characteristics can sometimes work restrictively against those who can profit the most from them.

Political failures that cause political isolation and political disrespect can also create antagonistic and authoritarian masculinities.

In addition to that, the small size of a political group or organization within a certain institutional site or the marginal political power of the party to which a youth group is attached to can lead to an underestimation of the political power and social influence of these groups. Often, male members of small groups are discriminated by members of larger political groups as if their inferior political presence equals a 'female weakness'. They are often 'in contempt' and 'left out' of fights, debates and events.

4.6.4 Practicing Masculinity in Politics

In the framework of organized political action there are some alternative ways to 'perform' or 'make public' subjected forms of masculinity through the use of violent language or through extreme popularity that is embodied and incorporated in language and performance. As D. Cornell notes, 'the very rhetoric of the political world reflects the 'macho' language that serves a compensation of masculine anxiety and fear' (1997:220).

'Elitist', 'technocratic' or 'theoretical' ways of speaking and expressing through words, terms, concepts, etc., complicated ways of thinking, in combination with authoritarian ways of fulfilling duties, and secretive or exclusive ways of operating and communicating with others in the group, are practices through which subjectivities create or establish positions and sites that are exclusive for other gendered subjectivities. Through this exclusion, they are enabled to secure their own position in the 'masculine' landscape. This exclusion/inclusion has an impact on the formation, destabilization and negotiation of embodied masculinities and is often demonstrated through (un)official fights for leading positions inside the hierarchical organizational mechanism of the youth organization. These conflicts are not analogous to those inside the official political parties but bare some similarities, through the formation of sub-groups, pacts, platforms or fractions and through the constant confrontation with certain ideological or organizational issues (e.g 'hard-core' against 'conciliatory' groups or traditionalists versus modernists) or the support of certain leading figures. All these are ways of performing and simultaneously negotiating different, complementary, antithetical – and always referring to certain hegemonic types –forms and patterns of masculinities to be found within political youth organizations.

The construction of an identity first as a 'citizen' and then as a political agent or 'politician' coexists and coincides with the construction of a hegemonic masculinity in a process of integration within a society and within a political culture, where the main purpose is the achievement of a higher position in the hierarchy of masculinities, the hierarchy of the political organization and the hierarchy of the social organization.

With the embodiment of certain models of hegemonic and alternative masculinities, the young men are in a way performing a critique on power and against powerful politicians and public figures, even from the same party.[9]

Stereotypes of western culture and political tradition equate hegemonic masculinities in politics with power, violence, aggressiveness, pragmatism, calmness, self-discipline, realism, heterosexuality and objectification of the Other (the political opponent, women or other men, gay, trans, etc.). J. Pleck, J. Sawyer (1974) locate the 'male role' in the binary stay cool/get ahead. Especially in younger groups it is almost the rule to avoid any feminine behavior, to be successful, to achieve status, social acceptance, to be

9 Very often, depending on their place of origin, young men refer to the local and regional masculine culture, so that hegemonic masculinities bear some elements of localism and regionalism. At this point it would be useful to consider and analyse the history and development of local communities, but that would transcend the framework of this research and lead to other research fields.

able to sustain the family, to gain power, autonomy, independence, to take risks, to implement violence and show aggressiveness. As S. Westwood (1990) has stressed, in a way the notions of calmness and self-control link masculinity to 'street-wise' strategies or strategies that play off 'street credibility', something that is valuable also in politics (politics is then identified with 'dirty business', immorality, etc.).

X: 'In organized politics, you learn to be cautious and careful with everyone and everything that is going on and unfortunately you have to adopt some 'immoral' behavioral strategies in order to survive the inner-organizational disputes.' (I, pasp, Communications, Panteio University, female)

Even if it is not always valid and actual in certain socio-political, economic and historical contexts, necessary for the negotiation of power positions for most members of political organizations is the achievement of a status of success, acceptance and popularity, the obtaining of a high(er) 'symbolic capital' (Bourdieu, 1977). Even by descriptions of a good 'politician' or a good 'political agent', there are references to stereotypes or typical patterns of hegemonic masculinities.

M: 'The good politician is smart, has a good education, has style, is not so arrogant, but always serious. He has to give a respectful impression. But most of all, he has to persuade, give quick and immediate answers, he has to be brave… A woman in politics has to adopt another style, to be more understanding and caring, show respect for the others and to pay attention to the problems of the people. Nobody wants a bitch who is shouting around and scares the people.' (d, dap/apox, Law School Athens, male)

Nevertheless, through typical processes of gender socialization, the various gender roles and the gender differences are referring to a net of prohibitions and commands that are characteristic of the dominant gender roles of a certain society (Bandura, 1977). F. Politis (2006) sees masculinity as a framework of discourses and debates in the dynamic context of organized social life. In organized political life, the 'performance' of a socially constructed masculinity is done through organized actions aiming for the acceptance of the performance by the audience (society) or the peer group, extracting material from the actual cultural context the performance is held in (political organization).

4.6.5 Collective Masculinities: the Negotiations of Hegemonic Masculinities in the Group

As mentioned above, the influence of the peer group on the individual is big, and, in the process of the (gender) identity construction, there is a constant negotiation and approving or disapproving relation between the young person and the peer group. Especially in all-boys/all-men environments, friendship is valuable for masculinity (Nardi, 1992). Within peer groups, the persons are participating in common meaning making processes that form perceptions about politics and masculinity, interacting within the site of political organizing and action. In most political groups (as well as in almost every peer group) there is a central person, 'leader' or 'central figure' and the 'supporters' or 'followers', people around him. Men within such sub-groups share the ideology of hegemonic masculinity, which is dominant in the certain context. As Walker (1997) stressed, usually men's friendships are developed in broader, looser networks and have a more fluid character. Therefore, the broad character of mass political organizations enables the formation of interpersonal relations between men. In this context, collective masculine identities are constructed referring to and simultaneously differentiating from the 'Other', which can be feminine identities or alternative, marginalized masculine identities.

Because of the ideology of antagonism that is dominant in political groups and very often in male groups, those men who are acting dynamically, competitively and fast are approved by the group. Other criteria for promotion within a political group include obedience, discipline, trustworthiness, communication skills, dominant presence, calm reaction in stressful or demanding situations, organizational skills, mobilization of others, all of which are usually acknowledged as male characteristics. The peer groups offer an institutional base in which a range of masculine and sexual identities are negotiating their positions and changing in a performative way, creating a very repressive and restricted space for gender formation, gender surveillance, observation and regulation. Within this space, a constant enforcement of hegemonic masculinities happens. Using their own perceptions of what it is to be a man, young men develop techniques for legitimizing and regulating the meanings and aspects of the notion.

Within universities, political involvement sometimes has a direct relation to the performance in academics. Politically powerful groups within a faculty have connections to professors and secretaries and often are better informed about upcoming exams or what is going on at the university. In certain cases, through connections, members manage better grades or get easier internships or other positions in the university, a privilege that others should gain through hard work. Even in the academic world, power and access to resources form certain elites, members of which are to be found among big youth organizations.

Also, within the political youth group, good academic performance is an element that adds to the status of the members but is not always a necessary characteristic of hegemonic masculinities in political groups. However, in other political organizations (especially left ones), the political education, the good knowledge of history and the classics of the ideological and political movements they belong to is highly respected. The 'intellectual' or 'theorist' has a different status in different political circles.

M: 'It is a fact that the Right does not have intellectuals, no ideological tradition. Do you know a good book written by a conservative? At least in Greece, I don't know, and I come from this side, you know.' (d, dap/apox., Law School Athens, male)

For working class men, intellectual work is linked rather with the social inferiority of a feminine occupation. Bodily work requires strength and skills that contain the social superiority of masculinity. Often they resist the alienation they suffered in school, criticizing the values and ideas that accumulated inside these frameworks as bourgeois and middle class and therefore alien to them (Willis, 1977:148).

K: 'We don't get to do a lot of theoretical schooling in our organization. And it is better that we don't, in my opinion, because we had enough lecturing in school and even now in the courses, although now we do a lot of technical stuff, too. We have to deal with other everyday problems. We in our faculty, we have the serious problem that we do not have permission to work as civil engineers, although we study this, but in a more practical way. So, we have to fight to achieve that. I guess this is much more important than reading books.' (c, pasp, Athens Technological Institute, male)

Concluding, we can say that 'political' masculinities are organized on the basis of social power. A way to gain this kind of status is through success in politics. The adoption of a political profile, like 'hard-core', 'orthodox', 'resilient', 'ideologist' or 'activist', is connected often with different types of masculinity and according to relevant political and gendered performance. The active construction of masculinity does not always lead to conflict and rapture with the institution, but usually moves within the limits of the given political culture and gender regime.

4.7 Violence as a Structure Forming Political Masculinities

For the analysis of political masculinities, 'violence' becomes a central structure and a basic tool for the analysis of the 'gendering' of politics within political organizations. Beyond the structural level, the spheres of activity and experience of the individuals and groups within organizations enable a constant 'being' in relation to violence, politicizing violence and even theorizing violence. For the researcher of political organizations, the 'seeing' of violence becomes a test of theory.

All through the analysis of the empirical material, I tried to understand and systematize my knowledge and the knowledge of my informants about the workings and the gendered character of violence in politics. As important as it is to not take people's narratives as objective truth, it is also important to always try to put them in the context of various discourses. I attempted to develop a matrix of connections between structures, identification processes and representations with patterns of masculinity construction processes within the certain organizational framework I am focusing on. The task is not simple, as violence has many visible and invisible aspects and in everyday political life in the Greek context takes forms of physical and sexual violence, emotional, psychological degradation, ideological manipulation and more.

What is striking about the character of violence and violations on an interpersonal as well as organizational level is that violence has a 'consensual' character. In contextualizing and talking about violence, individuals and groups undergo a 'normalization process' of violence, develop a political understanding of violence by defining what is deviant and what is normal in and about violence, producing and re-constructing often contradictory norms and discourses around violence (Lundgren, 2004).

As becomes clear, violence cannot be limited to men's violence, as there is the danger of isolating violence from the rest of social life, and although this particular work focuses on how violence forms masculine subjectivities, the development of a general understanding of violence in politics is a constant concern.

Many explanations about the gendering of violence have focused on individual male psychologies, on socialization experiences of boys and men, on sub-cultures of men, on societal patriarchal structures and trans-societal processes. In the case of violence in political youth organizations and its connections to the formation of male subjectivities, 'violence' can take all the above theorizations. What becomes even more crucial for the understanding of violence and its gendering character, however, is that it becomes a structural pattern of men's individual and interpersonal violence[10].

Individuals and groups within political youth organizations are subjected to state and institutional violence and are in the centre of structural relations of institutions that are historically violent, such as patriarchy and capitalism. Even if individuals have agency concerning the de-construction of dominant patterns of violence, this is indeed very demanding and often impossible, not least because this process is quite beyond individual control. At this point I might argue that certain moments of resistance and break with dominant violent practices, representations and discourses are constituting factors of various forms of masculinities within political youth organizations.

In the following table, I have tried to systematize the actors and the levels among which violence, intersecting with the Political and masculinities, is becoming normalized in contemporary politics:

STRUCTURES	**political system state political parties political youth organizations**	**masculinized political culture hierarchies organizational relations**
IDENTITY	**interpersonal violence physical, verbal**	**masculine subjectivities agents**
REPRESENTATIONS	**symbolic violence ideologies**	**hegemonic masculinities alternative masculinities**

Table 4.3 Contextualizing violence

Feminist, especially radical, materialist and structuralist analyses of men's violence emphasize the materiality and bodily effects of violence, violent acts and words, as violence is a matter of experience of embodiment

10 Jeff Hearn in a lecture titled, 'Thinking on men, masculinities and violence: personally, bodily, politically, societally, transnationally', in Linsköpping University, Sweden in June 2011.

and a matter of change in discursive constructions (Hearn, 2011). Through the process of analysing the discursive re-constructions of the informants, I consciously tried to view and conceive violence as a structure, process and agency and, parallel to that, to understand the process of 'masculinity construction'.

The issue of violence in politics get a class as well as a gender dimension and is clearly male dominated as well as an extremely 'masculinized' act. Gender and sexuality are significant in the explanation of violence but also other social divisions, such as age, are linked to the production of structural violations through the systematic creation of structural power differences (Hearn, 2001:88):

A: 'Violence is a classed notion.

G: Always. Violence is done also in the workplace. Where we go to distribute our leaflets, we see how the bosses look angry and accusingly at the workers if they dare to take the newspaper we give out.

A: Of course violence is not only psychological, but physical, too.

(question: In the violent incidents in demonstrations are women also participating?)

An.: In the demonstrations you are in danger every moment. And the class enemy sends men to seize a demonstration. So, in the front row we have men to cover up. A man biologically is stronger than a woman. A woman can train every day, be super sporty and still she cannot beat a man that never does sports. And as I said, if there are men on the other side, you have to fight with men.

A: But it is also an ideological issue. You can be 50 kilos and only 1.50 metres and still be stronger than a guy 2 meters tall, because you have the faith, you know why you are doing this. And so women can fight too. Sometimes we have to tie them to keep them back (laughter).' (e, pks, University of Economics, males)

The references to the structures of institutions that are violent, such as the state and the police, are linked to the social divisions that produce violence or reproduce structural violations such as class and gender. The references of the informants to violence and violent practices as part of everyday politics reveal how violence has been accepted and normalized by both individuals and institutions. Physical violence is connected with strength and physical power, male characteristics that automatically exclude women from political practices that entail different forms of violence. The narratives of the violent incidents in demonstrations, gatherings, sittings, to which members of organizations from the whole range of political spectrum referred repeatedly, get a character of heroic male narrations. Violence gets mystified, gains a symbolic importance and is a common reference point in discussions among male members. The narrations during the group interviews got a kind of boasting, a showing off that becomes part of a process that reveals the theatrical character of the combination of doing politics and doing gender.

The possible offence of women by 'others' (opponents or members of other groups) represents a strong symbolic, aggressive moment of violence. The gendered dichotomy of private/public becomes clearer when women are vulnerable and unprotected in the public domain and should be supported or helped by the constant attempts of surveillance and control by men. So, the control over and within the public sphere becomes elevated to a source of power and social status for men. The 'code of honour' (referring to the protection of women from other men in the public sphere during practices such as political debates, campaigns, demonstrations, etc.) links power with heterosexuality and gender relations.

When it comes to violence in politics, apart from physical strength and male biology, ideological fitness is stressed, a characteristic that is shared by both men and women, since biology does not play a role there. The involvement of women in fights, verbal or even physical, as indicated above, is a rare phenomenon that shows, however, the internalization of male attitudes by women, as necessary behavior in politics. In the female narratives, references to physical, verbal and psychological violence have a strong male character:

I: 'Clearly, the political youth organizations in the universities, they are not there to represent political ideas. Their role is to provide students with services, like material for the exams and to give them an alibi to kick each others' asses. Especially in male dominated faculties, as here in Marine Engineering, there is a violent tension in the air every day. There is this joke, well, I don't even know if it is a joke, it can be also true from my experience, that one day a group of members from the one big organization attacked members of the other, suddenly and without evident reason and they went like 'Wait for us to gather, so we can fight properly!'. Sometimes you think they are like boys playing and they take nothing seriously about politics.' (h, dap, Marine Engineering, Metsoveio University, female)

Various forms of violence, such as verbal violence but also violence that comes not only from the political opposition but from the State and the Law, have been established as necessary and unavoidable parts of politics by both men and women, becoming constitutive parts of the personal and gender relations within youth organizations:

F: 'Well, there is the formal violence we receive by the police and the state laws. The more active we are, the more violent suppression we receive. But of course nobody likes it, there is nobody who would say 'Give me some more of this tear gas!'. Now as for the verbal violence, it is often necessary and you cannot avoid it in politics.' (g, pks, University of Economics, female)

Organizational processes have an impact on the intensifying of organizational violence. Processes such as small group interactions, management styles of control, flows of information and the reproduction of a culture, such as the hegemonic masculine culture we try to analyse, belong to everyday practices that sustain the oppressive character of political institutions. In political youth organizations, the managerial power and control that is expressed through organizational hierarchies, task allocation (intellectual/activist, leadership/mass), as well as the physical and verbal violent acts and pressure between groups, can lead to violence and violations on an everyday level. As H. Kelman (1973 in Hearn, 2001:94) notes, an important part of these organizational processes is the reproduction of transcendent and mundane authorizations that consist of an organizational ideology, which can lead to forms of exclusion and oppression.

Looking at organizational structures, trying to link them with gender, often means looking at how organizational structures and processes are dominated by culturally defined masculine meanings (Alvesson; Billing, 1997:83). According to D.L.Collinson, J. Hearn (1994), there are five versions in the context of organizations: authoritarianism, paternalism, entrepreneurialism, careerism and informalism (men building networks on the basis of shared masculine interests and excluding women). D. Morgan (1992), suggests that different forms of masculinities are linked to each other, hierarchically, in terms of power (1992:45 in Alvesson; Billing, 1997). In an organizational context, D. Kerfoot and D. Knights (1996) view as the core of masculinities 'a preoccupation with a particular instrumental of 'rational control" (1996:79 in Alvesson; Billing, 1997:84), while femininity is often a matter of the prioritizing of feelings (Hines, 1992:314) and is characterized by nurturance, compassion, sensitivity, empathy (Grant, 1993), notions that also appear in discourses of female politics. M. Kimmel (1994) views masculinity as the antithesis of femininity. However, in everyday discourses and masculine representations, masculinity is linked to a profound unnatural form of masculine embodiment but also to gay masculinities. In political organizations, where the notion of hierarchy is more linked to power relations, individuals are involved in politics incorporating images, imaginaries and political models, with masculinity becoming a political discourse. The masculinity of the political agent depends absolutely on a network of informal circles around major personalities, well-funded campaigns and mainstream media discourses, and it relies heavily on a definitely recognizable political opponent.

The notion of sexuality (connected with notions of violence, Other-ness and devaluation of the political opponent) is very central within organizations, in which antagonism, power relations and hierarchies are constitutive variables. Masculinities become in such a context a mixture of discourses, practices and representations that mark individuals and institutional practices as masculine/male. Treating masculinities as forms of subjectivities (orientations in thinking, feeling, evaluating, making sense in body and mind) frees the notion from the boundaries of body and of certain categories and makes them appear in all persons and all genders in different forms and degrees.

Among peer groups and also in political youth organizations, another constructive process of collective identities are the narrations or even reanimations of real or fantastic situations that get a new collective meaning and are part of the history or mythology of the group (Kehily; Nayak, 1996 in Politis, 2006). Members of political groups narrate stories of political conflicts between political opponents and themselves or other members of their group, violent conflicts with the police, legendary debates on bigger meetings, election campaigns, all sites where competition and conflict on an ideological, collective and personal level get various forms.

Narrations of ritually 'orchestrated' conflicts, where violent fights between different groups (usually from opponent organizations) happened in certain moments of stress or boredom, usually in male dominated environments, offer moments of male bonding, a verification of collectiveness and a securing of power and masculinity. Parallel to that, extreme physical violence among men in certain institutional environments, such as universities, is a practice of 'mocking' institutional power that is often received as suppressive or restrictive. These collective behaviors, which are also subjects of narrations, are influenced by a 'spirit of masculinity', showing a 'constructed' collective toughness and absence of respect towards social rules. Through these kinds of 'prohibited' or 'politically incorrect' actions, certain individuals are usually get and gain respect from the others, in a process of emerging leadership. Through these practices and the relevant narrations that give a vague, often exaggerated picture of the real event, the involved persons prove their ability to stand physical pain, distress and danger by demonstrating physical and moral strength and political strength to defend their organization, values and ideas in any way.

Part of the narrations are also erotic and sexual adventures which, when shared, unite the young men around heterosexuality and misogyny, creating a coherence in the certain group and excluding others (Lazos, 1997 in Politis, 2006):

I: 'Not only women are seen as a kind of attraction for the group, so that the others get interested in meeting them and in doing so they come near to our organization. Also men play this kind of flirting game. I have heard someone boasting 'I am only dating her to get her to vote for me'.' (h, dap, Marine Engineering, Metsoveio University, female)

4.8 Concluding

Behind, in between and within the discourses, we see a constant 'gendering' of the public and private spheres in relation to citizenship, political engagement and political agency. A continuing identification of gendered spheres with different actors and their relations to the structures of the spheres reveal that politics remain a strongly gendered domain. Political youth organizations appear to be formed by what Connell (1990) referred to as an European equation between authority and a dominating masculinity (Arnot, 2009:88). The male character of the language of the discourses as well as of the images that appear when referring to leadership, ideology, political practices associates politics with the male notions of responsibility, duty, active public participation and radical resistance. Female politics are attributed to family or community, without these spheres being regarded as particularly political. However, the presence of women in politics is considered as a positive contribution to the common good without spreading the frame of established law and masculine order of parliamentarian liberal democracy. The most political, egalitarian, participatory discourses appear to apply to public spheres and to imply a direct relevance to men and the major role of men in terms of 'civic action' (Arnot, 2009:88). Although political action is categorized as definitely public rather private action, the discourses of political resistance appear to imply a unity between public and private, even if the public is promoted. Resisting discourses also have a female character, especially from women on the left, and appear to have been influenced by feminist and emancipatory politics. This reveals a tendency that politics of change, which are represented in the discussions through discourses of resistance, orientate more towards a deconstruction of the divisions public/private and male/female, at least on a political level.

Moving from the discourses to the practices, the picture looks a little darker regarding the presence of alternative characteristics other than those of a hegemonic masculine order. Although in the discourses there do appear some references to a greater range of accepted behaviors, a non-threatening masculine status within the organizations and a conscious reduction of sexism (even if usually only in discourse), when it comes to everyday political practices, individuals seem unable to overcome the pressure of the existing dominant gendered and classed order. Antagonism, competition, struggle of interests, hierarchies and shifting power dynamics are setting the context of organized politics.

The institutions of political youth organizations create conditions for developing power relations and create space for different forms of masculinity that have different access to power.

5 Epilogue

It is difficult to write about gender. Gender serves an important role, from a structural category to a methodological tool, in the analysis of a variety of issues. Many theorists, in anthropology, sociology, psychology and even in political science, have turned to gender as a new way to look at structures and institutions, to view the subject, to talk about identity and collectivities. Feminist theorists have introduced gender in their critiques of state, patriarchy and institutionalized oppression. From the first wave of feminism, where theorists were thematicizing the normativity of gender, divisions of labor and gender roles in the public and private spheres, by demanding political rights (mainly the right to vote) and underlying the exclusions of the Political in western societies, to the second wave of the feminist movement, where sexuality became an issue, the personal became political and black women demanded their voices to be heard, scrutinizing the (until then) universal categories of woman and womanhood. From there to the post-structuralist and post-modern discourses on power, hierarchy and domination, gender realized in Discourse, in the domain of imaginaries, reflected in language, defined by laws and carved within institutional morphologies. Theory and research received a different polymorphous character, avoiding normative, essentialist and purely positivist ways of looking at people's realities.

The division of sex/gender was the first step away from biologisms that attributed certain roles to people as natural and that made the biological sex merely their social destiny. However, in the Political, the subject in front of the law remained the man, as men were ever present in the public domains, in and behind institutions, in the legislation, the execution of the law and the administration of the state. Even when women got accepted as citizens with 'equal' political rights, equality was equality on paper only and exclusion, discrimination and isolation remained the reality not only for women but for minority groups such as migrants, gay and lesbian people, transsexuals, etc.

After many decades of discussion on equal rights, on inclusion and on gender mainstreaming, we still can trace the androcentric character of political and social institutions. Gender becomes again an issue for political science. It becomes obvious that any analysis of any matter cannot overlook gender anymore, that gender is a constitutive category of any political and social institution in addition to being a main aspect of the 'citizen', the 'worker', the 'politician'.

Despite all the feminist critique on the androcentric character of theory and research, there was a recent turn to men and masculinities as subjects of analysis. This paradox reflects an attempt to go beyond gender as a subject of empirical research and use it rather as an analytical tool to describe and analyse phenomena of hierarchy, domination, exclusion and to introduce scenarios for social change. This kind of critical perspective, what N. Yuval-Davis and M. Stoetzler (2002 in Arnot, 2009:3) call the 'gender gaze', is developed in this work, too.

There are various reasons why this work concentrates on masculinities in politics. Even if men are not the only subjects of law, of institutions and the Political, political structures and institutions, as well as the subjects within, are still participating in the reproduction of a 'masculinized' political culture. To look at the construction of gender subjectivities means to look at men in relation to women (so that talking about men does not mean that we do not talk about women). The formation of masculinities in political organizations is a way to combine the subject with the structures, the practices and the discourses, all in one context, because structures form the individual and the individual accordingly reproduces and often re-shapes the character of institutions. Combining the subject with the broader social, political, economic and cultural context is a way to criticize hierarchies and domination. Furthermore, this work takes 'political identity' as formed within political youth organizations, which in this analytical framework is theorized as constructed actively[1] by political ideologies, organizational structures, collective practices and context-related representation, as a variable that influences the formation of gendered subjectivities. Accordingly, the gendered subjectivities formed within political youth organizations shape the character of the organizations, (re)produce related representations and ideologies and form the political culture of a certain society at a

1 Ch. Mouffe analyses the active construction of a political identity by underlining that although subjects have different conceptions of the 'good', they accept submission to certain authoritative rules of conduct, constructing a 'we' as a chain of equivalence among different demands that do not eliminate difference (Mouffe, 1992:31).

certain historical moment. This is assumed to be valid in the contemporary Greek political context.

This work has as a point of departure the assumption that the hegemonic and other masculinities as constructed within political youth organizations are formed by power relations that reflect the power relations that are dominant in the broader political, social and economic structures in contemporary Greece. These structures are forming the social, economic, political and cultural realities of the individuals and of social groups and are generally accepted and internalized through hegemonic ideologies that cover all the range from the Political to the Cultural.

This hypothesis has been verified through the analysis of the collected empirical data, based on group discussions. The discourse analysis parallel to the theoretical analysis has shown that the individual and collective discourses on politics, utopias, state, violence and gender relations, as well as the relevant political practices within political youth organizations, reflect the dominant political ideologies, traditions and formal lines of the parties. These formal ideologies and party lines influence accordingly the formation of masculine subjectivities within political organizations.

Through the analysis, it also becomes clear that male subjectivities as developed in the framework of political youth organizations are influenced not only by official political ideologies, but also by the level and area of political involvement, by the positioning on the hierarchical ladder and the situation of individuals in the matrix of power relations. Political ideologies form relevant gender ideologies and views on gender relations accordingly. Gender consciousness is in relation to political consciousness and ideology.

The male subjects consciously position themselves towards models of hegemonic masculinities, dominant in the framework of the organized politics they are in. The claiming of political power requires in many ways the compliance with hegemonic masculinity. As the power equilibrium changes within various political organizations, the forms of masculinity also change. Not one type of masculinity is hegemonic for every political organization, but there is always one in each context that sets the relations of the other forms of masculinities in that framework, securing the gender regime of each organization. The various gender regimes are always in relation to the general gender order, with some space for alteration and some sites of resistance, which nevertheless do not manage to threaten and question the general highly masculinized, homophobic and sexist political culture.

Talking about masculinities, we have to talk about femininities in the context of political youth organizations. As becomes clear, the notions of masculinity and femininity are not always antagonistic and antithetical. Masculinity is not the negative of femininity, but it is certainly very often the negation of it and the limitation to it, in Discourse and Practice.

Male subjectivities are formed through the intersection of structures, representations and processes of identification[2]. In the framework of political organizations, class, sexuality, education, division of activity, ethnicity, body and age influence deeply the construction of masculinities.

Understanding this, one can understand how complex but also how important it is to think and write about gender constructions in a real social and political context at a certain historical moment. To capture 'masculinities', we have to follow their relation to femininities, the relation of both notions to time and space, meaning history and society, and to de-construct them as universal norms[3].

By focusing on masculinities in political youth organizations, this work has attempted to reveal not only some of the workings of gender and power within organizations, but also the character of the Greek political culture. I consider it to be the first phase of a broader study with a more global perspective on politics and gender.

---

2 For the process of 'identification', analysis in Brubaker, R.; Cooper, F.(2000). On identity. *Theory and Society*, 29:1, 1-47.

3 Although this is just a suggestion and not fully represented in this work, the method of Adorno's 'configuration' would be useful to understand gender subjectivities in a further research. For an analysis of the method regarding the concept of 'kaleidoscopic dialectics' see Rehbein, Boike (2010).Kritische Theorie nach dem Aufstieg des globalen Südens. Antrittsvorlesung, Humboldt Universität zu Berlin. http://edoc.hu-berlin.de/ovl

Bibliography

Adams, R.; Savran, D. (eds) (2002). *The masculinities studies reader.* Massachusetts: Blackwell Publications.

Almond, G.; Verba, S. (1963). *The civic culture*. Princeton: Princeton University Press.

Althusser, L. (1969). *For Marx*. London: Allen Lane.

Althusser, L. (1971). *Ideology and Ideological State Apparatuses. Lenin and Philosophy and Other essays.* London: Monthly Review Press.

Alvesson, M.; Billing, Y.D. (1997). *Understanding Gender and Organizations.* London: Sage Publications.

Anderson, E. (2002). Openly Gay Athletes: Contesting hegemonic masculinity in a homophobic environment. *Gender & Society*, 16: 6, 860-877.

Araujo, H.; Deliyanni, K.; Invison, G.; Tome, A. (2009). Teachers, gender and the discourses of citizenship, in M. Arnot (ed) *Educating the gendered citizen.* London: Routledge.

Archer, L.; Pratt, S.; Phillips, D. (2001). Working class men's onstructions of masculinity and negotiations of (non) participation in higher education. *Gender & education*, 13: 4, 431-449.

Avdela, E.; Psarra, A. (eds) (1994). *Siopires Istories. Gynaikes kai fulo stin istoriki afigisi.* Athina: Alexandria.

Badie, B. (1986). *Culture et politique*. Paris: Economica.

Bandura, A. (1977). *Social Learning Theory*. New York: General Learning Press.

Barkty, S.L. (1990). *Femininity and domination: Studies in the phenomenology of oppression.* New York: Routledge.

Barrett, F.; Whitehead, S. (2001). The sociology of Masculinity, in F. Barrett; S. Whitehead (ed) *The masculinities reader*. Cambridge: Routledge.

Barthes, R. (1994). *The Semiotic Challenge.* Berkeley: University of California.

Beck, L.; Trombetta, W.; Share, S. (1986). Using focus group sessions before decisions are made. *North Carolina Medical Journal*, 47: 2, 73-74.

Becker-Schmidt, R.; Knapp, G.A. (eds) (1995). *Das Geschlechterverhältnis als Gegenstand der Sozialwissenschaften*. Frankfurt, New York: Campus.

Bereswill, M.; Meuser, M.; Scholz S. (eds) (2007). *Dimensionen der Kategorie Geschlecht: Der Fall Männlichkeit.* Münster: Westfälisches Dampfboot.

Bochmann, K.; Haug, W.F.; Jehle, P. (eds) (1991-2002). *Antonio Gramsci: Gefägnishefte. Kritische Gesamtausgabe* (Vols 1-10). Berlin: Das Argument.

Bottomore, T.; Marshall, T.H. (1995). *Idiotita tou politi kai koinwniki taxi.* (O.Stasinopoulou, Trans.). Athina: Gutenberg.

Bourdieu, P. (1977). *Outline of a Theory of Practice*. Cambridge: University Press.

Bourdieu, P. (1999). *The weight of the world.* (P. Ferguson et al, Trans.). California: Stanford University Press.

Braidotti, R. (1994). *Nomadic Subjects: Embodiment and sexual Difference in Contemporary Feminist Theory*. New York: Columbia University Press.

Brannen, J.; Collard, J. (1982). *Marriages in trouble: the process of seeking help*. London: Tavistock.

Britton, D. (2000). The epistemology of the gendered organization. *Gender & Society*, 14: 3, 418-434.

Brod, H.; Kaufman, M. (eds) (1994). *Theorizing Masculinities*. London: Sage.

Butler, J. (1993). *Bodies that Matter. On the Discursive Limits of 'Sex'*. New York, London: Routledge.

Butler, J. (1997). *Excitable Speech: A Politics of the Performative*. New York: Routledge.

Carrigan, T.; Connell, R.; Lee, J. (1985). Towards a new sociology of masculinity. *Theory & Society*, 14, 551-604.

Chenut, H. (1996). The Gendering of Skill as Historical Process: The case of French knitters in Industrial Troyes, 1880-1939, in L. Frader; S. Rose (eds) *Gender and Class in Modern Europe*. Ithaca and London: Cornell University Press.

Chodorow, N. (1978). *The reproduction of mothering: Psychoanalysis and the sociology of gender*. Berkeley: University of California Press.

Code, l. (1991). *What can she know? Feminist theory and the construction of knowledge*. New York. Cornell University Press.

Connell, R. W. (1983). *Which way is up? Essays on sex, class & culture*. St: Leonards: Allen and Uwin.

Connell, R.W. (1987a). *Gender and Power*. California: Stanford University Press.

Connell, R.W. (1987b). Why the 'Political Socialization' Paradigm Failed and What Should Replace It. *International Political Science Review / Revue internationale de science politique*, 8: 3, 215-223.

Connell, R. W. (1990). The state, gender and sexual politics: theory and appraisal. *Theory & society,* 19: 5, 507-44.

Connell, R.W. (2000a). *Gender*. St.Leonards: Allen and Unwin.

Connell, R.W. (2000b). The men and the boys, in S.M. Whitehead (ed.) (2002). *Men and masculinities: key themes and new directions*. Malden, Massachusetts: Blackwell Publications.

Connel, R.W.; Messerschmidt, J. W. (2005). Hegemonic Masculinity. Rethinking the Concept. *Gender & Society,* 19: 6, 829-859.

Cornell, D. (1997). Gender Hierarchy, Equality and the possibility of Democracy, in J. Dean (ed) (2001) *Feminism and the New Democracy. Resisting the Political.* London: Sage.

Dalla Costa, M.; James, S. (1975). *The power of Women and the Subversion of the community.* Bristol: Falling Wall Press.

DD aka Dr.Limit (2010). Oi taxeis tis epithumias. *Container,* 5, 18.

Degele, N. (2008). *Gender/Queer Studies*. Paderborn: W.Fink.

Delphy, C. (1977). *The main enemy: a materialist analysis of women's oppression*. London: Women's Research and Resources Centre.

Delphy, C. (1995). The Invention of French Feminism: an Essential Move. *Yale French Studies*, 87, 190-221.

Demertzis, N. (1989). *Koultoura, neotwrikotita, politiki koultoura.* Athina: Papazisis.

Demetriou, D. (2001). Connell's concept of hegemonic masculinity: a critique. *Theory & Society*, 30: 3, 337-361.

Denzin, N.K.; Lincoln, Y.S. (1994). Introduction: Entering the field of qualitative research, in N.K. Denzin; Y.S. Lincoln (eds) *Handbook of Qualitative Research.* Thousand Oaks: Sage Publications.

Diamantouros, N. (2000). *Politikos duismos kai politiki allagi stin Ellada tis metapoliteusis.* Athina: Alexandria.

Donaldson, M. (1993). What is hegemonic about masculinity? *Theory & Society*, 22: 5, 643-657.

Eisenstein, Z.R. (ed) (1979). *Capitalist Patriarchy and Socialist Feminism.* New York, London: Monthly Review Press.

Erhart, W. (2001). *Familienmänner. Über den literarischen Ursprung moderner Männlichkeit.* München: Fink.

Erhart, W.; Hermann, B. (1997). Der erforschte Mann?, in W. Erhart; B. Hermann (eds) (1997) *Wann ist der Mann ein Mann? Zur Geschichte der Männlichkeit.* Stuttgart/Weimar: Metzler.

Erikson, R.S. (1979). The SRC Panel Data and Mass Political Attitudes. *British Journal of Political Science*, 9, 89-114.

Fenstermaker, S. (2002). Work and Gender, in S. Fenstermaker; C. West (eds) *Doing Gender, Doing Difference.* London: Routledge.

Firestone, S. (1971). *The dialectic of sex.* London: Paladin.

Foucault, M. (1997). *Ethics: Subjectivity and Truth.* New York: The New Press.

Frader, S. (1996). *Gender and class in modern Europe.* Cornell University Press.

Frank, B.(1993). Straight/strait jackets for masculinity: educating for real men. *Atlantis*, 18:1&2, 47-59.

Fraser, N.; Nicholson,L.J. (1997). Social criticism without Philosophy: An encounter between feminism and postmodernism, in D.T. Meyers (ed.) *Feminist Social Thought: a reader.* New York: Routledge,

Friedan, B. (1963). *The feminine mystique.* New York: Norton.

Gerhard, U.; Schwarzer, A.; Slupik, V. (eds) (1988). *Sozialstaat auf Kosten der Frauen.* Weinheim, Basel: Beltz.

Giroux, H. (1980). Critical theory and rationality in citizenship education. *Curriculum Inquiry*, 10, 329-36.

Gordon, C. (ed) (1980). *Michel Foucault. Power/Knowledge: selected interviews and other writings, 1972-1977.* New York: Pantheon.

Gordon, H. R. (2008). Gendered Paths To Teenage Political Participation: Parental Power, Civic Mobility and Youth Activism. *Gender & Society*, 22: 31, 30-54.

Gouws, A. (1999). Beyond equality and difference: The politics of women's citizenship. *Agenda*, 40, 54-58.

Gramsci, A.(1971). *Selections from the Prison Notebooks.* New York: International Publishers.

Gramsci, A.(1995). *Philosophie der Praxis, Gefägnishefte 10 und 11*, W.F.Haug (ed). Hamburg: Argument

Grant, J.(1993). *Fundamental Feminism*. New York: Routledge.

Greenstein, F.I.(1986). *Children and politics*. New Haven: Yale University Press

Grusec, J.; Hastings, P.(2007). *Handbook of socialization. Theory and Research*. New York: The Guilford Press.

Halberstram, J. (1998). *Female Masculinity*. Durham: Duke University Press.

Haraway, D. (1997). A manifesto for cyborgs: science, technology and socialist feminism in the 1980s' in D. T. Meyers (ed) *Feminist Social Thought: a reader*. New York: Routledge.

Harding, S. (1992). Rethinking standpoint epistemology: What is 'strong objectivity ?. *The centennial review*, 36:3, 437-470.

Harding, S. (1993). Rethiniking standpoint theory: what is 'strong objectivity' ?, in L. Alcoff; E. Potter (eds) *Feminist Epistemologies*. London: Routlegde.Harnecker, M. (1976). *Basic concepts of historical materialism*. Athens: Papazisis.

Harrison, J. B. (1978). Warning: The male sex role may be dangerous to your health. *Journal of Social Issues*, 34: 1, 65 – 86.

Hartmann, H.I. (1979). The unhappy marriage of Marxism and Feminism: Towards a more progressive Union. *Capital and Class*, 3:2, 1-33.

Hartsock, N.C.M. (1983). *Money, sex and power: Toward a feminist historical materialism*. New York: Longman.

Hartsock, N. (1997). The feminist standpoint: Developing the Ground for a specifically feminist historical materialism, in D.T. Meyers (ed) *Feminist social thought: a reader.* New York: Routledge.

Hartsock, N. (2004). The feminist standpoint: developing the ground for a specifically feminist historical materialism, in S.Harding; M.Hintikka (eds) *Discovering Reality*. New York, Boston, London: Kluwer Academic Publishers.

Haug, F. (2005). Gender relations. *HIMA* 13: 2,279-302.

Haug, F. (ed) (2001). Zur Theorie der Geschlechterverhältnisse. *Das Argument*, 243: 6, 761-87.

Haug, F.(2005). Gender Relations. *Historical Materialism*, 13:2, 279–302.

Hearn, J. (1987). *The gender of oppression. Men, masculinity and the critique of Marxism*. Brighton: Wheatsheaf.

Hearn, J. (1996). Deconstructing the Dominant: Making the One(s) the Other(s). *Organization*, 3, 611-626.

Hearn, J. (2004). From hegemonic masculinity to the hegemony of men. *Feminist Theory*, 5:1, 49-72.

Hearn, J. (2011). Male bodies, masculine bodies, men's bodies: the need for a concept of gex, in B.S. Turner; K. Davis; M. Evans; V. Pitts; D. Weinberg; W. Soon-hee (eds) *Handbook of the Body*. London, New York: Routledge.

Hearn, J.; Collinson, D. L. (1993).Theorizing Unities and Differences Between Men and between Masculinities, in H. Brod; M. Kaufmann (eds) *Theorizing Masculinities*. Thousand Oaks: Sage.

Hearn, J.; Parkin, W. (2001). *Gender, Sexuality and Violence in Organizations: the Unspoken Forces of Organization Violations*. London: Sage

Heater, D. (1990). *Citizenship: a civic ideal in work history, politics and education*. London: Longman.

Henze, B. (2000). Who says who says? The epistemological grounds for agency in liberatory political projects, in P. Moya; M. Hames-Garcia (eds) *Reclaiming Identity. Realist Theory and the predicament of postmodernism*. Berkeley: University of California Press.

Herzfeld, M. (1985). *The poetics of manhood: contest and identity in a Cretan mountain village*. Princeton: Princeton University Press.

Hines, R. (1992). Accounting: Filling the Negative Space. Accounting. *Organisation and Society*, 17: 3-4, 313-341.

Hoore, Q.; Smith, J.N. (eds)(1971). *Selections form the prison notebooks from Antonio Gramsci*. New York: International Publishers.

Howson, R. (2006). *Challenging hegemonic masculinity*. London: Routledge

Howson, R., Smith, K. (2008). Hegemony. Studies in consensus and coercion. New York: Routledge

Howson, R. (2009). Deconstructing Hegemonic Masculinity: Contradiction, Hegemony and Dislocation. *norma*, 4:1, 7-24.

Irigaray, L. (1979). *Das Geschlecht, das nicht eins ist*. Berlin: Merve Verlag.

Irigaray, L. (1989). *Le temps de la difference*. Paris: Livre de Poche.

Jackson, J.; Scott, S. (2002). Introduction: The gendering of sociology, in S. Jackson; S. Scott (eds) *Gender. A sociological reader*. London: Routledge...

Kerfoot, D.; Knights, D. (1998). Managing masculinity in contemporary organizational life: a managerial project. *Organization*, 5:1, 7-26.

Kimmel, M.; Thomson, E. (1994). *Older Men's Lives.Research on Men & Masculinities*.Thousand Oaks: Sage Publications.

Kimmel, M. (2000). *The gendered society*. New York, Oxford: Oxford University Press.

Kreisky, E.(1995). Der Staat ohne Geschlecht? Ansätze feministischer Staatskritik und feministischer Staatserklärung, in E. Kreisky; B. Sauer (eds) *Feministische Standpunkte in der Politikwissenschaft. Eine Einführung*. Frankfurt/M, New York: Campus.

Leaper, C. (2000b). The social construction and socialization of gender, in P. H. Miller; E. K. Scholnick (eds) *Towards a feminist developmental psychology*. New York: Routledge Press.

Leaper, C. (ed.) (1994). *Childhood Gender Segregation: Causes and Consequences*. San Francisco: Jossey-Bass Publishers.

Leaper, C.;Friedman, C. K. (2007). The socialization of gender, in J. Grusec; P. Hastings (eds) *Handbook of socialization: Theory and research*. New York: Guilford.

Lenz, I. (1995). Geschlechtssymmetrische Gesellschaften. Neue Ansätze nach der Matriarchatsdebatte, in I.Lenz; U.Luig (eds) *Frauenmacht ohne Herrschaft.*

Geschlechterverhältnisse in nicht patriarchale Gesellschaften. Frankfurt/M: Fischer.

Lister, R. (1990). *The Exclusive Society: Citizenship and the poor*. London: CPAG.

Ludwig, G. (2007).Gramscis Hegemonie und feministische Staatstheorie. *Das Argument*, 270: 2, 196-205.

Lundgren, E.(2004). *The Process of normalizing Violence*. Stockholm: ROKS.

Lyotard, J.F.(1984). *The Postmodern Condition: a report on knowledge*. Manchester: Manchester University Press.

Mac an Ghail, M. (1996). *Understanding Masculinities: Social Relations and Cultural arenas*. Buckingham&Philadeplphia: Open University Press.

Mac an Ghail, M. (2003). *Men and masculinities: Theory, Research and Social Practice*. Buckingham: Open University Press.

MacKinnon, C. (1979). *Sexual harassment of working women: a case of sex discrimination*. New Haven: Yale University Press.

MacKinnon, C.A. (1982). Feminism, Marxism, Method and the State: An agenda for theory. *Signs*, 7:3, 515-44.

Malouta- Pantelidou, M. (1990). Elliniki Politiki Koultoura: Opseis kai Proseggiseis. *Epithewrisi Koinwnikon Epistimon*, 75a, 18-57.

Marshall, T.H. (1977). *Class, citizenship and social development*. Chicago: University of Chicago Press.

Marshall, T.H (1981). *The right to welfare and other essays*. London: Heinemann.

Marx, K. (1977). A Contribution to the Critique of Political Economy. Moscow: Progress Publishers.

Marx, K.; Engels, F. (1970). *The German Ideology*. New York: International Publishers.

McIntosh, M. (1978). The State and the Oppression of Women, in A.Kuhn; A-M. Wolpe (eds) *Feminism and Materialism*. London: Routledge and Kegan Paul.

McKinnon, C. (1982). Feminism, Marxism, Method, and the state: an agenda for theory. *Signs*, 7: 3, 515-544.

Mellström U. (2007). Men, Masculinities and Gender Research in the Welfare Stateism of Sweden, in M. Bereswill; M. Meuser; S. Scholz (eds) *Dimensionen der Kategorie Geschlecht: Der Fall Männlichkeit*. Münster: Westfälisches Dampfboot.

Mellström, U. (2006). New Fatherhood at the Junction between production and reproduction?. *Socialvetenskaplig tidskrift'*, 13: 2, 114-128.

Metaxas, A. (1979). *Politiki Methodologia*. Athina: Sakoulas

Meuser, M. (2006a). Hegemoniale Männlichkeit- Überlegungen zur Leitkategorie der Men's Studies, in B. Aulenbacher et al. (eds) *FrauenMännerGeschlechterforschung. State of the Art.* Münster: Westfällisches Dampfboot.

Meuser, M.; Scholz, S.(2005). Hegemoniale Männlichkeit. Versuch einer Begriffserklärung aus soziologischer Perspektive, in M. Dinges (ed) *Männer-Macht-Körper. Hegemoniale Männlichkeiten vom Mittelalter bis heute*. Frankfurt a.M., New York: Campus.

Mies, M. (1993). Towards a methodology for feminist research, in M. Hemmersley (ed) *Social Research: philosophy Politics and Practice*. London: Sage

Millett, K. (1970). *Sexual Politics* .New York: Doubleday.

Millett, K. (1971). *Sexus and Herrschaft. Die Tyrannei des Mannes in der Gesellschaft*. München: Deutsche Taschenbuch Verlag.

Mitchell, J. (1971). *Women's Estate*. New York: Random House.

Mohanty, S. (2000). The Epistemic status of cultural identity: on beloved and the postcolonial condition, in P.Moya; M. Hames-Garcia (eds) *Reclaiming Identity. Realist Theory and the predicament of postmodernism*. Berkeley: University of California Press.

Morgan, D. (1992). *Discovering men: Sociology and masculinity*. London: Routledge.

Mouffe, Ch. (1985). *Hegemony and Socialist Strategy. Towards a Radical Democratic Politics*. London, New York: Verso.

Mouffe, Ch. (1992). Citizenship and Political Identity. *October*, 61, 28-32.

Nagel, J. (2005). Nation, in M. Kimmel; J. Hearn; R.W. Connell (eds) *Handbook of studies in men and masculinities*. Thousand Oaks: Sage.

Neuman, S. (1975). *Modern political parties: Approaches to comparative politics*. Chicago: University Press.

Offe, C. (1984). *The contradictions of the welfare state*. London: Hutchinson.

Offe, C. (1985). *Disorganized Capitalism*. Cambridge: Massachusetts: MIT Press.

Ouzgane, L.; Coleman, D. (1998). Postcolonial Masculinities: Introduction. Retrieved from http://english.chass.ncsu.edu/jouvert/v2i1/INT21.HTM, last visited 9.8.2011

Pantelidou-Malouta, M.(1987a). *Politikes staseis kai antilipseis stin arxi tis efiveias*. Athina: Gutenberg.

Pantelidou-Malouta, M. (1987b).Gynaikes kai Politiki/Gynaikes kai Politiki Epistimi: H anaptuxi mias feministikis politologikis theorisis. *Epitheorisi Koinwnikon Ereunon*, 65, 3-38.

Pantelidou-Malouta, M. (1989). Politiki uper tis Isotitas i Isotita uper tis Politikis: H ideologiki leitourgia tis diekdikisis tou 35%. *Dini*, 4.

Pantelidou-Malouta, M. (1990). Elliniko politiki koultoura: opseis kai proseggiseis. *Epitheorisi Koinonikon Epistimon*, 75a, 18-57.

Pantelidou-Malouta, M. (1993). *Politiki sumperifora*. Athina: Sakkoulas.

Pantelidou-Malouta,M. (1992). *Gynaikes kai politiki*. Athina: Gutenberg.

Papageorgiou, G.(2010). *Fulo kai ereuna*. Athina: Gutenberg.

Patak, Z. (2001). A pedagogy for postcolonial feminists, in D.Jobling; T. Pippin; R. Schleifer (eds) *The postmodern bible reader*. Oxford: Blackwell.

Pateman, C. (1988). *The sexual contract*. Stanford: Stanford University Press.

Pateman, C.(1970). *Participation and democratic theory*. Cambridge: Cambridge University Press.

Patrick, G.M (1984). Political Culture, in G. Sartori (ed) (1994) *Social Science Concepts*. Beverly Hills, Sage Publications.

Patton, P.; Pool, R. (eds) (1985). *War/Masculinity*. Sydney: Intervention Publ.

Perrigo, S. (1988). Women, the State and Democracy. *Interlink*, 8.

Pleck, J.(1981). *The myth of masculinity*. Cambridge, Massachusetts: MIT Press.

Pleck, J.H. (1987). The theory of male sex-role identity: Its rise and fall, 1936 to the present, in H. Brod (ed) *The making of masculinities. The new men's studies*. Boston: Allen and Unwin.

Politis, F. (2006). *Oi andrikes tautotites sto sxoleio*. Thessaloniki: epikentro.

Poulantzas, N. (1973). *Political Power and Social Classes*. London: Humanities Press.

Poulantzas, N. (1978). *State, Power, Socialism*. London: NLB.

Poulantzas, N. (1994) *To kratos, i exousia, o sosialismos*. (G. Kritikos, Trans). Athina: Themelio.

Pyke, K. (1996). Class-Based Masculinities: The Interdepedence of Gender, Class and Interpersonal Power. *Gender & Society*, 10:5, 527-549.

Ramazanoglou, C.; Holland, J. (2002). *Feminist Methodology: Challenges and Choices*. London: Sage.

Rehbein, B. (2010). Kritische Theorie nach dem Aufstieg des globalen Südens. Antrittsvorlesung, Humboldt Universität zu Berlin. Retrieved from http://edoc.hu-berlin.de/ovl, last visited 9.8.2011

Rösing, I. (1999). *Geschlechtliche Zeit – Geschlechtlicher Raum*. Heidelberg: Universitätsverlag Winter.

Rowbotham, S. (1985). *Hidden from History*. London: Pluto.

Sauer, B.(2001). *Die Achse des Souveräns. Staat und Demokratie in der Geschlechterdebatte*. Frankfurt/M., New York: Campus.

Schmidt, H.; Schmerl, C.; Krameyer, A. et al (eds) (1973). *Frauenfeindlichkeit: Sozialpsychologische Aspekte der Mysogynie*. München: Juventa.

Schössler, F. (2008). *Einführung in die Gender Studies*. Berlin: Akademie Verlag.

Scott, J.W. (1986) (1997). A Useful Category of Historical Analysis. *The American Historical Review*, 91: 5, 1053-1075.

Scott, J.W. (1997). Deconstructing Equality-Versus-Difference: or, the Uses of Poststructuralist theory for feminism, in D.T. Meyers (ed) *Feminist Social Thought: A reader*. New York: Routledge.

Seidler, V.J. (1991). *The moral limits of modernity: love, inequality and oppression*. New York: St.Martin's Press.

Seidler, V.J. (1997). *Man Enough: Embodying masculinities*. London: Sage.

Sewell, T. (1997). *Black masculinities and schooling*. Oakhill: Trentham Books.

Shaver, S. (1983). Sex and Money in the welfare state, in C. Baldock; B. Cass (eds) *Women, Social Welfare and State in Australia*. Sydney: Allen and Unwin.

Silverman, K. (1992). *Male subjectivity at the margins*. London: Routledge.

Sombart, N. (1996). Männerbünde und politische Kultur in Deutschland, in T. Kühne (ed) *Männergeschichte – Geschlechtergeschichte. Männlichkeit im Wandel der Moderne*. Frankfurt/ New York: Campus.

Spourdalakis, M (1998). *Komma-Kratos-Koinonia*. Athina: Patakis.

Spourdalakis, M. (1990). *Gia ti theoria kai ti meleti ton politikon kommaton*. Athina: exantas.

Stanley, L (2002). Should 'sex' really be 'gender'- or 'gender' really 'sex'?, in S. Jackson; S. Scott (eds) *Gender. A sociological reader*. London: Routledge.

Steedman, C. (1986). *Landscape for a good woman: a story of two lives*. London: Virago.

Tolson, A. (1977). *The limits of masculinity*. London: Tavistock.

Tsaousis, D. (ed) (1983). *Morphologia tis neoellinikis koinwnias*. Athina: Estia.

Varika, E. (1995). Epanidrusi I epidiorthosi tis Dimokratias; To aitima tis isarithmis antiprosopeusis ton fulon. *Sugxrona Themata*, 55, 42-58.

Ventouris, N.(1978). *Themata sugxronis politikis epistimis: politiki filosofia, politiki psuxologia, eurwpaiki oloklirwsi*. Athina: Papazisis.

Vlachou, A .; Wolff, R.D. (eds) (2005). *Political Economy of Capitalism*. Athens: Athens University of Economics and Business.

Walby, S. (1994). Is citizenship gendered?. *Sociology*, 28 :2, 379-95.

Weber, M. (1988). *Gesammelte Aufsaetze zur Religionssoziologie*. (Vols. 3). Tuebingen: Mohr.

Wetherell, M. (ed) (2005). *Identities, groups and social issues* (N.Mpompatzis, Trans.). Athens: Metaixmio.

Whitehead, S. (2007). Men's practices, individual and collective, in M, Flood; J.K, Gardiner; B. Pease, K. Pringle (eds) *International encyclopedia of men and masculinities*. London: Routledge.

Whitford, M. (ed) (1991).*The Irigaray Reader*. Cambridge: Basil Blackwell.

Widdig, B. (1997). Ein herber Kultus des Männlichen: Männerbünde um 1990, in W. Erhart; B., Herrmann (eds) *Wann ist der Mann ein Mann? Zur Geschichte der Männlichkeit*. Stuttgart/Weimar: Metzler.

Wilkinson, S. (1999). Focus groups: a feminist method. *Psychology of Women Quatterly*, 23:2, 1-8.

Wilkinson, S.(1998a). Focus groups in feminist research: Power, interaction and the co-construction of meaning. *Women's Studies International Forum*, 21:1, 11-125.

Williams, R. (1980). *Problems in Materialism and Culture*. London: Verso.

Young, I.M (1997). Is male identity the cause of male domination?, in E. Meyers (ed) *Feminist Social Thought: a reader*. New York: Routledge.

Young, I.M; Jaggar, A.(1998). *Companion to feminist philosophy*. Oxford: Blackwell Publ.

Yuval-Davis, N. (1992). Women as citizens, in A. Ward; J. Gregory and N. Yuval-Davis (eds) Women and Citizenship in Europe. Stoke-on-Trend: Trentham Books.

Gender-Diskussion

Hella Ehlers; Gabriele Linke;
Nadja Milewski; Beate Rudlof;
Heike Trappe (Hg.)
Körper – Geschlecht – Wahrnehmung
Sozial- und geisteswissenschaftliche Beiträge zur Genderforschung
Der Körper spielt notwendigerweise in allen Diskursen um Geschlecht eine Rolle, doch diese kann mehr oder weniger zentral sein. Dieser Band versammelt Beiträge, in denen die widersprüchlichen Zusammenhänge von Geschlecht, Körpern und Körperbildern aus sozial- und geisteswissenschaftlicher Perspektive betrachtet werden. Beiträge zur Vergeschlechtlichung von Körpern in Geschichte und Gegenwart sowie zur medialen und literarischen Repräsentation des Spannungsfeldes von Körperlichkeit, Geschlecht und Sexualität stehen im Zentrum. Der Band enthält darüber hinaus Texte zur Inszenierung von Frauen- und Männerkörpern in verschiedenen Musikszenen und zur Zuschreibung geschlechtsspezifischer Erwartungen in der Erwerbsarbeit.
Bd. 19, 2013, 272 S., 29,90 €, br.,
ISBN 978-3-643-12154-7

Gottfried Lorenz
Töv, di schiet ik an
Beiträge zur Hamburger Schwulengeschichte
Der vorliegende Band enthält Aufsätze zur Verfolgung homosexueller Männer während der NS-Zeit, zur mann-männlichen Prostitution, zum Schicksal schwuler Schauspieler und Musiker an Hamburger Theatern, zu homosexuellen Rechtsradikalen in der Hansestadt während der 1970er und -80er Jahre, zu der Homosexuellenzeitschrift „Die Insel" / „Der Weg", zu Gustav Wyneken sowie zur Schwulenverfolgung in der Belletristik. Der abschließende Beitrag beschäftigt sich mit Dr. Heinrich Mock, vormaligem Direktor des Lindenau-Museums in Altenburg.
Bd. 20, 2013, 560 S., 49,90 €, br.,
ISBN 978-3-643-12173-8

LIT Verlag Berlin – Münster – Wien – Zürich – London
Auslieferung Deutschland / Österreich / Schweiz: siehe Impressumsseite